The Democratic Genre

Fan fiction in a literary context

Also by Sheenagh Pugh

Poetry

The Movement of Bodies
The Beautiful Lie
Stonelight
Id's Hospit
Selected Poems
Sing for the Tax Man
Beware Falling Tortoises

Translation

Prisoners of Transience

Fiction

Folk Music

The Democratic Genre

Fan fiction in a literary context

Sheenagh Pugh

seren

Seren is the book imprint of
Poetry Wales Press Ltd
Nolton Street, Bridgend, CF31 3BN
www.seren-books.com

First published in 2005

ISBN 1-85411-399-2

The publisher works with the support of the Welsh Books Council

Printed in Plantin by Bell and Bain Ltd, Glasgow

Contents

Acknowledgements

Chapter 1, 'Puppeteers', and Appendix 3, Kristi Lee Brobeck's paper 'Under the Waterfall' have been previously published in Vol 5 of *Refractory*, ed Angela Ndalianis, the online media culture journal of the University of Melbourne (http://www.refractory.unimelb.edu.au//journalissues/index.htm)

Author's Note

There are several book-length studies of fan fiction in the context of women's studies or media studies, as a social or cultural phenomenon. I have quoted and acknowledged them but I did not wish to repeat them. I am a writer (of published poetry and fiction) and a tutor of creative writing, and my interest in fan fiction is literary, not sociological. I wanted to investigate it as writing, as I would any genre. Hence how the writers do it matters more to me than why – the 'why' is relevant only in so far as motives influence the way writers work.

The argot of fan fiction (*aka* fanfic) is quite specialised and I have included a glossary at the end. Throughout this book, rather than repeating the clumsy formula 'he or she', I have generally written 'he' when speaking of characters in general, because those most popular with fanfic writers still tend to be male, and 'she' when speaking of fanfic writers, because most of them are female. (There are always exceptions: *Doctor Who* is and always has been a mainly male fanfic universe).

I should stress at the outset that I am not claiming an exhaustive knowledge of fan fiction in print and online. Nobody could; the quantities of material involved render it impossible. I have read extensively in five fandoms, from which I took most of the examples in this study, and have a working knowledge of perhaps half a dozen more. My experience as a reader is partial; in some ways it may be typical, in others not. One has to start somewhere.

Fan fiction is published both online and in fanzines (sometimes known as printzines these days to distinguish them from webzines). Fanzines are quite expensive and many older ones are out of print. Some people do have large collections of them but most readers of fan fiction these days have read far more online than they ever have in printzines and I am no exception. Indeed in many newer fandoms the fan fiction exists only on the web, whereas in the days when people like Henry Jenkins and Camille Bacon Smith were writing about it from a more sociological viewpoint their material was mainly in print. Therefore many of the references cited are from the Internet. I have tried, however, to ascertain whenever a story quoted is still available in a printzine and cite that as a reference too.

There is also the matter of attribution. Many fanfic writers do not use their full or real names, preferring to be known by their pseudonyms (pseuds, in fanfic terms). Also some of the mailing lists on which they correspond and post views and stories are unarchived – this applies particularly to slash writers – and it is not normally etiquette in the community to quote or attribute posts from such lists. Where I have done so, I have obtained permission, but have not always been able to use more than initials in connection with the quote. I should also mention that many pseuds are non-gendered and a few are misleadingly gendered. Whenever I have referred to an individual fanfic writer as "she" or "he" it is because I know the sex of the writer in question; where I do not, I have not presumed to guess.

Fan fiction writers, readers and editors have given me immense help with this project and if I were to thank them individually I should rival an Oscar-winning speech (though I must make special mention of Kel, who kindly sent me the entire story archive of *The Bill's* Jasmine Alley website while it was temporarily offline). I am also most grateful to Kristi Lee Brobeck and to Executrix, both of whom allowed me to reproduce their essays as Appendices 3 and 4. I am the more grateful for this co-operation from fanfic writers, since they are people who sometimes have reason to feel patronised and misunderstood and can be justifiably suspicious of being written about in consequence. Fandom itself sometimes draws mockery from those not involved in it, and I have heard fan fiction dismissed automatically by those who have never read any and would be hard put to it to create fiction of any kind. I would like to thank the fan fiction reading and writing community collectively and to say that I hope what comes through this book is, firstly, an interest, from a literary point of view, in what they do and how they do it, and secondly an admiration for their inventiveness, their collaborative skills, their determination to do what they do well and, in many cases, for their sheer writing talent.

The sabbatical term I was granted by my employer, the University of Glamorgan, enabled me to write this book.

Introduction

When my children were young, they had a set of Robin Hood figures. We would set them out on the floor, with plastic trees to represent Sherwood Forest, build Nottingham Castle out of Lego, and I would act out the stories I recalled from my childhood. When I ran out of stories, I and my audience would invent new ones. Sometimes they were simple variations on the formula: Robin goes into town, or the Sheriff comes hunting for him; there's a battle and all ends well for the good guys. Sometimes we explored aspects the canonical stories didn't touch on – the Sheriff's childhood, (in my version he was a comically awful brat) or life in the forest when the outlaws were taking a day off. Now and then, we departed from the canon altogether to produce a "what if". This tended to happen when the children, or I, didn't like some aspect of the canon. They disliked the sad ending of Robin's betrayal and death and preferred alternatives, while I got bored with the canonical Marian and liked to speculate that she was herself a mean hand with a bow and arrow and joined in the battles. And every now and then they would want other toys to take part, and I would have to find a storyline that could accommodate some space-men or a polar bear.

What we were doing, in essence, was writing fan fiction – i.e. fiction based on a situation and characters originally created by some-one else. We had a canon of stories invented by others, but we wanted more, sometimes because the existing stories did not satisfy us in some way, sometimes because there are simply never enough stories and we did not want them to come to an end. So we invented the ones we wanted. In this we were part of a very long tradition. Hero-figures like Robin, Arthur and the characters of ancient myth have always accreted stories to themselves through the generations and their legend grows and changes according to what each set of new readers and listeners needs from it. In the earliest Robin Hood stories, for instance, Marian does not appear. She was added later by French writers who wanted a romantic interest. At first she was no more than that, generally gazing wistfully from the castle walls and waiting to be claimed or rescued. When vapid heroines fell out of favour, she began to play a more positive role, culminating in Tony Robinson's TV series *Maid Marian And Her Merry Men*, a feminist version in which Marian is the outlaw chief trying to make something of a fairly useless bunch of male outlaws.

It may not immediately be obvious that this is fan fiction in the way the term is now understood, because the oldest original Robin Hood stories have no named author. It is therefore difficult to decide what is canon (i.e. part of the original source material) and what is not. Marian once wasn't canon; now she is accepted as such, but it is doubtful if Robinson's version would be so accepted yet. She is a "what if", an AU or AR (alternate universe or alternate reality), as some fanfic writers would term it. In the Arthurian canon, there are several named authors – Chrétien de Troyes, Thomas Malory, Wolfram von Eschenbach, just for starters. Since these authors contradict each other wildly, however, there is no rigid, generally accepted canon, much to the relief of later authors who can use the elements they want to create their own take on the legend. To quote Catherine Fisher on her fantasy novel *Corbenic* (Red Fox, 2002), a version of the Grail legend for young readers:

> The book is a contemporary fantasy based on only the earliest Grail stories, i.e. Chrétien de Troyes' *Le Conte du Graal* and its Welsh version *Peredur* from the *Mabinogi*. Also some very early and obscure Merlin poems and no more than a touch of Wolfram's *Parzival*. [1]

It is generally felt that the materials of myth and folk-tale belong to all, and are for each author to interpret and develop as he or she sees fit. Many, I am sure, would quarrel with defining Tennyson's *Idylls of the King* or Scott's *Ivanhoe* as fan fiction, merely because they use material from a common myth-kitty, and perhaps they would similarly not accept that Robinson's TV series and my inventions for my children were such. But what of respected writers who do use as their taking-off point the creations of other, named, writers? What of Jean Rhys's alternative take on *Jane Eyre* from the viewpoint of the first Mrs Rochester, *Wide Sargasso Sea*? Or the published "sequels" to Austen's *Pride and Prejudice* and du Maurier's *Rebecca?* If George Macdonald Fraser takes Hughes' Flashman and writes a series of novels on his later adventures, or Will Self sets a version of *The Picture of Dorian Gray* in the present (*Dorian*, 2002), how does what they are doing differ materially from what fan fiction writers all over the world do every day when they invent new episodes for ITV's *The Bill* or new stories for Pratchett's *Discworld?*

One answer, of course, is that Fraser, Self, Rhys etc got paid for it. It is a distinction often made by fan fiction writers themselves, between "fanfic" (unpaid, done for love) and "profic" (professional writing, done for money). But this distinction is not very satisfactory from a literary point of view, because it has very little to do with any difference in genre. For one thing, there is such a beast as paid, official fiction based on TV series (e.g. the *Star Trek* novels and the BBC series of *Doctor Who* novels) and whatever it is called, it is often indistinguishable from unpaid fan fiction – indeed, the same writers are sometimes involved.

Equally unsatisfactory, to my mind, is the notion that there must naturally be some intrinsic difference in *quality* between what Rhys, Self et al do and what pseudonymous, unpaid fan fiction writers do. In the first place, even if there were, it wouldn't mean they were writing in different genres, merely that some people were handling the genre better than others. But when I began to read fan fiction, it soon became apparent to me that its spectrum of achievement, in literary terms, was actually very wide. There is certainly a great deal of poor writing in fanzines and on the Net, but also some work which is ambitious and interesting by anyone's standards – much as is the case with any kind of fiction. Paul Magrs writes literary fiction and gets respectful notices for it in literary journals. Those same journals did not review his BBC *Doctor Who* novels, but he was the same writer when he produced them and there is no evidence that he turned off half his talent expressly for the purpose. He wrote differently, rather than worse.

There have been several studies of fan fiction as a sociological phenomenon, usually in the context of women's studies or media studies. I do not want to repeat these, but rather to consider fan fiction from a literary point of view, as one might any other highly successful, popular genre. I want to investigate what *kind* of writing this is, how its particular conventions and history have shaped it, what needs it tries to satisfy, how it has developed and is developing. A quick Google search with the words "fan fiction web sites" throws up over a quarter of a million answers, and that is without considering printed fanzines. And when the film *Pirates of the Caribbean*[2] had been out about two months, I checked on the umbrella website fanfiction.net and found upwards of 1,500 fanfic stories already written about it. It seems worth trying to find out what it is that so many people want so much.

NOTES

1. quoted on Catherine Fisher's website at http://www.geocities.com/ catherinefisheruk/corbenic.html 14.11.02
2. dir. Gore Verbinski, 2003

1. Puppeteers

For most people, John F. Kennedy Jr was a character in a play, a character in a story, just the way Sherlock Holmes was. When he's lost, then people react very emotionally. Constantly rehearsing the details of somebody's life and death shows that people are trying to continue the story. We always try to do that when the story ends before we're prepared for the ending.

– Neil Postman, chairman of the Department of Culture and Communication at New York University[1]

I do not allow fan fiction.

The characters are copyrighted. It upsets me terribly to even think about fan fiction with my characters. I advise my readers to write your own original stories with your own characters.

It is absolutely essential that you respect my wishes.

– The official Anne Rice website[2]

Until relatively recently in the history of fiction, this would have seemed a very odd message from writer to reader. For a start, the idea that there is some intrinsic virtue in using an "original" character or story would have puzzled most ancient or mediaeval writers. They did do that sometimes, but they plundered the vast resources of myth and history just as happily – indeed there is a mediaeval convention of authorial modesty whereby writers routinely claim that they found the story they are about to tell in some ancient book. Thus Robert Henryson, the fifteenth-century Scottish poet, tells how, one winter night by the fire, he read a book

writtin be worthie Chaucer glorious,
Of fair Cresseid and lustie Troilus.[3]

And he tells us that when he had finished Chaucer's *Troilus and Criseyde*, which ends with Troilus mourning his faithless love but does not say what became of her, he took another book, in which he found

...the fatall destinie
Of fair Cresseid

This second book, of course, does not exist, though it will: he is about to write it. *The Testament of Cresseid* is his sequel to Chaucer's poem, using the characters both poets had borrowed from Greek myth and made their own, though neither would have thought to call them "my characters". However individualised by each successive poet who used them, they were still Troilus and Cressida, part of a resource that belonged to all.

History is another such resource and Shakespeare, his contemporaries and successors happily plundered classical, English and European history for plots and characters. But they don't seem to have regarded the "original" plots and characters of other writers as sacred either. Sir John Vanbrugh did not, when in 1696 he wrote *The Relapse*, a response to Colley Cibber's *Love's Last Shift* in which he uses some of Cibber's "own" characters and takes their story further. This is a sequel, in as much as it starts where the earlier play leaves off, but it is also a subversion of Cibber's happy ending. Cibber leaves us with a reformed rake vowing to be the most faithful of husbands; Vanbrugh plainly thinks this an implausible outcome and his sequel has a far darker ending.

Nonetheless, Cibber seems not to have minded, given that he acted the lead in Vanbrugh's play. Presumably he saw it in the context of a long tradition of writers responding to and developing on each other's work. (Nor would this be the end of it: in the next century Sheridan, writing, he claims, for changed tastes, adapted *The Relapse* as *A Trip to Scarborough* (1777) and put the happy ending back.)

But nowadays this form of dialogue attracts the notice of lawyers. At the end of 2001, in the wake of the Twin Towers attack, John Reed wrote an alternative version of Orwell's *Animal Farm* called *Snowball's Chance*[4] in which the exiled Snowball returns and turns the Stalinist collective capitalist. This gives Reed the chance to explore whether a capitalist solution is any better than the one Orwell was condemning. In an article in the online New York Press[5], John Strausbaugh outlines Reed's position:

> To Reed, *Animal Farm* represents "an outdated, hyperbolic allegory [...]. Right at the end of World War II, Orwell weighed in on interpreting the first half of the century." Reed believes that Orwell's vision of the Stalinist Soviet threat to the West expressed in the book was very influential on the Cold War mindset. In a real sense, Reed says, 9/11 marks the very end of that Cold War epoch; the realities, and enemies, have irrevocably shifted, rendering Orwell's vision irrelevant and obsolete.

In *Snowball's Chance*, Orwell's famous slogan becomes "All animals are born equal – what they become is their own affair". The farm becomes a sort of Disneyfied theme park; conspicuous consumption and expansion create tensions with the neighbours and out in the woods the fundamentalist beavers eye the farm's twin windmills with hatred which will soon turn violent. Orwell's estate was emphatically not amused by Reed's use of Orwell's original characters and setting, yet it is very hard to see how he could have written the book otherwise. Part of his stated aim was to refute Orwell and what he saw as the simplistic, one-sided world view of *Animal Farm* which, like so many students, he had been fed in school and which he felt had long outlived any relevance it had to the modern world. Any updated fairytale which satirised capitalism as Orwell had done Stalinism would necessarily have to engage directly with the earlier work, and in an earlier age it would have been expected to.

Anne Rice's website itself alludes to one reason that this state of affairs no longer obtains: the advent of copyright. The earliest licensing acts, in the 17th century, were mostly concerned to protect the interests of church and government and the commercial rights of printers. Only with the passing into law of the Statute of Anne in 1710 did the concept of the author as owner of copyright for a fixed term come into being – the notion, if you like, of intellectual property. "The characters are copyrighted." To be strictly accurate this isn't possible, though the embodiment of a character can be trademarked. But the copyright holder, in this case the author, though it need not always be, has the right to control derivative works and it is the unauthorised creation of these to which Rice is objecting. The way she phrased it, though, is indicative of the central point in her argument. In her view "her characters" belong to her; they sprang fully formed from her head and only she has a right to play with them, to decide what they would or would not do and how they shall develop – even, indeed, whether they shall live or die. There is of course a perfectly understandable commercial angle to this. Rice makes a lot of money from these characters and if anyone could legally write and sell books about them, her commercial interests could be badly damaged, both by the market being flooded with imitators and by substandard imitations being taken for her work

But these are not, interestingly, the reasons she gives for her hatred of fan fiction. Indeed, neither could really come into play. Fanfic authors don't normally make money. Fanzines (the magazines in which fan fiction is printed) do not pay their authors for contributions and are priced to recoup production costs: if a fanzine should happen to go into profit, this tends to be hastily donated to some convenient charity to avoid this very accusation. Nor do fanfic authors seek to be confused with the real thing: their stories bristle with acknowledgements that these are not their characters but the property of such and such an author, film-maker or TV company. It is true that if writers are known to read fan fiction they can theoretically be accused of plagiarising it, and this has happened at least once. But again this is not the objection Rice states. Her objection is more emotional than commercial: it "upsets" her to think of "her characters" being manipulated by any other puppeteer. It is a visceral reaction which many authors would share. In fact some other authors, like the fantasy writer Anne McCaffrey, are equally averse to fan fiction and, like Rice, actively try to get it stopped, though as far as I can see, new web sites spring up as fast as the lawyers close them down.

Readers, however, have not always been content to play as passive a role as Rice would assign to them. Most of us can recall feeling vaguely bereaved by the end of a book, wishing it could go on and continuing the action in our heads – maybe even on paper. Or perhaps we have wished to change something about a book, feeling we actually understood a character better than the author did (presumably anathema in Rice's mind). One of the more amusing examples of this is an afterword by V S Pritchett to a Signet Classic edition of *Vanity Fair*[6]. Pritchett, who is plainly more than a little besotted with Becky Sharpe, states outright "It is apparent that Thackeray is wronging her, and at three points he is actually lying". This is a fascinating concept. Thackeray is, after all, lying throughout the novel, from the moment he pretends that Becky ever existed at all – as, at moments, he cheerfully admits. He *created* her; she is, in his own words, the "famous little Becky Puppet" whom he, the puppeteer, will put back in her box when he is done with her. Thackeray, by the sound of him, would have had no truck with "death of the author" theories; this is the Author as God.

But Pritchett, as reader, does not accept that she can be put back in the box. Once created, she has her own reality, which her creator does not necessarily understand perfectly, or even better than a reader. He has not, after all, created her out of air. As we shall see in a later chapter, fanfic readers and writers themselves are sometimes disparaging of characters with an autobiographical element, and in her review of Colum McCann's novel about Nureyev, *Dancer* (Weidenfeld 2003), Nicola McAllister alludes to a more widely held notion that creating "original" characters is somehow more of an achievement than drawing them from life:

> Any notion that McCann's fictional account of Rudolf Nureyev's life is a novelistic shortcut, an easier task than creating an original character, is swiftly dispelled.[7]

As indeed it should be, for how much actual difference is there in the two processes? Even if a character like Becky Sharpe had no one real-life model, in what sense can she be "original"? Thackeray cannot invent character traits for her that did not already exist in the world, any more than he can invent a totally new colour for her hair or dress. He is stuck with materials that already exist in the world and all he can do is reassemble them in different combinations. Becky will be partly himself perhaps, and people whom he has known; maybe she will even inherit something from fictional characters he himself has read about.

In fact it is possible for her creator, by understanding her imperfectly, to make her say or do something which goes against that reality, against the essence of herself, and thereby "lie" about her. Pritchett's fervour about this non-existent woman verges on the comical, yet most us have at some time thought "this doesn't ring true" even when reading the best authors. When Darcy has been accepted by Elizabeth, Austen has him at one point use the phrase "dearest, loveliest Elizabeth". I have never been able to read this without the words jarring: even allowing for unusual emotion, I cannot make the phrase sound right in his voice.

No doubt many would feel differently, just as many would disagree with Pritchett about Becky. In a way, that is the point; it is also the greatest possible compliment to the writer's trade. That a writer can create fictional characters who come alive so fully that readers feel they *know* them, can understand their motives, predict their actions, continue their stories and grieve when they "die". That, surely, is as close to God as any author can come.

But once that has happened, they can no longer be solely "my characters".

When, in the December 1893 issue of the *Strand* magazine, Arthur Conan Doyle killed off Sherlock Holmes[8], he may have expected to cause some disappointment among the readership. But he could not forecast 20,000 cancelled subscriptions, mourning bands worn on the London streets and hate mail beginning "You brute"[9]. Conan Doyle remarked "If I had killed a real man I could not have received more vindictive letters than those which poured in upon me" – but then, in the fans' eyes, he had. Nor should it really have come as much of a surprise, given that he had for some time not only been receiving letters addressed to Holmes as if he were real, but now and then replying to them and signing himself Watson[10].

Doyle, at the time he killed him off, was by his own account very tired of Holmes and ready for his story to end. The fans were not, and some at least were prepared to continue it if he would not. In 1899 the American actor William Gillette acquired the rights to a Sherlock Holmes play by Conan Doyle and extensively rewrote it, with Doyle's agreement. When he asked Doyle's permission to have Holmes get married in the drama, Doyle replied by telegram "You may marry him or murder him or do whatever you like with him".[11]

The play was massively popular – touring in it as Holmes kept Gillette in work for the rest of his life – and Doyle himself seems to have softened towards his creation, remarking that it was good to see the old boy again. He would himself in 1901 write a new Holmes story set before the detective's "death" (*The Hound of the Baskervilles*). In 1903 he unequivocally brought Holmes back and cancelled his canonical "death" in the short story 'The Adventure of the Empty House',[12]. Doyle continued Holmes's adventures until 1927, three years before his own death. It was perhaps significant that even when tired enough of Holmes to kill him off, he had not done so in a way that admitted of no resurrection: in 'The Adventure of the Final Problem' there had been no eyewitness to Holmes' plunge over the Reichenbach Falls.

Back in 1893, before Doyle's attempt to kill Holmes, his friend J M Barrie had tried to cheer him up, after the failure of a musical comedy the two had co-written, by sending him a Holmes pastiche, *The Adventure of the Two Collaborators*. (Booth, p174). In it he forecasts what Doyle was about to do to his creation – perhaps Doyle had confided his intention:

> Holmes grew less and less, until nothing was left save a ring of smoke which slowly circled to the ceiling.
>
> The last words of great men are often noteworthy. These were the last words of Sherlock Holmes. "Fool, fool! I have kept you in luxury

> for years. By my help, you have ridden extensively in cabs, where no author was ever seen before. Henceforth, you will ride in buses!"

It must be one of the earliest pieces of Sherlockian fan fiction extant. Doyle loved it so much that he included it in his autobiography.

A fan fiction writer of my acquaintance once remarked, on an unarchived mailing list, that people wrote fanfic because they wanted either "more of" their source material or "more from" it. The early Sherlock fans plainly wanted "more of". However many cases the great man solved, it would never have been enough for them; they would never have been ready for the story to end. They did not particularly want Conan Doyle to do anything differently, just to carry on with what he was doing, and when his death intervened they stepped into the breach. As Neil Postman remarks, they were simply trying to continue the story.

But that is not the only motive for fan fiction. When fan fiction began, and how it is defined, are matters of debate, as we shall see in the next chapter. But it is undeniable that a new era began in the late 1960s, with the first published *Star Trek* fan fiction[13]. Obviously the emergence of TV shows with mass international appeal was a major factor in the 70s explosion of fanzines (fan fiction has no national boundaries; the nationality of the source material has far more impact on the writing style than the nationality of the writer). But it is interesting that many of the TV shows which inspired fan fiction in the 70s and early 80s were science fiction and police shows – *Star Trek*, *The Professionals*, later *Miami Vice*, *Starsky & Hutch*, *Blakes 7*. It is even more interesting that though the fan base for such shows was traditionally more male than female, the fan fiction writers were nearly all women.

Other writers have discussed this issue at length, notably Camille Bacon Smith in *Enterprising Women: Television Fandom and the Creation of Popular Myth*[14] and Henry Jenkins in *Textual Poachers*[15]. Since my primary interest in fan fiction is literary rather than sociological I don't want to discuss it in depth yet again. But to summarise very briefly, I think it is true to say, as these writers did, that though women found aspects of these series that attracted them, they also found much wanting. Generalisation is perilous: among female SF and cop-show fans there are, as I know from experience on mailing lists, many practising scientists who are perfectly happy with technobabble about alien viruses and forensics (though they frequently complain that the writers don't get the science right). But by and large, what the women liked were the characters (at least the male ones, for back in the 70s female characters in such series tended to be awfully vapid) and the relationships between them. What they wanted was the development of that; what they got from most scriptwriters was space battles, car chases and other assorted frenetic "action". (And there does seem to be a sex divide here, to judge by the discussions of the fan forum for the British police show *The Bill.* This went through a stage of being purely crime drama, then became more relationship-based, a development which seems to have been far more popular with women than with men.)

This was, I think, a case of wanting "more from" rather than "more of". Some fans, often female, wanted the action to slow down enough to give the characters and relationships time to evolve; they wanted more overt emotion and personal interaction than the scriptwriters were giving them. They wanted vulnerability in the characters too, so that they could feel with and for them. And this has persisted – there was a filk song (see Glossary) in 1989, set to the tune of *Try to Remember*:

> Those who seek action can stay with their faction
> The same for hardware wars and monsters.
> Give us dejection, rejection, compassion,
> Attacks with guilt instead of blasters[16]

And what they wanted but weren't getting from official sources they invented for themselves. In fact, they invented whole fanfic genres for it. One was hurt/comfort (h/c), the point of which was to take some hero-figure, the tougher the better, completely apart either physically, emotionally or preferably both, before having him rescued and consoled by some other character. (It almost inevitably is a "him" in this scenario, both because fanfic writers tend to be more interested in male characters and because extreme h/c can feel uncomfortable for both reader and writer if it happens to a female character.) There were "missing scenes" – i.e. scenes which could have happened in canon and sometimes must have, but which were not shown, generally because they would have consisted of characters talking or reflecting rather than rushing around zapping something. And PWP, standing for "Plot? What plot?" – because there wasn't one. This was the riposte to the frenetic action screenplay: a story, instead, in which little or nothing happens, but plenty changes – usually in a relationship.

The viewers who became fanfic writers had obviously decided that there was more potential in these characters and situations than met the eye of their original creators, and that given the chance, they could do as well or better. Trends in the TV series of the 70s, 80s and 90s would seem to support them. Series did alter. *Star Trek: The Next Generation* was far more relationship-oriented and thoughtful than its parent; tough cops who drove red Torino cars like maniacs were allowed to emote all over each other when not causing a traffic hazard (*Starsky & Hutch*). Above all, the vapid female characters whom fan fiction writers loathed so much that they practically wrote them out of fanfic were replaced by the Buffys and Xenas of the 90s. I don't mean to suggest that fan fiction writers brought this about, rather that they were more in tune with the zeitgeist than their official counterparts writing the scripts at the time. I don't doubt, though, that marketing men took note of what they obviously wanted – the development of *Starsky & Hutch* from pretty basic fights-and-car-chases in Season 1 through to sustained angst-fests in later seasons does suggest some tailoring to perceived audience preferences. And when audiences didn't get what they wanted, they had quicker ways of letting the programme-makers know. In an uncharacteristic lapse of 1999, one of the *Hornblower* TV films, 'The Frogs and The Lobsters', featured an irritatingly ineffectual woman called Mariette who captured the hero's heart and duly died at the end of the episode. She was widely vilified on the show's fan message boards: "stupid French hussy" was the least of it.

And if there was awareness that audiences wanted stronger female characters and more emotionally vulnerable male ones, then the audience, as well as the official writers, directors and actors, had played some part in shaping those characters. (So, of course, did the make-up department and the wardrobe mistress: even now, souvenir Starsky figures include his trademark cardigan). These days, fans are far more aware of their power to shape ongoing series. To quote a fan on the unarchived mailing list Britslash, when a storyline in the TV series *The Bill* wasn't progressing to the liking of some of the fans:

> I say if they won't give us the ending we want now, maybe they will give it to us when Luke leaves later in the year. They won't have filmed his leaving yet and if we make enough noise they might relent and give us the proper and right conclusion
>
> – Tracy

Whether or not the fans' pester power could have influenced the eventual ending of the storyline cannot be known (at the time of writing, June 2003, it seems to have ended inconclusively, with Luke transferring stations but no indication of what might happen to him in the future). What is interesting is the participatory, rather than passive, attitude to the fiction shown in this post. If fans like this *don't* get "the ending they want", they will certainly go ahead and write it themselves. So many people play a part in bringing a TV series or a film to life that it is hard to see who could speak of "my characters". It is sobering to find, on an internet reviews site, a review of the recent TV serialisation of *Pride and Prejudice* "by Jane Austen and Andrew Davies"[17]. But the review's author (Don Harlow) was surely right, in essence. For many who have read the book, Davies' adaptation has added something to their understanding of the characters; perhaps Mr Bennett, in their minds, will forever have the face and voice of Benjamin Whitrow. Sherlock Holmes, for very many years, had the face and voice of William Gillette, and has had others since (to echo the words of a current *UK Gold* programme trailer, "Jeremy Brett is Sherlock Holmes"). And for all Anne Rice wrote the screenplay for *Interview with the Vampire* (1994), even she doesn't own the copyright on Tom Cruise's face.

For those who have not read Austen's *Pride and Prejudice*, or who read it after they saw the series, some of the purely Davies elements may well become indispensable to their vision of the story. Who knows, perhaps one day in the far future, Darcy's plunge into the Pemberley lake will, like Maid Marian in the Robin Hood stories, become accepted as canon. Already some fans of the 1990s *Hornblower* TV series are sorely disappointed when, on reading the C S Forester books on which it was based, they find that the character Archie Kennedy does not, beyond a name and a couple of lines, exist in Forester. (Though it is only fair to add that others, faithful to the book canon, always opposed the character's presence in the TV version.)

This erosion of the author's control over "her characters", once they are out in the world, would probably horrify most writers; there are moments when it horrifies me. But though a writer of books, especially one who does not get involved with film or TV adaptations, can more easily speak of "my characters" than most, I can't help feeling that even he or she, in the days of widespread literacy, internet access and participatory culture, may have to come to terms with seeing these characters slip away from them and lead a life of their own.

After all, fan fiction has gone beyond fictional characters now. There is a relatively recent category of "real person" fiction which uses real, named people as fictional characters out of reluctance to let their stories end. In the epigraph to this chapter, Neil Postman remarks that " for most people, John F. Kennedy Jr was a character in a play, a character in a story". I have not, so far, seen any JFK Jr fan fiction. But there is plenty of Princess Diana fiction, Beatles fiction, and Bill Clinton fiction. Later I will discuss what was, I think, the first Plath and Hughes fan fiction. It has not been the last; since the film came out, we have seen an exponential increase in Ted & Sylvia fandom. If people cannot keep complete editorial control of their own personalities these days, what price fictional constructs?

And if real people can become characters in a story, fictional characters can acquire a considerable degree of reality, via their fans' belief in them. If people can be consumed with interest in their lives, feel love and grief for them and find their own lives and actions influenced by them, then they are "not real" only in the fairly limited sense of having no physical presence. (Even that is not quite true in the case of TV characters, who have the face and body of the actor who portrayed them.) The *Hornblower* character Archie Kennedy, referred to above, was eventually killed off in the TV series, in early 2001. The message boards of A&E, the programme's producers, were filled with anguished reactions – see the archive board[18], of which this from "Fluteface" is fairly typical:

> I keep telling myself, you're an adult, he was a fictional character, but it just doesn't help. I still find myself bursting into tears with absolutely no warning.

The consolatory rejoinder from "Avid" suggests that active rather than passive consumption of the fiction will help:

> Here is one absolute truth; Archie does exist, in our minds... he will have only died for me if my mind makes it so.

"My mind", not that of anyone with an author's, screenwriter's or producer's claim to call him "my character". And "make it so", the naval confirmation of a command, which, as Herman Melville once pointed out[19] implies an unusual degree of control of the universe:

> It is not twelve o'clock till he says so. [...]

> "Twelve o'clock reported, sir," says the middy.
> "Make it so," replies the captain.
> And the bell is struck eight by the messenger-boy, and twelve o'clock it is.

Needless to say, fanfic writers have been resurrecting Archie ever since he died. In fact a schism has occurred in *Hornblower* fan fiction between the mainstream fans, still writing to the now Archie-less TV canon, and the "Crumpeteers", the specific Archie-fanciers, who in many cases have left to play and write in their own alternative universe. This is the LKU (Live Kennedy Universe), where Archie lives on because their minds make it so.

NOTES

1. *Christian Science Monitor*, 23.7.1999
2. http://annerice.com 12.8.02
3. *Poems*, ed Charles Elliott, Oxford University Press 1963
4. Roof Books, 2002
5. http://www.nypress.com/15/40/news&columns/publishing.cfm 27.11.02
6. pub. New American Library of World Literature, 1962
7. *Independent on Sunday*, 12.01.03
8. *The Adventure of the Final Problem*
9. *The Doctor, the Detective & Arthur Conan Doyle*, Martin Booth, Hodder & Stoughton 1997, p190
10. Booth, p180
11. Booth, p243
12. first published in *Colliers* magazine and collected in 1905 in *The Return of Sherlock Holmes*
13. in the magazine *Spockanalia*, 1967
14. University of Pennsylvania 1992
15. Routledge 1992
16. "Wallow", Zen Nine Productions, http://www.fortunecity.com/tatooine/halojones/75/blakes/wallow.html 13.10.02
17. http://donh.best.vwh.net/Esperanto/Literaturo/Recenzoj/pride.html/ 13.9.02
18. http://www.aande.com/perl/wwwthreads/wwwthreads.pl?action=list&Board=Horatio 24.11.02
19. *White Jacket*, 1850

2. The Knowledge

Writing with a Canon

I have a lot of sympathy for ex-President Clinton, who, when asked "is such and such an allegation true?" replied "It depends what you mean by 'is'." The world is full of concepts which seem easy to define until you try.

The preceding chapter indicated that there is a very long tradition of writing that depends on a pre-existing canon of events and characters. But where exactly on that timeline "fan fiction" begins is a matter of debate. Some would take it all the way back to myth and legend: Robin Hood, Arthur and beyond. Some hold that it cannot predate copyright. Most, I think, would count in the Conan Doyle fanfic of the 30s and 50s, though some only reckon from the start of *Star Trek* fanfic in the 1960s. Then there are questions not of time but of type. One can identify a category of "authorised fanfic", like the BBC *Doctor Who* novels and the stories written after Conan Doyle's death by his son, working from Doyle's notes. Some will not admit "profic", i.e. fiction published for money like the sequels by Emma Tennant and others to Austen's novels; others would say it is so like in kind to non-profit fanfic that it too is a sub-category. Then there is fiction which uses someone else's plots and characters to veer off in a new direction (Will Self's *Dorian,* Jean Rhys's *Wide Sargasso Sea*, George Macdonald Fraser's *Flashman* novels). It may seem ludicrous to class these as fanfic until you realise that taking characters into another time or place, as Self does, or telling the story from the viewpoint of a minor character, like Rhys, are things fanfic writers do so routinely they have even evolved genres for them. (Perhaps we have here a case of one of those irregular verbs: my novel makes creative use of literary reference, yours is derivative, hers is fan fiction.)

Myself I would go along with those who define fan fiction as writing, whether official or unofficial, paid or unpaid, which makes use of an accepted canon of characters, settings and plots generated by another writer or writers. This source material may come from books, films or TV, and in the latter two cases it will not derive purely from writers but also from directors, producers and even actors, all of whom have a hand in the creation of characters. There is a relatively new sub-category using named real people as fictional characters, to which I will come later. But even in this branch, I hope I can show that one thing all fanfic has in common is the idea of "canon", the source material accepted as authentic and, within the fandom, known by all readers in the same way that myth and folk-tale were once commonly known. A good fanfic writer's familiarity with and ability to use her canon is comparable with "the knowledge" required by a London cab driver, a small encyclopaedia in the head (and in the case of an open canon, a constantly updated encyclopaedia).

This knowledge can be increased and honed by re-reading, in the case of a book canon, or re-viewing in the case of film or TV, thanks to the VCR. But unlike most of the taxi-driver's knowledge, it is also open to interpretation. What was the implication of a particular phrase, or the tone in which it was spoken, or the expression on the man's face and the attitude of his body when he said it, or the reactions of those characters who heard it? These are the aspects that will be constantly discussed and re-interpreted in the writer's fan community – again the VCR has made a great difference to this. The image of someone watching a tape again and again, as a fanfic writer would do, has become part of the vocabulary of fanfic writing: it crops up in any number of different contexts. In Gill's *The Bill* fic "Aftermath"[2], Sgt Gilmore replays events in his head:

> It was like a favourite film with a sad ending that he played to himself over and over. [...] Craig switched off the tape.

As far as possible, I am trying to keep the special argot of fan fiction, and fandom generally, to the glossary in appendix A, but some will inevitably need to be explained as we go along. Earlier I referred to an "open canon". A canon may be "closed" or "open", depending on whether it is still possible for it to be expanded by the originator. Sherlock Holmes is a closed canon; there isn't going to be any more fiction from the original source. Terry Pratchett's *Discworld* is at the time of writing (2004) still open; it can be added to by him and no-one yet knows in what direction it might go. This can make a difference to fanfic writers, depending on how much reverence they afford canon constraints (and that varies widely). At one stage for instance, it would have been possible, without contradicting canon, for a fanfic story to assert that Esme (Granny) Weatherwax had never had a love life of any kind. Then, in *Lords and Ladies*[3], Pratchett revealed that she'd once had an affair with Archchancellor Ridcully, thus instantly rendering any "untouched Esme" story uncanonical. Having said all this, of course the phrase "never say never again" comes to mind regarding closed canons. It is not impossible, though highly unlikely, that something unpublished by a Wodehouse or a Conan Doyle might turn up (as I write, in 2004, a collection of "lost" Conan Doyle papers is about to go on display at Christies). And TV series which unequivocally ended sometimes get a visit from the resurrection man, like *The Man from UNCLE*, 25 years after it finished.

Because when discussing fanfic stories it is necessary to know something of the canon on which they are based, I am as far as possible going to try to draw examples from five particular fandoms, to obviate the need to explain reams of back-story every time something is quoted. I have chosen these five partly because they do not generate quite such daunting quantities of fiction as some, partly because they represent between them very different writing problems and characteristics – past and futuristic settings, different genres, closed and open canons. I also freely admit to more personal reasons – four of the five canons feature several strong female characters and they all happen to be British canons: anyone who has read many studies of fan fiction has spent long enough on the bridge of the Enterprise to last them a lifetime. I will here outline a little of the background to each, though that should hardly be necessary in the case of the first.

1. Jane Austen

The Austen fandom was one of the first to generate fan fiction, and in its earliest days it was based on her books. But nowadays it is a multimedia fandom; fiction is as likely to be based on the Ang Lee film of *Sense and Sensibility* (1995) or Andrew Davies' TV adaptation of *Pride and Prejudice* (1995). These two books, and especially the latter, inspire much more fan fiction than the rest of the Austen canon. But it lives purely on the web – only the relatively large TV and film-based fandoms can support fiction in printed fanzines. As we shall see, it also tends to have more of an agenda than other fanfic universes, and the agenda in question is not about personal fulfilment as a writer.

2. Discworld

With book-based fandoms it is not always clear whether the book, or some screen adaptation of it, is the inspiration. Though much Holmes fanfic is still based wholly or mainly on the books, Holmes has been many times portrayed on screen and the various adaptations have themselves inspired fics. Fanfic based on *The Lord of the Rings* and the Harry Potter books existed before they became hit films, but expanded out of all recognition when they did. And writers who may never have read a word of P G Wodehouse were inspired by the 1990s ITV series *Jeeves and Wooster.* But Terry Pratchett's Discworld, barring the odd stage adaptation and made-for-TV animation, lives on the printed page, which makes it an unusual and interesting fanfic universe for my purposes. Again its fanfic exists only on the web, though I suspect this is more out of concern for the author's known wishes than because it couldn't support printzines.

For non-addicts, Discworld is an imaginary universe populated by, among others, witches, vampires, dwarves, elves, dragons, trolls and talking dogs. Most bits of it, nonetheless, are reminiscent of bits of our own – the Closed Continent is very like modern China, while Überwald is recognisably the Middle Europe of Dracula and the Prisoner of Zenda. The witch-ridden rural landscape of Lancre may possibly not be a million miles from Lancashire. But the most popular Discworld location, both for Pratchett himself and the fanfic writers, is the polluted, violent and politically unstable city of Ankh-Morpork, perpetually kept from chaos by the machinations of its devious but highly efficient ruler, Lord Vetinari, and the efforts of its police force, the Watch. This body, commanded by the ex-alcoholic detective Vimes, boasts in addition to its human personnel a dwarf, a troll, a zombie and a female werewolf.

3. Blakes 7 (aka B7 – n.b. grammatically the title may need an apostrophe but historically it never had one)

This is at once an example of a closed canon and of how hard it is to close a canon. A BBC science fiction series (1978/81) set in the far future, it postulated a totalitarian world government, the Federation (its creator, Terry Nation, once admitted pessimistically that all his visualisations of the future involved fascist governments). Blake himself is an idealist with a dream of freedom, falsely accused and convicted of child abuse, who manages to steal a spaceship and conduct a minor rebellion. His companions are a mixed bunch of idealists and criminals (in some cases both at once) and the tone of the series was basically dark: there never really seemed much chance of the rebels succeeding and they were by no means angels themselves. Almost uniquely for the time, it ended with the good guys (though their moral purity was by then distinctly grey) defeated. At the end of the final episode, most of the rebels, including Blake, appeared to be quite unequivocally dead.

This has never hindered any writer who wanted them resurrected. (It didn't hinder the BBC either, since they later broadcast two radio plays set, in an echo of Conan Doyle's *Hound of the Baskervilles* device, before the heroes died. Some fans accept the radio plays as canon, some do not.) *B7* fanfic lives both on the web and in printzines.

4. The Bill

A long-running ITV police series (1983 to date) set in present-day London, still at the time of writing an open canon, this has been through a lot of changes. At first, though always open to humour, it was grittily realistic (apart from the language, which, since the programme went out before the 9pm "watershed", could not reflect the casual profanity that would have been natural in that milieu). It was firmly set in the station, Sun Hill, and on the streets; it was strong on point of view – at one time there was never a scene in which a police officer did not appear – and it hardly ever went into the private lives of the officers. With the advent of a new producer, this changed: characters suddenly acquired private lives, especially love lives, which sometimes seemed more prominent than their jobs. There was resistance to this among some of the fans, and another volte-face (under another new producer) saw a return to the station as the focus. But the love-tangles and melodramas did not disappear; rather the characters simply took them into work.

The Bill fandom, like most, crosses national boundaries; many of its fanfic writers are Australian and because they see episodes far later than British fans the two groups are sometimes working with different situations and sets of characters. Furthermore, Australian fans may want to write about the latest plotlines before they have aired over there. They can do this by getting friends to send tapes, but sometimes they simply go ahead and write the fanfic from their knowledge of the characters, without actually depending on having seen the source episodes and plotlines it sprang from. The fanfic is web-based.

5. Hornblower

In this fandom there are certainly purists whose canon is the C S Forester books about life in the British navy in the time of the French wars – among them C Northcote Parkinson, whose *The Life and Times of Horatio Hornblower* (Little, Brown 1970), based on non-existent "documents", was surely a forerunner of, and influence on, G M Fraser's *Flashman* books. But by far the most fiction is written to the canon of the screen adaptations by A & E Meridian from 1998 onwards. Because of this, it is still at the time of writing (2004) an open canon, with the latest pair of made-for-TV films having aired in early 2003. In some ways the films are faithful to the books, in others not, and the most obvious departure was the elevation of a bit part from the books to, effectively, an original character (OC, in fanfic terms) in the person of Archie Kennedy. I was not originally going to make this one of my fandoms for discussion, until it became evident that I could not discuss certain topics, notably angst and character death, without Kennedy intruding at every turn.

In one respect *Hornblower* is odd for an open canon; it is intermittent. *Discworld* fans can be reasonably sure of a book each year; *The Bill* airs twice weekly, but *Hornblower* fans get a couple of longish made-for-TV films and then have to wait, sometimes years, for their next fix. Not surprisingly, they fill the gap with a lot of fanfic of their own, which lives both online and in printzines.

Many other fandoms will, however, need to be referred to in the course of the book, notably Tolkien, in which Henneth Annun, a website for book-based Tolkien fan fiction, has taken unusual steps toward establishing a critical apparatus for the fiction it hosts, and LotR (Lord of the Rings), based on the films, with its offshoot LotRiPS, which concerns the actors rather than their roles.

Pratchett's Granny Weatherwax, who sometimes goes into deep trances for magical purposes, takes the precaution of leaving on her comatose body a notice reading "I ATEN'T DEAD". It should perhaps be pointed out that the fact that some TV series ended 20 or 30 years ago does not mean the fandom is dead, any more than Austen or Holmes fandom is, or that fanfic has ceased to be written in it. It may slow down; there may not be the amounts generated by the Latest Thing (at the time of writing, *Lord of the Rings* and Harry Potter). But the fiction goes on; that is the whole point, after all. Fan fiction happens because people are not ready for a story to end. To their fans, Solo and Illya are no more dead than Elizabeth and Darcy are, which is why new writers, who are not old enough to have been fans when the originals aired, spend time mugging up Sixties and Seventies argot and style in the interest of authenticity.

And there can be debate as to when exactly the story canon did end and what belongs to it (what, as Mr Clinton might ask, do you mean by canon?) Some *B7* fans will not accept as canon the two BBC radio plays produced long after the original series and set before the massacre at Gauda Prime. They were from the same source, i.e. the BBC, but they were not written by any of the original series writers and no-one who had been an important part of the original concept, like Terry Nation himself, or Chris Boucher the script editor, was involved with them. (I can't help suspecting, however, that some fans would be readier to accept them as canon had they not been by common consent pretty awful.) Most fans of any series, I think, would not count as canon any scenes that were filmed but then cut and never shown. But when a series airs in different countries, scenes are sometimes cut because of different cultural sensibilities or an earlier viewing time, and such scenes will still be canon. And what of something never shown in an episode but featured in a trailer? In 2003, *The Bill* ran a trailer in which Sgt Gilmore told PC Ashton he loved him. In the episode, for whatever reason, the words did not appear – but by then they had been heard by fans and were, I suspect, most definitely part of the canon.

It can also happen that a canon is internally inconsistent – in fact it happens more often than one might think. Sometimes this is carelessness on the part of the source. David Croft and Jimmy Perry, who wrote the BBC sitcom *Dad's Army*, were apparently incapable of remembering the Christian names they had bestowed on minor characters and several have at least two in the course of the long series. Mrs Fox, who eventually marries Corporal Jones, is Marcia at one point and Mildred at another. Sometimes it is due to writers being given incomplete or out of date information. The chronology of the *B7* episode 'Harvest of Kairos' is impossible because when the writer,

Ben Steed, was working on it, the plan was for one character to be aged about 35 and he wrote some back-story with that in mind. In the event a much younger actor was cast and either the series producers did not notice that he would have to have been a child space captain or they hoped the viewers would not. And in early 2003 PC Luke Ashton appeared on duty in *The Bill* when he was, quite unequivocally, meant to be on his honeymoon. When this happens, the fanfic writer has to decide which truth to accept – though some get a lot of fun out of trying to reconcile the impossibilities.

So what effects does working to a canon have on writing? Perhaps the most obviously important is that fanfic writers not only have their own knowledge of the canon but can assume a similar knowledge on the part of their readership. Like most constraints on writing, this is at once a restriction, since those without such knowledge will not be able to relate to canon-based stories in the same way, and an opportunity, since it facilitates a lot of shorthand, allusion and irony. If I might illustrate by a comparison with literary fiction, the 19th-century Scottish-born writer Francis Lauderdale Adams (1862-93) has a poem about a young mother, out on the streets, so malnourished that she has no milk for her infant child. In desperation she commits infanticide on Christmas Eve. The poem's title is "Hagar". This is not, of course, the unfortunate girl's name but an allusion to a Biblical character, the handmaid of the patriarch Abraham and his wife Sarah, who bears her master a son and is later thrown out, with her child, by her jealous mistress. They nearly starve, and would do but for the last-minute intervention of God, who is markedly absent from Adams's poem.

Because his audience was Bible-literate, Adams could effectively use Hagar's name as a form of shorthand. A nineteenth-century audience reading that title, followed by the opening lines

> She walked along the road,
> Her baby in her arms.

would at once have in its mind the picture not just of a mother but an unmarried, destitute mother. Indeed the further suggestion would be of someone – a housemaid, perhaps – who had got into that situation courtesy of some patriarch, some eminently respectable pillar of the community. Adams is using shared information, which he can rely on as being shared, to condense his utterance and convey his meaning more quickly and powerfully.

And there is more. For any reader who knows the Bible story, Adams is also setting up an expectation, that at the moment of the girl's greatest despair, something – God or someone acting on his behalf – will intervene to set matters right. This expectation Adams will brutally disappoint: nobody, this time, will intervene to prevent tragedy and in this respect Adams is not just using his Biblical canon but subverting it, perhaps making his readers see it in a new light. It would be hard to read the poem without certain questions occurring: why does God not intervene to prevent this, and if he does not intervene this time, can we trust the story which asserts that he did in Hagar's case? And if so, why did he let things get so desperate for her in the first place? Adams does not raise any of these questions directly in the poem: he trusts the reader's knowledge to make comparisons and draw conclusions.

Fan fiction writers do the same, both relying on their readers' knowledge of their shared canon and sometimes making them rethink it. At the simplest level, it is convenient shorthand, though a good fanfic writer will be careful not to rely on it too much. Every time Terry Pratchett writes a new book set in Ankh-Morpork, he has to bring the city alive for the benefit of readers who, for all he knows, may not have read the earlier Discworld books. But it's a fact that because he has done it so often, the mere name now conjures up an immediate picture for those of us who have been there before, and of course that is also true for the fanfic writers who play in his universe. In the following extract from "Bugs in the System" by Marduk42[4], the Watch Commander Vimes is asking one of his officers, Angua, if she knows a certain person:

> "Sir, I do not know Miss Sto Helit personally, but I do occasionally see her at Biers."*
>
> Vimes inhaled sharply.
>
> "What is she? What reason does she have to drink at Biers?" Angua turned away.
>
> "Sergeant, if you don't answer me in the next ten seconds, I will make you take the Shades for the next week." Carrot made a move as if to say something, but Vimes cut him off.
>
> "Sergeant?"
>
> "It's not what she is, but who she is," Angua said, and then dashed from Vimes' office, slamming the door behind her.
>
> * [Biers was in one of the worst sections of the Shades, and was a bar open to the undead and the honorary undead. It was best for the

squeamish to order clear drinks, because like most non-human races, Igors had difficulties with metaphors like 'Bloody Mary'.]

Here the writer adopts Pratchett's own technique of using footnotes as part of the text. Pratchett's footnotes are part of the comedy but also enable him to get in a bit of quick exposition or comment without interrupting the narrative flow too much. And the context makes it fairly clear what kind of area the Shades is. But the fanfic writer is relying on the reader to be familiar, via the canon, with 'the Igors', a bunch of cloned Ancient Servants from horror movies, and with the fact that Miss Sto Helit is Death's granddaughter. Most Pratchett fans would be. Readers who weren't, however, would not be completely lost, since Vimes at this point doesn't know who Miss Sto Helit is either, only that if she drinks at Biers she can't be completely normal. They would presumably simply take his viewpoint on the scene rather than Angua's.

Alluding to what your reader knows but your characters may not yet know is also one way of investing your tale with irony, pathos or humour, and fan fiction writers often use their canon to do so. In the *B7* canon, for a long time Avon believes that he caused the death of a young woman named Anna Grant, who having been his accomplice in a crime was arrested and died while being tortured to reveal his whereabouts. In fact, as he and the audience find out in the Season 3 episode 'Rumours of Death', Anna is alive, well and a government agent, who betrayed him. Any story set pre-'Rumours' which involves his feelings of guilt is therefore charged with what we know and he, at that point, does not. Fanfic writers are conscious of the benefits of having an audience that shares a lot of their background knowledge, so that they can allude without spelling out in the same way Adams did. The condensed utterance enabled by this shared knowledge sometimes leads them to very pared-down forms, like the drabble (a story of exactly 100 words, named for the author Margaret Drabble and popular in many fandoms).

> "What I like about fan fiction is that you still get that very highly trained audience that can understand very, very complex and allusive things [...] I love that I can write a couple of simple words [...] and they come already heavily pre-packaged with a whole host of connotations and associations and emotional resonances for the audience I'm writing for."
>
> – Ika, in a radio interview with Radio National, Australia.

Writers have always used shared historical, folkloric and mythological information – what Philip Larkin called the "myth-kitty" – in this way. The difference with fanfic writers is that they do it all the time; also that their canon is restricted to a smaller audience than the canons of religion, history and myth. At least, this has been the traditional view, which may no longer be quite so accurate. Nowadays, when I read Adams's "Hagar" to students of English Literature, I have to explain the title. I would expect to do the same for references to Circe's swine and the Tolpuddle Martyrs. But a quote from Elizabeth I's Armada speech ("I may have the body but of a weak and feeble woman...") drew instant recognition, because it had been parodied on the TV programme *Blackadder II*.

This does not suggest that my students are less intelligent than those of former generations, nor even less well-informed in general. Rather, they live in an age overloaded with information, and with more varied sources of it. They draw far more of their information from mass media than was the case in Adams's day, or even 50 years ago, and they are less steeped in the traditional canons of myth, religion and history.

None of this stops them actually appreciating Adams's poem. They do not get that frisson of recognition from the title, which is a pity. But the poem as a whole does not depend on knowing who Hagar was, since it is not "about" Hagar. It is about a woman failed by her community and driven to extremes, and it can be appreciated as such by those who have never picked up a Bible.

Is fan fiction, by contrast, "about" the characters and universes it uses to the extent that it only has something to say to those with the necessary background knowledge? There is certainly an element of being an insider in fanfic reading which can enhance the experience. One reader who is also a writer remarks:

> It's always been high praise in fannish circles to be told that you wrote a story so good it should be published, but sometimes, the highest praise is that it can't be. Its very uniqueness, what creates it, makes it impossible to be anything else. Lots of people can write stories that fall into readable (more than you think, actually, but I'm flexible on the idea of readable), and many can write stories I'd pay to read, and even some write stories that could be published and be great. But there's this small, fascinating group that write a story that belongs only to the fandom that created it. It's like having a treasure you never have to share. It wraps itself in the canon and fanon and the author's own mind that created it and takes it as its own so perfectly that you

> are so damn glad you went into that fandom, just *grateful,* just absolutely *thrilled,* because you get to read *this.*[5]

Again, though, generalisation would be fatal. Most fanfic readers are in it because they love either the universe in question or – in the case of "character junkies" – a character or characters within that universe. Because of this, some do not wish to read fiction which is heavily reliant on original characters (OCs) rather than on the canon characters. Some have canon characters they like reading about better than others; some will not knowingly read stories in which characters are killed off, or in which they are treated humorously if they weren't in the original. No fanfic reader I know likes or approves of fiction in which the canon characters are made substantially different from their originals, doing things that seem out of character for them ("character rape", as the term is).

Again, some readers do not care for departures from the facts of the canon universe, i.e. such genres as "alternate universe" (AU) where the story at some point diverges from the events of the canon, or "crossover", in which universes get mixed up, with characters crossing into each others' stories. Many fan fiction web libraries have preference settings, where potential readers can stipulate elements they want and don't want when selecting what to read. They may want to avoid particular characters, "character death" or certain genres like humour, crossover or adult/slash (overt sexual content, and in the case of slash homoerotic content).

Yet these genres do exist, and are popular. Those writers who don't like them do still have other ways to avoid being totally restricted by the canon. They can write prequels and sequels to it, or "missing scenes", which fill in times or events that were ignored or skated over in canon – eg Darcy's boyhood or the four years of Heathcliff's life unaccounted for in *Wuthering Heights.* These scenes need to be compatible with the canon (otherwise they are AUs), but apart from that, they are at the mercy of the fanfic author.

Some things about writing with a canon – like the shared knowledge – are the same whatever the individual canon is like. But in other ways the nature of the individual source property can make a difference to the kind of fanfic generated, and not always in the ways that would seem obvious. It isn't always clear whether fanfic writers gravitate naturally towards fandoms which facilitate their preferred kind of writing or whether they choose them for other reasons (like a fascinating character or handsome actor) and then ignore the parts of their canon that do not interest them to concentrate on those that do.

One would think, for example, that a police series like *The Bill* would generate a lot of plot-driven, action-packed writing, and so it does, but a writer like Kel, who has almost no interest in plot and is fascinated by mood, angst and the inside of people's heads can work perfectly well within it. *B7* writers are not necessarily science buffs intrigued by how a teleport beam might work – some are, others couldn't care less. What often matters more is the pattern of relationships within the canon source. Some, like *X-Files* and *The Man from UNCLE*, contained a central pairing that was all-important (the One True Pairing or OTP as it is sometimes known by those who like to explore them in depth), while others like *The Bill* and the Discworld have ensemble casts in which the relationships have potential to be more various and more shifting.

The extent to which canon controls fanfic writing varies wildly, even within individual fandoms. At the extreme of faithfulness stands one of the web-based groups devoted to Jane Austen fandom, the Republic of Pemberley[6]. Their fan fiction section, Bits of Ivory, contains a "vision statement" and guidelines for writers. Many fan universes provide similar writers' guidelines. Some requirements from the Pemberley statement would be familiar to any profic writer: "Your document should have spelling, punctuation and grammar checked and corrected. The editors will not correct your document for you." (Actually some will. Wolfie, the co-ordinator of *The Bill's* former fanfic site, would edit first-time submissions and, like the Republic of Pemberley, provided a grammar guide for authors; spelling and grammar are important to zine editors, whether print or web-based.) But in other ways, Pemberley's guidelines are more prescriptive, and restrictive, than most. To quote:

> The stories at Bits of Ivory are intended to present Jane Austen's characters behaving as she wrote them in scenes we might wish she had an opportunity to write herself. We may describe what happens before or after the events in the novels, re-tell parts from the point of view of another character, or elaborate scenes which she, in her wisdom, did not describe in great detail. In this, the guide is Jane Austen's own sense of taste and humanity. [...]
>
> Your story must be about Austen characters and must present them in a manner faithful to their original conception. "What if" stories are acceptable if the premise is plausible within the world

> created by Jane Austen. Your synopsis will help us decide whether or not your story meets this criterion.
>
> Your story must have no profanity, violence or "adult" content.
>
> Your story must take place within the same historical era as Jane Austen's novels. Characters of your own creation may appear in the story, provided that the primary focus of the story rests on Jane Austen's characters rather than your own.[7]

The rule about "adult" (i.e. overtly sexual) content is sometimes made by web editors for convenience, so that the site need not ask visitors to go through cumbersome "age statements" and avoid certain pages. It is for this reason that The Bill had two main fan fiction sites, one for gen fiction (i.e. with no overtly sexual content) and one (known as the Jasmine Alley) for slash fiction, which does have such content. But in the Republic of Pemberley the reason is that "Jane wouldn't have done it" (this form of words was actually used in an earlier version of the guidelines). Ditto the profanity and violence: they don't fit "the world created by Jane Austen". Combined with the requirement that "the story must take place within the same historical era as Jane Austen's novels", this rules out most crossovers and any story which might want to explore not just how Austen wrote in her own time but how she might have written in ours.

This is, as I said, an unusually prescriptive set of guidelines and it is probably fortunate for Austen fan fiction that much of it takes place elsewhere than in the Republic. The "Hyacinth's Garden" site[8], for instance, welcomes adult fiction and contemporary treatments, as does the Darcy-oriented "Firthness"[9].

The reason for the rigour of the Republic's guidelines lies in the mission statement:

> The Republic of Pemberley is designed and intended to allow members of the Pemberley community to honour Jane Austen, appreciate her genius, and share this with others who feel the same. The Bits of Ivory board is a part of Pemberley whose purpose is exactly the same as the rest of the site [...]
>
> Bits of Ivory [...] is not, nor do we ever intend to allow it to become, a writers' forum. We do not have the space for writers to discuss their own writing process. We have never envisaged BOI to be a teaching tool, or a resource and repository for academic writing available to the public at large. BOI is simply yet another, very Pemberlean, expression of the delights to be found in Jane Austen's genius.

The focus, in other words, is Austen; the fan fiction may be used as a way for fans to express their own creativity but is primarily there to celebrate *her*. This would seem to be a recipe for pastiche and little beyond it – "more of", and ersatz "more of" at that. And in truth, a lot of the fiction on this site does strike me in that light. But the authorial spirit is surprisingly resistant. Elspeth's 'At the Club'[10] is, despite the odd faltering in the period language, a genuinely funny and inventive "missing scene" from several Austen novels. It is inspired by Darcy's cry "I shall conquer this!" in the Davies adaptation, which, as Elspeth points out, has no parallel in the book. Austen does not tell us exactly how Darcy copes with his rejection. Davies has him fight his love for Elizabeth by fencing and swimming. Elspeth supposes he might instead have gone to a London club with the equally heartsick Bingley to drown his sorrows. But that is not the end of it. Where we are going becomes clear quite soon:

> [...] I tell you, Darcy, there's no other girl has caught my fancy like her! Why – why she's like...like.... Like Spring itself!"
>
> Darcy was not moved. "If your poetry is any indication of your heart, Bingley, you're in a very poor way all round. If you've any desire to take lessons in the manner of your writing, I could direct you to a certain Captain Wentworth of my acquaintance.... Ah, Knightley! I'd no idea you were in Town!"

In fact just about every Austen male protagonist turns up during the course of the evening – Brandon, Ferrars, Henry Tilney and Edmund Bertram are not far behind – and all hopelessly lovelorn. It is one "missing scene" Austen would never have written, since it involves only men. By using her style in relation to them, in effect imagining how a scene of intimate, agonised confidences like those between Elizabeth and Jane or Elinor and Marianne might play if enacted by a group of men, the story manages to be not just funny but oddly thought-provoking. Putting characters who never met in the same room is a fanfic speciality and often gives the reader a new light on them; in this case Tilney's utter refusal to be impressed by Darcy's loftiness was an insightful observation on both of them.

In general though, I would have to say that the Republic's rigid criteria work against creativity and quality in its fan fiction. Their effect is to highlight even further the importance of the single most difficult task in Austen fan fiction, namely capturing her idiom consistently. It is not easy to sound like Austen for page after page, but if you have to set your story in the same historical era and present the characters "in a manner faithful to their original conception" you have little option but to try. And if you are simply writing pastiche, every perceived departure from the idiom will jar your readers ferociously and convince them that they would be better reading the real thing. If on the other hand you are doing something more than pastiche, then parrot-like authenticity will matter less. In a fanfic sequel to *Pride & Prejudice*, which focused on the Rev. and Charlotte Collins and sent them out to India as missionaries (it seemed unlikely to him, too) I have temporarily been fascinated enough by the premise and the plot to live with American spelling and idiom[11].

The writing guidelines on *The Bill's* gen fanfic site[12] were considerably less prescriptive as regards canon:

> **Who can I write about?**
> Anyone you want! Providing it's in TB universe, of course. You can write your story in any era, from Galloway to Supt Chandler and beyond, if you wish. As long as the main focus is on a TB character then that's great. For tips on writing the popular characters, click on the PROFILES links on the top navigation bar.

The point of the last sentence is that the unforgivable sin in any fanfic universe is getting the facts wrong, departing from the canon not deliberately but accidentally by giving someone an accent, appearance or opinions that the canon plainly states didn't belong to him. The site gives character profiles and an index of streets in Sun Hill to help get it right. Otherwise the writing guidelines on this site are almost all connected with literary quality, with how to structure a story and make it work. There is a no-slash rule, partly so that under-18s can access the site and partly so as not to usurp the territory of the dedicated *Bill* slash site, The Jasmine Alley. But there is no objection to AU stories, crossovers or OCs, and stronger language than the series used is allowed as long as a warning is posted.

Canon is a framework to write against. It contains inherent restrictions, though sequels, prequels, missing scenes and AUs can get around most of them. Anyway restrictions, as all writers know, are not necessarily a disadvantage; they can help to focus writing. But I have heard fanfic writers suggest that the more sophisticated, complete and internally consistent the canon, the harder it is to write originally and creatively within it – in much the same way that mediocre books sometimes make better films than great ones, because they give the film-maker more scope for his own imagination and interpretation.

If the original scriptwriters fail to explore ideas or relationships adequately, they leave space for fanfic to do it; if on the other hand they spell everything out, there is little space left. Holes and inconsistencies in plot lines tempt fanfic writers to try to resolve them. Similarly, aspects of the canon universe obligingly left open to debate by the writers are a gift to fanfic. The politics, social relationships and details of daily life in futuristic universes are generally fruitful ground. In the first episode of *B7*, we hear about the Domes, the indoor complexes on earth which citizens cannot leave without permission. We hear very little about these places afterwards, in the canon, but in fanfic, whole novel-length universes have been constructed around life in the Domes – eg M Fae Glasgow's 'Dome Cycles'[13].

Now and again, a fanfic writer's addition to canon seems so apposite to other writers in that fanfic universe that it becomes "fanon" – i.e. although it was never part of the canon it is generally accepted and used by other writers. In *The Bill* fanfic, it seems to be accepted by several writers that John Boulton had a violent father, though to my knowledge this was never said in the series. In Austen fanfic, characters whose physical appearance was never described in detail by the author are beginning to acquire the features of actors who played them in film (*Sense and Sensibility*) or on TV (*Pride and Prejudice*). And in *Hornblower* fan fiction it seems to be widely accepted fanon that Archie Kennedy has been sexually abused by Jack Simpson in the past, though again it is not explicitly said in the canon, where Simpson has certainly mistreated him in some manner but not necessarily sexually. One irony here is that Kennedy, a central character for Hornblower fans, is no more than a name and a couple of words in the C S Forester books. In terms of the book canon he is effectively an original character (OC) invented by the screenwriters of the TV series, but for the fans of the series there can be no doubt that he is canonical.

The logical end of this process is entire fanfic "universes" spinning off the source canon and it frequently happens. In *The Bill*, Nat and Wolfie created the "Father and Son" universe, effectively a prequel universe for the character John Boulton. In *B7* there is Executrix's "Avoniad", S Lewis's "Legends" universe, Manna's "Administration" series and the late Pat Jacquerie's Fargone; in *Hornblower* the multi-authored "Life of Duty" alternate universe. Even when these have a prequel or sequel element they are not quite the same thing as prequel or sequel fics. Either there will be something about them that is not totally compatible with the existing canon or their universe will be constructed with far more detail than would be needed just to fit in with the said canon. Often their main interest is some aspect not fully developed in the canon (political, in the "Administration" series, social in the Domes Cycles). And their time scale often extends over too wide a period to classify as either prequel, sequel or missing scene from the canon. Some are more like extended "alternate universe" stories (see chapter 3), but some go still further away from the canon – see Manna's explanation of her "Administration" stories:

> These stories are not *Blakes 7* fan fiction. They are not even really AU fan fiction. At best, they are avatar stories, featuring a character not unlike Avon, but also definitely not canonical Avon; he is perhaps Avon as he might have been if he'd been born in a different time and place.[14]

"Avatars" are characters who aren't quite someone else's but are heavily influenced by someone else's; they feature in profic too (see chapter 7). In Austen fanfic the creation of non-Austen universes is effectively discouraged by the rules of the two main homes for fics, Pemberley and the Derbyshire Writers Guild, and in the Discworld one doesn't really have to invent them, merely add to the multifarious Discworld itself as Pratchett periodically does. But these are exceptions; most fanfic universes have their spin-offs. Once these satellite universes are created they too have their canon of knowledge, which binds both their author and any others who want to use them, and stories based in a particular spin-off universe will be identified as such so that readers and potential writers know which set of rules is in operation. These universes often end up being epic-length; those who suppose that fanfic writers who habitually play in someone else's world cannot create one of their own would find them instructive. It happens in profic too, of course, as admirers of George Macdonald Fraser's *Flashman* books have good cause to know.

It comes back in the end to "more from" and "more of". There is canon material which creates a world so entertaining and congenial to the readers that they cannot bear to leave it even when it comes to its natural end – they want "more of" it. They might prefer to let the original writer make it live on for them, but if that cannot be, all they can do is take it into their own hands. To quote the mission statement of another Austen fanfic site, the Derbyshire Writers' Guild[15]:

> The Derbyshire Writers' Guild is an ever-growing archive of writings based on the characters and stories created by the immortal Jane Austen. We make no claims to be able to reach the literary heights of Miss Austen, but, because we all wish that she had lived longer and written more, we feel the need to expand on the world, the characters and the stories that Miss Austen created. We sincerely hope that we will not offend her ghost or the spirit of her works in so doing.

And then there is canon material which, though it draws its readers or viewers in, strikes them as being far from perfect or fully realised; they see possibilities in it which were never explored as they might have been. They want "more from" their canon, and again, who else will give them that if not themselves? Sometimes, indeed, there is something they cannot accept about the canon as it stands and want to "fix" by finding an explanation for it, which, for them, makes it fit the canon better. It might be a straight canonical inconsistency of dates or facts, or it might be someone behaving in a particular episode in a way that strikes the fans as out of character for him, and therefore needing an explanation.

One other aspect of canon-based writing should perhaps be mentioned here. Because they are so used to basing writing on the shared material of their own canon, many fanfic writers become adept at using other shared material too. It will be noted how many titles of fanfic stories, and sometimes of fanzines, are themselves quotes from books, songs or other sources. Fanfic readers share this tendency – after all, the two groups overlap considerably. After the fictional "death" of Archie Kennedy in the Hornblower fanfic universe, his fans, the "Crumpeteers", were given the chance to post elegies on the "Requiem" page of the website "Archieology 101"[16]. Apart from their own poems, they posted quotes from Sassoon, Shakespeare, Byron, John Ford, Henry King, Auden, Longfellow, Edna St Vincent Millay, Kipling, John Donne, Langston Hughes, Delmira Agustina and various singer-songwriters including Sting, Loreena McKennit and Sarah McLachlin.

Not many writers can be assured of an audience which recognises material from so many fictional sources, but fanfic writers can, and they drop literary references as casually as Adams used Hagar's name. They are also fond of parallels between their canon universe and others. They may put the characters of their universe into the narrative of a song lyric, film, novel, poem, TV series or play which strikes them as somehow being appropriate or casting a new light on their own canon. I have myself, while researching this book, had the eerie experience of seeing a poem of mine quoted in an *X-Files* fanfic, 'We, the Living'[17].

In Executrix's 'Stuff and Nonsense', a partial Austen pastiche from the *B7* fanzine *Fire & Ice 7*[18], Blake and Avon express their relationship (prickly and laden with misunderstanding but, in this slash story, also passionate) via the words of Darcy and Elizabeth, roles which they have been alternating throughout the story:

> Kerr-Avon spoke, with a remarkable ability to draft rhetorical periods; "But why, Blake? Or why, rather, at this time? My beauty you had early withstood, and as for my manners – my behaviour to you was at least always bordering on the uncivil, and I never spoke to you without rather wishing to give you pain than not. Now, be sincere; did you admire me for my impertinence?"
>
> Oh gods, man, belt up, Blake wanted to say, but instead groaned "For the liveliness of your mind, I did."
>
> Kerr-Avon [...] enfolded him in an embrace.
>
> "You may as well call it impertinence at once," he whispered. [...] "It was very little less." His teeth closed on Blake's earlobe [...]
>
> "The fact is, that you were sick of civility," (nibble) "of deference," (nibble,) "of officious attention. You were disgusted with the followers who were always speaking and looking and thinking for your approbation alone." [...]
>
> "I roused..." he began again, and Blake moaned, "Jesus, yes..."
>
> "And interested you," Kerr-Avon continued implacably. "Because I was so unlike them. Had you not been really amiable, you would have hated me for it, but in spite of the pains you took to disguise yourself, your feelings were always noble and just." [...]
>
> "And in spite of the pains you took to make yourself appear heartless, nevertheless your actions have often been thoughtful and even generous," Blake conceded.

And in Grey L Bloom's Discworld fic 'Tyger, Tyger'[19], Vetinari, the Patrician of Ankh-Morpork, is wandering his palace worrying about the idea of kingship. (It is a recurring plot in Discworld that Vetinari, a capable and basically decent ruler, is constantly threatened by romantic idiots who want to bring back the True King.) Vetinari is wondering why such a dangerous and useless idea has such a hold on the human imagination and the concept of kingship takes shape for him in the words of William Blake's poem:

> He probably shouldn't worry; it would calm down in a week, two weeks at the most. Commander Vimes would clonk a few heads, curse a few Guild leaders, mess up the whole thing terribly, and then probably get a promotion. Then it would be over.
>
> Until the next time, when some insane Royal-Fanatic, like that poor d'Eath boy, got the idea into his head that Ankh-Morpork needed a king.
>
> It was like someone had said once. Somewhere in mankind's subconscious, some invisible hand had written the words "Kings. What a good idea." And mankind had run with the idea.
>
> Fools.
>
> Lord Vetinari stepped carefully over what was apparently six inches of empty air.
>
> What the hammer? what the chain?
> In what furnace was thy brain?
> What the anvil? what dread grasp
> Dare its deadly terrors clasp?

Since fanfic writers are usually writing for like-minded people who share some of their genre preferences, they can often rely on this wider knowledge too being shared, but not always, and then it becomes important to construct a story in which, though preferable, this shared knowledge is not actually essential. The feedback most desired from readers in those circumstances is "I'd never heard of [the film, play, poem etc in question], but it didn't stop me enjoying the story." Which is what my students generally tell me about "Hagar".

NOTES

1. produced by the Sherlock Holmes Literary Society and its successor the Sherlock Holmes Society of London
2. http://www.savegilmore.co.uk/aftermath.htm 20.01.03
3. Corgi 1993
4. archived at fanfiction.net http://web.archive.org/web/20021024190208/http://www.fanfiction.net/read.php?storyid=1023894 30.03.02
5. Jenn, in an online journal
6. http://www.pemberley.com
7. http://www.pemberley.com/derby/guidenew.html 6 Oct 02
8. http://www.geocities.com/tinker_belladonna/main.html
9. http://www.firthness.com/

10. archived at http://www.pemberley.com/derby/elspeth4.atc.html 12.9.02
11. 'An Unlikely Missionary', by Skylar, archived at http://www.literatureclassics.com/ancientpaths/jane3.html 4.01.05
12. http://212.67.202.77/~tbff/index.html
13. in the Oblaque series of fanzines
14. http://www.mannazone.org/zone/admin.html 31.12.02
15. http://www.austen.com/derby 18.11.02
16. http://members.tripod.com/archieology101/requiem.htm 09.04.03
17. Rhiannon's Fiction Lair, http://www.ejai.org/eyrie/living.html 06.01.03
18. ed. Kathleen Resch, 2002
19. fanfiction.net, http://www.fanfiction.net/s/826031/1/ 04.01.05

3. What Else and What If

Sequels, Prequels, Crossovers, Missing Scenes and AUs

Whenever a canon closes, someone somewhere will mourn it enough to reopen it. The wish to find out "what happened next" – or invent it if it didn't – is familiar to most of us from our childhood reading and it is responsible for a lot of fanfic. Even though we may feel that the canonical ending is "right" artistically, if we liked the story we may still not be ready for it to end, for the characters and milieu that have become real to us to be folded up and put back in the puppeteer's box.

Nothing else makes sense of the fact that anyone could want sequels to Jane Austen's books. They consist, after all, of sustained unresolved emotional and sexual tension between a man and a woman who are meant for each other but must overcome various misunderstandings and difficulties to end up together. Once they do, and are happily married, what is there to write about? Yet people do, constantly, write sequels, above all to *Pride and Prejudice*. Quite apart from unpaid fanfic sequel stories, it has inspired several published profic sequels – e.g. Emma Tennant's *Pemberley*[1], *An Unequal Marriage*[2] by the same author and Julia Barrett's *Presumption: An Entertainment*[3]. Tennant and others, including Joan Aiken, have published sequels to *Emma*. There is a searchable database of published Austen sequels on thc Republic of Pemberley web site[4]. It lists 26 sequels to *Pride and Prejudice* alone.

Pride and Prejudice is the most popular and the most frequently screen-adapted of Austen's books, but I think another reason it inspires more sequels than the rest is that, despite Austen's assurances at the end that all is well, it is easier to see something going wrong for Elizabeth and Darcy than for most of Austen's married couples. They are the most unevenly matched in terms of wealth and status; Darcy has friends and relatives who bear his wife a grudge and only at a distance will he ever be able to abide his mother-in-law. When we read the book, none of this need occur to us; we can happily go along with the ending we wanted and accept the author's assurances. But anyone who wants the story to go on can find ways to make it do so, more easily perhaps than with her other books. Lou's 'The Cure for the Common Marriage'[5] is an attempt to engage with Darcy's potential problem in getting on with Elizabeth's family. They visit, en masse, and he must try to overcome not only his innate shyness and social awkwardness but also his quite understandable dislike of some of their manners and behaviour. It is made clear that without a lot of tolerance on both sides this could become a serious problem in the marriage. By the end of the story things are well, for the present, but one would not necessarily lay bets on peace at the next family gathering.

There are also several characters in *Pride and Prejudice* whose stories evidently have the potential to go on after the end of the novel, either because they are unattached – Kitty, Mary, Anne de Bourgh – or because their circumstances are not unreservedly happy – Lydia and Wickham, the Collinses. A surprising number of fanfic writers are consumed by sympathy for the pallid and characterless Anne and manage not only to invest her with something of personality but to match her with her other cousin Colonel Fitzwilliam, which always strikes me as hard luck on the Colonel. Many too find it hard to believe, in the long term, in the professed contentment of Charlotte and her expectation of reasonable happiness in wedlock with Mr Collins.

The endings of Austen's novels, heralded by the tell-tale compression of the pages before us, at least do not come as an untimely shock to the reader. The end of the TV series *Blakes 7* on 21 December 1981 was violent, unexpected and disconcerting to most of those who saw it. True, the series had always been dark, more pessimistic than most. The rebels had scored odd successes but had seldom seriously threatened the totalitarian Federation they opposed. Blake himself had disappeared after Season 2 (when the actor, Gareth Thomas, returned to the RSC). His crew had searched for him intermittently through the third Season, only to hear in its last episode that he was dead (though since the character who said so was a noted liar, one couldn't be sure). Two other crew members were definitely dead (three if one counts the talking computer Zen) and throughout Season 4 the tone grew darker, the rebels more desperate and disunited.

But the final episode, 'Blake', still came as a shock to the system. Avon, in Blake's absence the crew's increasingly paranoid and unstable leader, tracked him down to a planet called Gauda Prime and took the crew looking for him. Avon's attitude to Blake had always been ambivalent. He didn't share Blake's idealism or his enthusiasm for the revolution but seemed susceptible to his personal charisma. At least, throughout the first two seasons he had sniped at and challenged him verbally, yet constantly backed him up when it came to action, and at the end of Season 3 his fruitless search for Blake lost the rebels their space-ship Liberator and one of its crew members. Now he went looking again, and found him. But when they met on Blake's new, secret rebel base, Avon misinterpreted what he saw and heard, thinking Blake had betrayed him, and shot him, three times and with a great deal of blood. (Gareth Thomas had agreed to come back and do the episode on condition his character ended up clearly dead.) Then it emerged that Blake's base had been penetrated by Federation troops, who shot all the remaining rebels except Avon, last seen raising his gun and smiling enigmatically as a number of shots rang out against a dark screen. To anyone who'd been subconsciously supposing the forces of evil could not finally triumph in a popular TV series, it was a hell of a run-up to Christmas.

If the death of Archie was a shock to his devotees among the *Hornblower* fans (see chapter 1), this was the sudden annihilation of a whole fictional universe. A fan, twenty years later, reminiscing on an unarchived mailing list:

> I remember being 12 years old, and feeling the stun and shock of what I would later come to learn was grief. Discussing our disbelief at school the next day. The futile letters of protest to the BBC. They took my friends away.
>
> – PW

Fans were divided, and still are, between those who thought the bleak, chaotic ending had a great rightness and inevitability and those who thought it had to do with the BBC's lukewarm attitude to any programme, however successful, which was vaguely SF or futuristic. Nothing, of course, prevents both from being true. But even those who basically approve of the ending sometimes like, when writing fan fiction, to find ways around its bleak finality. This is not all that difficult. Chris Boucher, the programme's script editor, had written the episode so that if it did turn out to be the ending, it would be a fitting one, but if the BBC (and Thomas) did relent, all would not be lost. The troopers could have been using stun-guns, the shots might not have been fatal. Blake himself was definitely meant to be dead, but then again, who could tell what futuristic medical technology might be able to do?

From this developed a considerable archive of sequel stories, known in this fandom as PGP (post-Gauda Prime). The technical details of How People Survive are perhaps the least important – there are any number of possible ways, from the quite simple, as outlined above, through to far more elaborate ones. It's all a chemically-induced hallucination in someone's head; the figure which appeared to be Blake was in fact a clone of him (at least one exists in the canon); Avon, wandering in a grief-stricken haze afterwards, inadvertently does a favour to an alien life form which can bring the dead back to life (Belatrix Carter's 'Bargaining Stage', as yet unpublished). What matters far more than how they survive is how the survivors are then going to come to terms with what has happened – in particular how Avon and Blake, if they survive, can come to terms with the fact that Avon shot Blake. The possibilities are many. Jenner's 'Swept and Garnished', from the fanzine *Tales from Space City 5*,[6] plays on Avon's canonical penchant for extreme remorse, taking both its title and its inspiration from Kipling's Great War story about a woman haunted by the ghosts of slaughtered children. (Kipling himself of course had borrowed the phrase from the Bible.) This fic also has a slash element, since it assumes there was a sexual relationship or the desire for one:

> At first he simply lay there, his eyes fixed upon me. It was difficult to clean up the blood with him in the way but I did my best. Now that they have moved me to the white room it is easier. He sits in the corner, knees drawn up. I am no longer distracted by the holes in his guts and can get on with my work. He will approve of me when every speck is gone.
>
> Of course I was at somewhat less than my best to begin with, using my clothes and my hands to soak up the larger pools. Now that they have provided me with mop and buckets I go much faster. So many particles to find. If I had Orac I would not have to plan vectors and trajectories in my head. A gushing flood from the first shot, less from the second, a slowing trickle from the third. Remember to think in three dimensions. The blood flew up and out. Check the walls and ceiling. Look for flesh and keep it separate. When I am done I will take the blood to him and put it back. My hands will fit the jigsaw of his torn flesh together, piece by piece. What I have always dreamed of will be mine. My palms sliding down his chest, making a pathway for my lips. I will tongue him to completion, body and soul. I will close his eyes with kisses.

> The others come and go, talking, always talking. I do not know them. The sounds are garbled, incomprehensible. I ignore them. There is only one voice I shall ever hear again, one light in my darkness.
>
> I am very tired.

The proportion of PGPs in *B7* fan fiction is high, which probably reflects not only the abruptness but the bleakness of its canonical end: artistically satisfying as it might have been, it was hard to live with. There has recently been a book-based parallel to this in the sequel fics written to Philip Pullman's trilogy for young people, *His Dark Materials*[7]. At the end of this, the young hero and heroine, Will and Lyra, are literally worlds apart, trapped in their alternate universes and without the prospect of ever meeting again, though they have strong feelings for each other. When the book came out, opinion on fan message boards was divided, some protesting bitterly at the sad ending, others arguing that it was right for the book. Fanfic writers on the whole seem to go with the latter: at least they are not writing AUs which would change the actual ending, but sequel fics, set in some cases years later, which try to find a way for Will and Lyra to meet again. See, for example, 'The Game' by Green Eyes, 'Bonds of Love' by Allyson Potter, and 'The Silver Portal' by Snoopy, all at fanfiction.net[8]. What these writers are saying, basically, is that they feel the ending is artistically right for the book but can't live with its lack of hope.

Another strong possibility for *B7* sequels was what would happen if Blake not only survived but actually won his war. The more politically-minded *B7* fanfic writers like to speculate on how his idealism would survive the transition to power (often not well, in this most pessimistic of universes). In Una McCormack's 'The Last Days of Roj Blake', published in the fanzine *ttba*[9], Blake, having overthrown the president of a corrupt government, has become a Cromwellian figure, on the brink of allowing himself to be declared (rather than elected) president as a temporary measure to restore order. His followers (here, Cally and Avon) are concerned that temporary will turn to permanent:

> "Look up, Avon."
>
> I shook my head in irritation but did as she asked. The moon was full but the sky was clouded. The domes had been badly damaged during the fighting. As an emblem of federation control, they had quickly become a focus for the sort of mindless violence that appears

> to grip crowds as soon as they're given the chance. Blake hadn't seen any problem in it, arguing that the domes were a better target for people's anger than each other – and I rather suspected that he liked the symbolism. Of course, it was sheer stupidity. It was senseless to open up the population to the elements. Winter was coming on, and the weather was getting colder in corridors and levels that had once had their climates completely controlled. No wonder the natives were getting restless.
>
> "Yes, Cally, the sky is still there. Now can we get back to the matter at hand?"
>
> She smiled at me and I had to work hard to hide my irritation.
>
> "I was brought up on a planet without domes. [...] I can't imagine what it must be like to feel rain for the first time, or hear a thunderstorm and watch lightning. These events must seem extraordinary, almost out of control. Rather like everyday life."

Sequel universes can often become novel-length or longer, eg S Lewis's *B7* sequel 'Careless Whispers' on the Liberated site[10] or Flamingo's *Starsky & Hutch* slash sequel 'Total Eclipse of the Heart'[11]. Though set in a pre-existing universe with pre-existing characters they leave more scope for the fic writer than stories set within the time-line of canon, because the characters and relationships can quite plausibly develop beyond anything that happened in canon. 'Total Eclipse of the Heart', for instance, starts, as several other sequels to that series have done, from the assumption that in the final episode of the canon, 'Sweet Revenge', where Starsky nearly dies, he and his partner realise that they are or want to be lovers. Watching the episode, one might be forgiven for supposing that the canon writers (Joe Reb Moffley and Steven Nelevansky) were dropping frantic hints to that effect, but it never unequivocally happened and is thus fertile territory for fanfic writers.

Only closed canons can have sequels, as such. But prequels can happen in any universe. Very often, they take the form of "how did such-and-such a character get to be the way he is?" Nat's 'Lost Boys', archived on *The Bill's* gen fanfic site[12] supposes that *The Bill's* hard-as-nails DS John Boulton came from an abusive background; the narrator is his elder brother, who ran away from their violent father and feels guilty for having left John behind. With rather more canonical evidence, *Hornblower* prequel fics sometimes focus on Archie Kennedy's assumed abuse at the hands of Jack Simpson.

In *B7*, the focus may be on prequel relationships between the characters (since the show obligingly made it clear that one at least had had part of his memory chemically expunged, there is much scope) or on the politics of the universe. How, for instance, does Blake, canonically born into the privileged Alpha class, become a rebel? Executrix's 'Purple Haze' (*ttba*), a sort of AU-ish prequel, suggests a violently suppressed campus protest with strong and intentional echoes of the sixties Kent State protest in the USA:

> "We set the guns to stun, eh? one of the troopers had asked, earlier. You couldn't tell which one – they'd removed all ID from their uniforms and because there'd be tear gas, they all had their helmets on.
>
> "Fuck, no," the section leader said.
>
> "Then we fire over their heads," another trooper said confidently.
>
> "I see anyone doing that, sunshine, and there'll be a court martial – that is, unless they find him with the big hole in the front and the little'un in the back."
>
> "Section Leader, we can't shoot them – they're just a bunch of kids like us."
>
> "They're nothing to do with us. When we're out in the colonies up to our necks in slime and lasers, they're getting puking-drunk on beer and spending Daddy's money on drugs."
>
> "Sounds all right to me," another trooper said. "Throw in the free sex and I'll be filling up the application form."
>
> "This place isn't for the likes of us. It's for Alphas, and a Beta or two who can lick boots and pass exams."
>
> At first there were a few students in the centre of the plaza and a lot hanging around the edges. The groups interchanged some of their members. the viscast teams arrived, and the protest signs and the banners came out. Somebody walked up to the line of troopers, and stuck a daisy into a gun barrel.

Austen prequels are not that common. Her main characters tend to be quite young in the first place, though "how Mr and Mrs Bennett came to get married" has possibilities, as in Kara's 'Beauty and Folly'[13]. So does the shared boyhood of Darcy and Wickham and how their once-friendly relationship went so disastrously wrong. One rather moving *Emma* story is Dee Dee's 'Poor Miss Taylor', archived on the Republic site[14], which begins as a prequel in Miss Taylor's early days as governess to the Woodhouse girls. Mr Knightley, then aged 20, calls, and Miss Taylor is much taken with him but knows nothing can come of it because of the gap in their social status. Emma, at this point only four, has a brief conversation with him which not only sounds very like Emma at four but has a curious and slightly uncomfortable edge for us, knowing as we do how his affection for this child will turn into something else as she grows:

> "How do you do, Mr. Knightley?" Isabella greeted him shyly.
>
> Emma, on the other hand, broke away from her governess and ran to him, her short blond curls bouncing and her cheeks flushing with excitement. "Mr. Knightley!" she cried, flinging herself into his arms. She pressed her small red lips against his cheek.
>
> Mr. Knightley laughed and situated the child on his lap. "How are you today, Little Emma?" he asked with a broad grin.
>
> "I was finding husbands for all my dolls."
>
> "Ah! I see, and what was your success?"
>
> "They are not married yet because Miss Taylor came and took me away."
>
> Anne had returned to her seat, and watched this exchange with amusement and something like tenderness. She was very impressed with this Mr. Knightley – so tall and handsome and gentlemanly and...
>
> Her thoughts were interrupted when Mr. Knightley teased, "Miss Taylor, you should not have forced Little Emma to postpone such an important event for her dolls. One of the husbands-to-be might catch some ill wind and fall fatally ill before the wedding can take place."
>
> "No, Mr. Knightley," insisted Emma, "I decide what happens to my dolls. They only die if I make them die, and I shan't do that before the wedding."

Nor do prequels seem terribly popular in the Discworld universe. It is possible that book characters, by and large, have more back-story than characters from film and TV series, simply because there's more time to fill it in. Of course one danger of prequels, in any open canon, is that the original writers may suddenly decide to fill in gaps and render your story incompatible with canon, an AU. This doesn't bother all fanfic writers, but it puts off some, and because of the uncertain and shifting nature of time in the Discworld, it is more likely to happen there than in most universes. *Night Watch*[15] takes Vimes back in time to confront him with an alternative future and in the process shows us the past of half the major characters in Ankh-Morpork: it must have rendered many prequel stories uncanonical at a stroke. Rozi's prequel story 'Bad Influence'[16], written and posted before *Night Watch* came out, was actually partly rewritten in the light of it – presumably the author was not happy for it to become an AU.

Indeed this possibility puts some writers off working in an open canon at all. To quote an author from a closed canon, on an unarchived mailing list:

> Well, fanfic is in large part about filling in the gaps in canon. And for a series-in-progress, how do you know where the gaps *are?* A question that's unanswered now may be answered in great detail next week. The mysterious character back-story or dangling plot thread may not stay mysterious or dangling. [...] I think I'd feel a natural disinclination to spend my time filling in the gaps when canon is likely to come along and tell me I filled them in wrong. I mean, I'd find that kind of discouraging.
>
> – Belatrix Carter

There is even a word for it: a story wrong-footed by a later canon development is sometimes said to be "jossed", from the name of Joss Whedon, creator of Buffy the Vampire Slayer, whose unexpected plot twists and penchant for filling in gaps were particularly likely to make this happen. Not that scriptwriters are regarded as infallible when it comes to the canon. During *The Bill's* first seismic shift, under the producer Richard Handford, it suited the scriptwriters to decide that police officers Dave Quinnan and Polly Page had known each other before they joined the police; had in fact been childhood sweethearts. This was not so much filling in a gap as creating one that had never existed – Dave's and Polly's behaviour to each other up to then had simply not been that of people with a shared past and the fanfic writers, almost to a woman, refused to accept it as canonical. Sometimes an apparent canonical inconsistency like this will trigger "fix-it" fics that try to find a logic in the situation, as mentioned in Chapter 2, but this one seems to have been thought beyond fixing.

"Crossovers" involve a character or characters from one fictional universe crossing into another. This may be, and often is, done for humorous reasons but often it is making a more serious point. In a way it is an extension of the penchant of fanfic writers for using references and comparisons from other fictional sources; it is done because the author feels this can somehow cast light on the universe being explored, or perhaps, by putting a character in an unfamiliar world, help him see himself in a new light. Catbert's 'Origins'[17], a light-hearted *The Bill/Doctor Who* crossover fic, uses a *Bill* convention whereby bit-part characters have become collectively known to the fans as "Trev" and suggests that Trev is really a Time Lord, who has set up his Tardis in the station. The point the fic is making, in a satirical way, is one about the unacceptably fast turnover of officers in the show at the time, and the unrealistic explanations given for it by the scriptwriters:

> He had to admit, though, that he'd made a few mistakes. On several occasions now he had forgotten to close the inner door of the console room. He'd been quite startled one day to find Debbie Keane wandering through the seemingly endless inner corridors, although not as startled as she was – she'd only popped in for a new pencil, and certainly hadn't expected to find herself in a cupboard which was apparently many times larger than the building which housed it. He explained the situation to Debbie, and, when she demanded proof, took her on a quick spin around the beauty spots of the Universe. Unfortunately, Debbie hadn't wanted to come back. This had made things slightly tricky, but the Council allowed him special dispensation to alter the time-line. He did the work well; no-one at the station noticed she had gone, because she had never even been there.
>
> And she hadn't been the first. The excuses he'd had to think up for some of the others were harder than anything else he'd had to do here on Earth. Only once had he allowed an officer to think up his own cover story, and that had been so far fetched he wasn't going to take the risk again. After all, who could seriously believe Nick Slater was going off to work undercover?
>
> They'd been lucky to get away with that one.

Crossovers, like some other departures from canon, can also be a means of liberating the characters from their author and his specific voice. The way crossovers, or crossover elements, like one fic in the style of another author, work can be quite unexpected. One of the oddest I ever read was 'Green Eggs and Hamlet' by Sinclaire[18]. As the title might indicate, this is the conversation between Hamlet and his father's ghost, done in the style of a Dr Seuss poem, with its cumulative repetition:

> Would you stab him
> In his bed?
> Put a dagger through
> His head?
>
> I would not stab him
> In his bed.
> Or put a dagger through
> His head.[...]

I would not kill him
Here or there.
I would not kill
Him anywhere.

On the face of it, it sounds like something which could only be humorous. But the actual effect of the ghost's repeated badgering and Hamlet's resistance is more like angst than humour; it throws stress on his terrible anguish and helplessness in a way that is all the more chilling for its nursery-rhyme context.

One would expect to find differences between book-based and film/TV-based fanfic when it comes to "missing scenes", and I did. These are incidents, conversations, interactions, that take place within the timescale of canon and are compatible with canon, that might have happened and in some cases must have happened, but which are not seen on the page or the screen. Heathcliff's four years away is a "missing scene".

On the screen, missing scenes may well be missing because of time constraints in scripts which must be capable of playing out in an hour, or half an hour. In such situations scenes based on conversations and relationship development often lose out to action and plot. The early scripts for *The Bill* deliberately excluded much personal life, so there were tempting gaps to be filled. Some of the original *B7* scripts still exist, with canonical "missing scenes" which were cut for time reasons. The script for 'Rumours of Death' (Chris Boucher, extract archived at Judith Proctor's *Blakes 7* web site[19] shows the kind of scene that was liable to be cut. The two characters, Grenlee and Forres, are Federation soldiers guarding a presidential conference. Though they work for a totalitarian government they are not, in themselves, evil, just normal guys working for a living and obeying orders (which is true of a lot of Federation operatives). We are in fact being encouraged at this point to see through their eyes and come to know them, which will provide an interesting exercise for our loyalties when the good guys gun them down. While on duty with not much to do, they chat. Some of the conversation survived, but not this bit:

FORRES	What's the President like?
GRENLEE	Her own way mostly, why?
FORRES	No I mean what's she like as a person?
GRENLEE	She isn't a person. She's a president.
FORRES	And a woman.

GRENLEE	Idle speculation, Section Leader.
FORRES	I wonder what makes her so special, though? When you think about it there's thousands of men ready to die for her.
GRENLEE	Every man needs something to believe in, Forres. There are no exceptions to that. It's a universal rule.
FORRES	If you say so, sir.
GRENLEE	I do say so. Just be grateful you joined the service and you don't have to worry about what to believe in. It's all laid out for you.
FORRES	Oh I am grateful, sir.
GRENLEE	I mean it. Some men have to find their own faith.
FORRES	Tough.
GRENLEE	It can be, Section Leader. There's only one thing more dangerous than a man looking for something to believe in. And that's a man who thinks he's found something.

This little conversation may not have advanced the plot, but from an artistic point of view it's a shame it went missing. It is loaded with irony and portent: Grenlee, who has no illusions about the President, will die in defence of her (and in the process frustrate a justified revolt) because what he believes in is not her but his duty. Meanwhile Avon, who constantly denies having any ideals or faith whatever, is about to risk his life to exact revenge for something that never happened, because of his misplaced faith in someone else. Later in the series, he will twice court disaster, and both times find it, because he "thinks he's found something", both literally and to believe in.

It is this kind of scene which is very liable to turn up in fanfic. And it can shadow and deepen the canon in the same way this would have done. Una McCormack's 'Five Days' on the Aquitar web site[20] is a missing scene from 'Rumours of Death'. In the episode, Avon spends five days in a Federation torture cell as part of a plan to capture an infamous torturer and exact revenge on him. The fic shows these five days from the viewpoints of his crewmates and thereby explores their feelings about him and themselves. One of them, Cally, has opposed his actions with a personal bitterness which her professed motive, a distaste for revenge, would not seem to justify. The fic suggests that her attitude has to do with her canonical telepathy:

> He clearly has no idea that I can feel just about everything that they do to him. Three days it has been, and I have not slept either, and I have felt all his pain and his fear and his despair. I have not been able to leave my room for the last few hours because I am unable to focus on anything else, and I saw that Vila was starting to get suspicious. I do not want anyone to know what he is going through.

This is a missing scene that actually must have happened in some form: while Avon was in his cell his crewmates must have been doing something. A similar example from *Hornblower* involves the death of Archie Kennedy. In the canon ('Retribution'), Hornblower is accused of pushing a former captain down a hold and is in some danger of death. Archie, who is in the infirmary having been shot, and reckons he will die anyway, finds out what is afoot, turns up at the court-martial and himself confesses, probably falsely, to the crime (he dies of his wound before they can hang him). Between the point when he finds out the truth and the point when he turns up to testify, we are ourselves in the courtroom and elsewhere, so we do not see Archie make his decision. This is a gap to tempt any fanfic writer, especially since Bush is conveniently also present in the infirmary to witness and report, and many have provided their versions of the scene in question, focusing both on Archie's motivation for acting and Bush's for not stopping him.

Another example of a far longer missing Archie scene is Kathy Kirchner's 'The Ties That Bind'[21]. This is close to a "fix-it" fic in that it sets out to solve the question of why the Archie who turned up in the later *Hornblower* films is so much more confident and less defeatist than the same character had been in earlier appearances. In this fic, he suffers a seaboard accident resulting in temporary memory loss. This proves a blessing, since without the memories of abuse which have haunted him, his naturally chirpy and outgoing nature emerges, and by the time the memories come back he is confident enough to deal with them.

But novelists, unlike TV scriptwriters, do not have to make the story fit a certain time slot and leave out scenes which, from an artistic point of view, they might have preferred to keep. If a novelist chooses to skate over a certain scene it is liable to be *for* artistic reasons, because, in the writer's view, the book is better without it. (True, in *Barchester Towers*, Trollope candidly admits that we shall not see the Bishop enthroned because our author does not know the details of the ceremony and can't be bothered to find out. But we are probably rather grateful than otherwise for this. If the scene had for any reason been necessary, we may be sure he would have stirred himself to research it.)

In Austen fanfic, missing scenes sometimes involve exactly the kind of romantic scenarios which Austen preferred to leave out, or at least to render in reported speech or paraphrase. In *Pride and Prejudice* the only proposal in which we are allowed to hear the voices of both parties is that of Mr Collins to Elizabeth, and this is a comic scene. When Darcy first proposes to her, he is allowed four brief sentences in his own voice before the scene goes into reported speech. All we know of the substance of his proposal is that "he spoke well" but "was not more eloquent on the subject of tenderness than of pride". From Bingley's proposal to Jane we are absent altogether and on Darcy's second try we hear his voice – the three sentences there are of it – but this time Elizabeth has gone into reported speech and whatever emotion she may have expressed is buried in "gave him to understand that her sentiments had undergone so material a change... as to make her receive with gratitude and pleasure his present assurances". She only recovers her voice for the reader when, the proposal safely over, she can gently tease Darcy.

All writers play to their own strengths, and it is hard not to suspect that Austen really just didn't much like doing love scenes in which romantic sentiment could not be undercut with either humour or conflict. But her judgement was surely sound anyway. In this fandom, I have read some very treacly missing love scenes and some far better ones, in which the voices convince thoroughly. But I can't think of one "missing love scene" that actually adds anything to the story or gives a new perspective on it. "Bingley's Proposal" by Carolyn[22] is believable enough; it could well have happened that way and in more or less those words but there is nothing in it one couldn't live without, as Austen evidently realised.

The same, by and large, goes for missing scenes which do little more than spell out emotions where Austen herself did not choose to, though sometimes these can surprise or move. Martine's 'Le long retour vers Donwell', written in French and translated by Barbara and archived in both French and English at the Republic of Pemberley web site[23], is a missing scene from *Emma,* Mr Knightley riding home after the Coles' party. He is disturbed by Frank Churchill's attentions to Emma, but he does not yet realise his own feelings for her. Rather he sees her as a family member, a sister almost, whom he has known from a child, and he attributes his reluctance to see her and Frank as a couple to an unwillingness to acknowledge the passage of time. His mind goes back to a moment when he saw her unexpectedly, framed by a sunlit window, and realised she was not the child he still saw in his mind:

> "She might very well say that she never wishes to marry, but upon my word, such beauty and spirit will not long remain without admirers," he thought. And the place in which he kept all his affection for his sister-in-law was invaded by an unspeakable regret and awareness of the passage of time. There, imperceptibly, silently, and without a hope of return, the image of Emma the child, long a source of joy and sometimes pain to him gave way to that of Emma already a young woman, radiant in the disappearing sunlight.

This is a delicate parallel to Emma's feeling, in the novel, that "Mr Knightley must never marry", because it would upset the cosy situation to which she has become used. It takes her a long time to see that what she really means is "Mr Knightley must marry no one but herself". Their almost-brother-and-sister relationship and perhaps also the age difference between them have prevented them from recognising each other as lovers. In the novel we see this situation entirely from Emma's viewpoint and seldom if ever reflect that it must be the same for him, with the added complication that the difference in their ages cannot but be more painful to him, the elder. 'Le long retour vers Donwell', like Elspeth's 'At the Club', is a scene we would not get from Austen since it is all-male, and it is among the male characters and minor characters that Austen fanfic most often succeeds in creating a new perspective or deepening an old one.

AUs, in some fandoms, are known as "what ifs". They are deliberate departures from canon; what if this, and not that, had happened. They can be pure curiosity on the writer's part, a desire to go down a road not taken, or they can be attempts to alter something the writer really wishes hadn't happened in canon. The name "AU" comes from the idea, familiar in futuristic fiction, that there might be any number of parallel universes in which the same people live out different destinies. But the idea that one man might have different potential fates, and that there are turning-points in his life at which he goes down one of these paths rather than another, is a lot older than science fiction. In the 14th-century Icelandic *Grettir's Saga* the eponymous hero fights and defeats a fearsome ghost, Glam. Before he dies,

Glam makes it clear that for Grettir, this is such a turning point:

> ... I can tell you this, that you have now acquired half the strength and development that was intended for you if you had never met me... I can ensure that you never become any stronger than you are now... you have become renowned up to now for your deeds but from now on you will become guilty of crimes and deeds of violence."[24]

Charles Dickens, in *A Christmas Carol*, gives his hero more choice than Grettir: Scrooge is shown in a dream one of his possible futures and given a chance to avoid it and opt for something else. The fanfic writer Predatrix used this precedent as her conscious model for 'A Midwinter Carol', (unarchived at the time of writing), a *B7* AU on a favourite theme: what if Blake hadn't left the crew at the end of Season 2. In the series, he leaves more or less by accident, when the crew temporarily have to abandon *Liberator*; some get back but Blake does not. He is briefly in contact with the crew and they have a location for him, but somehow this comes to nothing and contact is lost. This is a temptingly unexplained gap, which has inspired many a missing scene. But one reasonable assumption is that Blake doesn't want to be contacted, because of the tension and apparent animosity there had been between himself and Avon just before he left, culminating in Avon's statement "I want to be free of him." If he stays away because of this, then Avon has effectively driven him away.

This is the situation at the start of 'A Midwinter Carol'. Avon, like Scrooge, is then sent a vision of what will happen if Blake doesn't return, culminating in the bloody debacle on Gauda Prime, and is given the chance, which he takes, to undo his actions.

An AU may also be a chance to make the reader think again about some aspect of the canon. A quite common AU in fanfics based on *Romeo and Juliet* is to alter the sex of one of the lovers. Some of the Romeo/Mercutio stories archived at the Slash Cotillion[25], such as 'Servants with Torches' by Jane St Clair and 'Mercutio' by Joram, play on the fact that a Romeo in love with Mercutio would have to practise much the same concealment as one in love with Juliet, and face even more certain death. 'Some Day', by mintyfreshsocks[26] has Romeo wake up in Tybalt's bed rather than Juliet's. Often enough, *Romeo and Juliet* fics (and other Shakespeare fics) are written by young people studying the play at school (in fact they frequently stem from classroom exercises), and this variation on "star-crossed" love seems to speak to them more directly than bitter family feuds and a situation where a girl had no choice in marriage. Modern profic versions of *Romeo and Juliet* have often placed the lovers in a more repressive culture or put new obstacles in their way in an attempt to recreate a situation which it is hard for us to appreciate in the same way that Shakespeare's audience did. In *West Side Story* the new barrier was race; in Alun Owen's *Progress to the Park*[27], set in the Liverpool of the Sixties, religion. These *Romeo and Juliet* fan fiction writers are effectively using homophobia in the same way. Such fics can also be used to make readers rethink their attitudes. 'Some Day' does not, until the next morning, identify Romeo's lover:

> He smiled down at the body that lay next to him, entangled in his arms.
> "Good morning," he said.
> Tybalt groaned and stretched, yawning widely.

From then on it is made clear that they are no different from the original star-crossed lovers, as innocent:

> "The sun is starting to come up." It was something that neither of them wanted to hear.
> "Don't leave yet," Tybalt said. He pulled Romeo closer. "I've missed you." He ran his hands through Romeo's hair, and then cradled his face.

and as persecuted:

> Tybalt kissed Romeo again. "Some day. . ." he said. "Some day." Romeo knew what he meant. Some day, we can be together without fear. Some day, we can lie in bed until noon, asleep in each other's arms. It was a day that Romeo wanted badly and knew would never come.

It isn't always obvious to a non-fanfic reader when a missing scene turns into an AU. Basically, to be completely compatible with canon, a missing scene must leave things in the same state they would have been if it hadn't existed, and that means not just facts but characters and their relationships. Otherwise the logic of their later behaviour may be destroyed. If, for instance, someone wrote a *Pride and Prejudice* missing scene which involved Elizabeth doubting Wickham's veracity earlier in the novel, it would be an AU, because it would alter her subsequent behaviour; she would not later speak as she does to Darcy. But a scene which made someone else (eg Charlotte) doubt him would not necessarily be an AU: even if Charlotte passed on her doubts, Elizabeth could still ignore them, just as in the canon she shrugs off her father's evident coolness toward Wickham.

AUs often involve something which readers and writers of fanfic wish hadn't happened in the source material, either because they feel it was bad writing or because it was emotionally upsetting (eg involving a character's death). *B7* fans tend to want to change the course of two episodes, 'Star One', where Blake leaves, and above all 'Blake', in which he and just about everyone else gets shot. In *The Bill* fanfic, a favourite "what if" involves the death of John Boulton at the hands of fellow-officer Beech. Catherine and Jayne have both written AU stories ('Queen of my Heart'[28] and 'Saying Goodbye'[29]) in which Boulton's girlfriend Claire Stanton goes to the fatal meeting instead of him. (By and large, female characters are less popular than male with fanfic's mostly female constituency, and *The Bill* fans would certainly rather have lost Stanton than Boulton.) The death of Archie Kennedy in *Hornblower* triggered umpteen AU fics and presented writers with an added difficulty: his canonical death had been a noble, self-sacrificial one, and preserving the nobility while altering the ending takes some ingenuity. Green's fic 'Unacceptable'[30] solves it, rather callously from the point of view of the fans of Lt Bush, by having Bush drug Archie and take his place. This would of course be every bit as unacceptable to Bush fans as the canonical version was to Archie fans, but that is the virtue of AUs: there is a world to suit everyone if you can either write it or find someone who has.

AUs, like crossovers, can also be a means of getting away from the original author's voice and showing "his characters" from an angle he did not. Executrix, on an unarchived mailing list, has pointed to "the reciprocal light that characters in one property can shine on those in another", and in her own fanfic has used different timelines and locations in much the same way, so that Blake turns up in the Thirties Berlin of *Cabaret* in 'Wanderjahr'[31]. Executrix likes her fics to be unclassifiable, and it's debatable whether this is an AU or a crossover; it uses the location of *Cabaret* but rather than having the characters of *B7* interacting with those of *Cabaret*, the first are assimilated into the second; this is how Blake might have acted had he been in this place at this time. The same could be said of some of the modern-day versions of *Pride and Prejudice* on the Hyacinth's Garden web site[32], like Amber Leah Marie's 'All That's Best of Dark and Bright', in which Darcy has become a detective on the homicide squad, and

Heather Lynn's 'Longbourn and Pemberley Go To War', which opens with the words "Elizabeth Bennet sat at her computer".

Discworld fans have more scope for AUs than most, since they are canonical fact in the series due to the Pratchett concept of the Trousers of Time. This is basically just a typically quirky Pratchett variant on the "turning point" concept of *Grettir's Saga*: every so often, life heads off down one leg of the Trousers of Time rather than the other. The difference is that in a universe full of magic, this can with any luck be reversed. An instance of Pratchett's own use of the Trousers of Time scenario occurs in *Jingo*[33], when Vimes has to choose one of two courses of action. Pratchett, deciding to have it both ways, contrives to show us not only the one he chooses but the one he doesn't choose, which would lead to Vimes' death and the loss of the city in battle. Several Discworld fics, like Miss Malice's 'Loose Ends'[34] and JD's 'The End'[35] explore the consequences for Vetinari and the city had Vimes indeed chosen this route.

The existence of the Trousers of Time may also be partly responsible for the fact that Discworld writers and readers seem slightly readier than those in other fandoms to accept "character death" in fan fiction. In most fanfic writing, it is still something of a taboo to kill off the canonical characters (unless of course they died in the canon). Some fanfic readers avoid reading character death and it is etiquette to post a warning on a story which contains it. Even granted that many readers are "character junkies", who may care greatly for certain characters, I have never entirely understood this. After all, fanfic stories are in essence an infinite number of AUs and what happens in one story need have no effect on all the rest. If a character is killed off in one fic, he can live on in the next (or indeed be resurrected: fanfic writers are more ingenious about that than Conan Doyle could have dreamed of).

Nonetheless, it still upsets some readers. Discworld writers, like those in other fandoms, warn of character death but they do seem readier to write it. This may be not only because, in this one universe, it is readily reversible but also because Death is himself a prominent character in the Discworld universe, frequently taking a hand in the action, and because characters who die in the canon seem to have some kind of afterlife.

The one aspect of canon that is not usually up for alteration is the nature of the characters. To some fanfic readers, these are the most important aspect of their fanfic universe and of any story set in it, which is why, as we shall see later, some do not like original characters playing any major part. But even readers who don't class themselves as "character junkies" and to whom the fanfic universe is as important as any of the characters who inhabit it will have a firm idea of what those characters are like and won't stand for interpretations that strike them as wildly off-beam. Some of the most vituperative reviews you will ever read are those written by Austen fans about the various Emma Tennant Austen sequels, and the reason for the animosity is that fans do not feel they are true to the characters. To quote from the reviews on the Republic website:

> Darcy metamorphoses completely from the Fitzwilliam we all know and love from Jane Austen. He changes into this cold, scheming, arrogant, haughty man that he appears to be in the beginning of Pride and Prejudice. This time, he really (supposedly) is that way.
>
> – Rachel Schneider on An Unequal Marriage[36]

> And where, dare I ask, is Georgiana? Apparently Georgiana has been abducted by aliens and everyone's memory has been wiped clean of her, because I remember no reference to her whatsoever in *An Unequal Marriage*. However, after Tennant's bad choice in making Georgiana a giggling protégé of Caroline Bingley in *Pemberley,* I suppose I should count that as a blessing.
>
> The one part of this book that did bring a short-lived smile to my face was seeing Caroline Bingley a lonely, dependent spinster, getting her jollies by talking about other people's misfortunes. This smile was promptly replaced by a frown when Elizabeth fails miserably in parrying her attacks—maybe the real Elizabeth has been abducted by aliens too, and is out in the universe somewhere with Georgiana.
>
> – Ree, on the same book, archived at the same reference

In the introduction to her *B7* fanzine *Bend Me, Shape Me*[37], Nova explained why she had chosen the title:

> It comes from a song by Amen Corner which is, IMHO, the slash writer's anthem:
>
> Bend me, shape me,
> Any way you want me.
> As long as you love me,
> It's all right...

Actually it could be an anthem for fanfic writers generally, not just slash writers. The canon is for bending and shaping according to the fanfic writer's preference, but the "love" – i.e. basic respect for it – is important. That doesn't mean supposing the canon to be perfect. Most fanfic writers are convinced they could improve on something about it; that is why many of them write. But because they care about it, they want it shaped rather than misshapen, bent rather than broken. And for no aspect is that more true than for the treatment of characters, for whom many fanfic writers and readers do quite genuinely feel love.

Fanfic writers do not speak or think of "my characters" as Anne Rice does in her anti-fanfic statement. But they do speak and think of "our characters", a shared resource that the whole community of that fandom feels it knows and cares about. You can set the story in a different timeline, cross it with other fictions, write before it began or after it ended or even make it go in a different direction. But in the end you must work with a particular set of people and whatever situation you put them in, they must behave and speak like themselves. Not that you will ever get a complete consensus among fans on that subject; naturally there are different interpretations of certain aspects of the canon characters, but if too many readers feel "that's not them", then the story will have failed as fanfic, however else it may succeed.

NOTES

1. Hodder & Stoughton, 1993
2. Sceptre 1995
3. University of Chicago Press 1993
4. http://www.pemberley.com/index.html 11.12.02
5. http://www.pemberley.com/derby/lou24.cfcm.html 18.11.02
6. ed. Helen Patrick, 2002
7. Random House, 1995-2000
8. http://www.fanfiction.net/ 9.12.02
9. ed. Tavia, 2001
10. http://www.liberated.org.uk 11.11.02
11. http://www.squidge.org/~flamingo/eclipse/index.htm 11.11.02
12. http://web.archive.org/web/20030626192330/212.67.202.77/~tbff/lost boys.html 2.10.02
13. http://www.pemberley.com/derby/kara2.baf.html 18.11.02
14. http://www.pemberley.com/derby/olde/dee1.htm 6.11.02
15. Doubleday 2002
16. http://www.fanfiction.net/s/658959/1/ 25.01.03

17. http://212.67.202.77/~tbff/origins.html 6.12.02
18. http://www.fanfiction.net/s/799155/1/ 31.12.01
19. http://www.hermit.org/Blakes7/Episodes/scripts/RumoursExtra.html 23.9.02
20. http://163.1.246.40/~rmb/Blakes7/ 8.11.02
21. http://www.fanfiction.net/s/1174176/1/ 20.04.03
22. http://www.pemberley.com/derby/olda/carolyn2.htm 18.11.02
23. http://www.pemberley.com/derby/oldc/martine1.htm 24.03.03
24. *Three Icelandic Outlaw Sagas*, tr. and ed. Anthony Faulkes, Everyman 2001
25. http://cotillion.slashcity.org 04.03'03
26. http://www.fanfiction.net/s/924723/1/ 27.05.02
27. *New English Dramatists Vol.5* Penguin, 1962
28. http://web.archive.org/web/20030626202305/212.67.202.77/~tbff/queenofmyheart.html
29. http://web.archive.org/web/20030421003650/212.67.202.77/~tbff/saying-goodbye.html 23.9.02
30. http://www.fanfiction.net/s/1009249/1/ 5.12.02
31. http://www.liberated.org.uk 31.12.02
32. http://www.geocities.com/tinker_belladonna/directory.htm
33. Gollancz, 1997
34. http://www.fanfiction.net/s/862223/1/ 25.11.02
35. http://discfanfic.tripod.com/jd/end.htm 10.01.03
36. http://www.pemberley.com/sequels/PandP/UnequalMarriage.html 4.11.02
37. ed Pat Fenech, 2000

4. Our Characters

From Canon to Mary Sue

So you have a cast of ready-made people (or aliens, trolls and werewolves), whom your readers already know and to whom they ascribe certain characteristics. In that respect, if in no other, you resemble Ancient Greek dramatists, working with the characters of myth, the writers of mediaeval morality plays with their cast of Bible characters, or some historical novelist bringing Queen Victoria or Napoleon into her pages. There are things you cannot do, and far more that you can. You cannot very easily tell your audience that Odysseus is a tall blond man with a speech impediment, but you can give him an unexpected streak of compassion, as Sophocles did in his *Ajax*. You cannot get away from the fact that Orestes killed his mother, but if you are Euripides you can make your audience re-examine that act, by presenting it not as justice inflicted by a champion of morality but as a sordid murder carried out by a sick, damaged man. You can re-interpret what your readers think they know. Indeed if you choose the more unfamiliar versions of myth, you can tell them that Helen was never at Troy at all; the gods created an illusion of her in order to start the war (Euripides again, basing his play on a poem by Stesichoros, the unlikely forerunner of many an SF plot).

If you are happy to regard canon, like history, as raw material for fiction, which can be tailored like any other raw material, you can create AUs and missing scenes. Dryden, in his play *All for Love*, could not resist an unhistorical set-piece confrontation scene between Cleopatra and Antony's wife Octavia, and from Schiller onwards, writers have been unwilling to accept that history was so poor a judge of drama as never to have arranged a meeting between Elizabeth I and Mary Queen of Scots.

And you can use minor characters, whose personalities and opinions are not so well established in the canon or known to your readers, to convey your own agenda, saying what might not sit easily in the mouths of your heroes. You can even invent your own characters and add them to the mix. Euripides uses the Greek herald Talthybios, little more than a name in myth, to suggest a dissenting view on the Trojan War, and no-one reading the 'York Realist's' Crucifixion play from the York mystery cycle can doubt that the frighteningly impervious workmen chatting over Christ's head and complaining about the quality of the nails are "original" characters, in so far as that is true of characters drawn from life.

All this is true of fan fiction writers, but it is true too that there are special circumstances and constraints, particularly on those whose canon is wholly or partly film or TV-based. We know very little about Achilles' looks or voice; we may have seen portraits of Elizabeth I but she does not, for most of us, have an individual presence – unless, indeed, it is that of Glenda Jackson from the 1970s BBC series *Elizabeth R*, or Miranda Richardson from *Blackadder II*[1]. For this is the big difference: the modern characters on whom fanfic is based are liable to have the face and voice of a particular actor whose interpretation is as much a part of them as was the original writer's concept.

With a book-based character, the author may or may not provide a detailed physical description. Austen, on the whole, tends not to. We know that Marianne and Elizabeth have dark eyes, but usually Austen prefers to give a general impression and let us fill it in. Mr Bingley is "good-looking" with a "pleasant countenance" and all we really know of Jane Bennet's appearance is that everyone considers her beautiful. But even a book-based character will have a distinctive voice supplied by the author; he or she will phrase things in a certain way and a fanfic author cannot decide their spoken idiom in the way that Euripides could for Orestes. These days, indeed, the name George Wickham is liable to conjure up for the reader not only a man who uses English in the way determined by Austen, but one who does so with the accent and mock-shy, dark-eyed glance of Adrian Lukis (who played the part in the Davies adaptation).

So fanfic authors are dealing with well-defined characters, whom readers and viewers think they know in far more detail than anyone ever knew Odysseus or Samson. Indeed for some readers, the so-called "character junkies", a particular character or set of characters will be key to their enjoyment, to the point that they may not want to read anything in which that character is not involved or where he acts in a way they can't see as true for him. So whatever other talents a fanfic writer has and wishes to practise, she must to some degree be mimetic, able to reproduce the character, created by writers, actors and others, who has become familiar, even real, to the reader.

However striking the ideas, however gripping the plot, if the voice is wrong nothing else will compensate for it. Fanfic readers are as appreciative of pure literary quality as any other group of readers, but one of the most complimentary pieces of feedback for a fanfic writer is still, referring to her re-creation of the characters, "that's so them". Not that she is liable to get that from everyone: there is naturally room for debate and disagreement about the characters in all fandoms, but she would probably be worried if too many readers objected "I can't see him doing this", or "he doesn't use that phrase".

This is probably why, until relatively lately in the history of the genre, fanfic was almost always written in the third person. To write first-person fiction from a character's viewpoint demands complete control of the voice. Not only in dialogue but throughout the story the voice must be kept up, and any lapse will be the more glaring. These days it is not so. Fanfic writers are more assured and more ambitious and in many fandoms you are as liable to read first as third person fanfic. Nevertheless, readers do not always like it. To quote a doubter:

> First-person pov used to be very rare in fandom. I'm not sure why that's changed. I think it makes it harder to "sell" a fanfic character from first person pov. The intimate nature of first-person means the writer and reader have to be on the same wavelength for the character to work.
>
> – Cami[2]

Cami suggests here that this is a problem specific to fan fiction, presumably because the reader feels she knows the pre-existing characters before the fanfic author ever gets at them. When, however, I raised this matter on a literary mailing list which had nothing to do with fan fiction, I got some unexpected feedback both from readers and writers of mainstream literary fiction. Many readers, it appears, simply would not pick up a novel written in the first person (a preference which must, one would think, somewhat restrict their reading). Among objections raised were that it was unrealistic; why would a person be telling his own story in this way, and that it tempted writers into telling you all the details of the character's motivation, rather than leaving his words and actions to speak for themselves. (This latter is probably true, though only of bad writers.) So the prejudice would seem to go beyond fan fiction, but nonetheless Cami has a point about the special character knowledge of the fanfic reader and the need for reader and writer to "see" the POV character in the same way.

As to why things have changed in this respect, I believe, as I said above, that it indicates increasing confidence and sophistication in fanfic writers. It is not the only respect in which fan fiction has become more adventurous, but that is for a later chapter.

I do still see a difference between book-based and TV-based fanfic when it comes to the use of first person. From what I have read, I should say it was far commoner in TV-based fanfic, which is hardly surprising. Screenplays consist of dialogue; the characters' voices are heard at every turn. Not only does this make them easier for a writer to assimilate; the reader, when she sees the words on the page (or screen, which is how web-based fanfic is often read), will "hear" them in the actor's voice. The ability of writers in some screen-based fandoms to write authentic dialogue for their character voices is truly astonishing, particularly with some characters. I have lost count of the number of times I have read Starsky dialogue which sounded as if the man were in the room speaking. This ability often transcends the boundaries of national speech: there are Americans who make *B7*'s characters sound as British as the Brits do and Australian fanfic writers who can catch the exact London cadences of *The Bill*. In a *Bill* fic by an Australian writer I was once puzzled by the use of the word "doris" as an adjective, plainly uncomplimentary. Thinking that the writer might for once have slipped up in idiom, I spent some time fruitlessly checking Australian slang. I should have known better. As soon as I checked *London* slang I found it: an 80s expression, apparently originated by city traders but now general London slang for an unattractive woman. I didn't know it, not being a Londoner and not being anywhere near as au fait with London slang as these specialists.

In a book, it makes some difference from the viewpoint of a fanfic writer whether there is a character-narrator (as in *Jane Eyre* or *Wuthering Heights*) or an authorial voice, as in Austen or Pratchett. In the former case the fanfic writer must imitate the character voice in much the same way she would that of a TV character. Even if she decides to tell the story from another character's viewpoint, this will apply. But in the case of a book with an authorial voice, it may sound very odd if she uses a character voice, since the voices of the characters will not be the authorial voice which told the original story. This is particularly so in the case of Pratchett, who has a very strong, individual authorial voice which is nothing like the voices of any of his characters. I have seen very little first person *Discworld* fanfic, and what I have read took some getting used to, because it lacked all flavour of the original. In a character voice all the dry comments, the footnotes, the conscious asides to the reader had to go missing or sound wrong for the character. Even when the character's voice had been perfectly well captured, it was not the *Discworld* voice. This paragraph from CorianderEisenhower's 'Purveyor'[3] is fairly typical of the kind of aside without which *Discworld* doesn't sound like itself but which will not go into any character voice:

> Events often hinge on little things we see from the corners of our eyes. Policemen learn to be very good at seeing out of the corners of their eyes; no self-respecting unlicensed criminal will stand in a policeman's direct line of vision. Though now, with the perversity of adaptation, the more intelligent criminals would walk cheerfully down the street, wave at the watchman patrolling, and be completely ignored by the dumb sod who was concentrating too hard on the periphery.

I came to the conclusion that the most important character in the Discworld is the authorial voice and that it would be very hard to write a successful *Discworld* fic without it. The best bet for character voices would be fiction in diary or letter form, for which there is some precedent in the canon. Captain Carrot, for instance, sometimes writes letters home in the novels, so his voice can be used in that way by fanfic writers and still sound authentic. In Wingleader Sora Jade's 'Good Luck and Goodbye'[4] Carrot is used as narrator – at this point he is trying to persuade his werewolf girlfriend Angua not to leave him:

> "That's right," she nodded, looking me in the eye finally. "We'll each find our own way into tomorrow. You here, in the Watch, and me, back home." I saw her wince slightly at the word 'home', and I wanted to hold her and tell her that it was alright, she didn't have to go, we'd make our own home here.
>
> But that wasn't what she wanted, and in a way, it wasn't what I wanted either. I wanted her to be happy. Even if it meant that she left me behind.
>
> She was searching for something, I realised. Something. I didn't know what. Maybe a way to control her wolfish outbreaks. Maybe a way to accept her family. I didn't know much about her past, but there were times, on full moons, I would hear her mumbling in her sleep. I got the impression that her home-life wasn't even nearly as good as mine.

There is nothing about this voice that is un-Carrot-like and the actual dialogue works well enough. The naïve understatement of the last sentence (Angua comes from a family of dysfunctional homicides) is particularly authentic. And using a different voice from that in the source property is one way to extend the canon and do something the original author did not. At least it is in most canons. But in the Discworld, though the story works well enough in itself, it no longer sounds to me like a *Discworld* fic, because there is an innocence and straightforwardness about Carrot that is the exact reverse of the authorial *Discworld* voice. Nor will any other character voice quite match it. Vimes has its humanity, Vetinari its barbed elegance, but there will always be some element missing.

First person Austen fanfic, though also uncommon, is somewhat easier than in the Discworld, since her voice is not so unlike the voices of some of her characters. What there is tends to be in the form of diaries or letters. 'A Clandestine Correspondence' by Mags[5], picks up on Austen's hint in the last chapter of *Northanger Abbey*, when Henry and Catherine are separated by the General's opposition to their marriage. "Whether the torments of absence were softened by a clandestine correspondence, let us not inquire". The two voices are convincing and there are touching moments, as when Catherine replies to a letter in which Henry imagines her in his drawing-room reading *The Mysteries of Udolpho*:

> I must take exception to your vision of me in the drawing-room. I do not mind that you are thinking about me, of course; but I want you to know that I no longer read novels such as Mrs. Radcliffe's. Although you kindly do not mention it, I am sure that you remember the mischief that such books caused, the mistaken assumptions that I made about your family. I do not wish to be tempted into such flights of fancy ever again, so I have resolved to read no more horrid books. I will go into my father's library and find a book of history, or sermons, directly I finish this letter.

Henry, evidently touched and amused, reassures her in his reply:

> So you have resolved to read no more horrid books! I am indeed saddened to hear that. I enjoyed *Udolpho* thoroughly. I do not wish to discourage you from reading history, my dear, or even sermons, but do not eliminate the stories that have previously given you such pleasure. You have learned that these stories are not real, and that such things do not occur in these modern times, and in such a Christian

> country as England. That does not mean that you cannot indulge yourself in fictional stories. There is nothing wrong with reading purely for pleasure, as long as you understand the difference between novels and reality.

To a fanfic writer or reader, this has a particular resonance, since people in fandom are conscious that many non-fans ("mundanes", as the term is) suspect them of not knowing fiction from reality. Their level of emotional engagement with the characters of their fictional universe can be misinterpreted by outsiders as a belief in the existence of these characters. Of course in one way they do exist, as a concept in the mind which may give both pleasure and inspiration, and as such they may be greatly valued. But fanfic writers and readers are well aware of the difference between that existence and the kind which enables one to walk down the High Street. Indeed their awareness of real life is often the reason they value their fictional universe as a bolthole and Henry is here speaking for harmless (and sometimes valuable) escapism.

It is not surprising that people who care so much for "their" characters should sometimes feel they know more about them than the original writers did – much as V S Pritchett felt about Becky. In particular it is not surprising in TV-based fanfic where, as indicated in the preceding chapter, time constraints have traditionally favoured plot and action over development of characters and relationships. This is no longer quite as true as it was in the Seventies, when TV-based fanfic really took off. The original *Star Trek* (1966-69 on TV, though for decades more in the cinema) had some characters who could potentially have been interesting, if they'd been allowed more time to develop and interact on a level beyond the casual and superficial. *B7* (1978-81) had characters and relationships that really were interesting, and were left tantalisingly unexplored. The characters of most Seventies police shows like *The Professionals* (1977-83) were too busy being all-action heroes to develop in other ways, though the contemporaneous *Starsky & Hutch* (1975-79), after starting out as another guns-and-cars based show, broke the mould by allowing its heroes not only a life outside the job but a distinctly emotional side.

These days, it would be an odd cult series that didn't have such a side. Partly, no doubt, this is due to the advent of more central and developed female characters, though *Buffy the Vampire Slayer* (1997-2003), with its strong cast of females, is still pretty much of a one-off. But male characters have changed too: even in SF and cop shows, all-action macho heroes are out of fashion. The British shows *The Bill* (ITV, police, 1983 to date) and *London's Burning* (ITV, firefighters, 1988-2001) began by concentrating almost wholly on the business and giving the characters very little personal life outside it; both changed in response to perceived audience tastes. What is perhaps strange is how long it took producers and scriptwriters to catch up with these tastes: fanfic writers were catering to them decades ago.

Kel, in comments on her *The Bill* fic 'They Also Serve'[6] explains why she wanted to write about a particular character:

> Look at the official character outline for DC Paul Riley. He's interesting. Complex. Individual. Brimful of possibilities. But did any of that actually make it onto our screens? Did it bollocks. He had enormous potential as a character. But he was *never used*. In two years, he puts Dave up, protects his brother, throws up at a wake, and dies. He's so non-existent the death episodes show people explaining who he was – *to his colleagues*!

Whole genres evolved to provide the character interaction and emotional content felt to be under-explored or missing altogether. Indeed the term 'shipper (from relationship) was coined to describe writers and readers to whom emotional relationships between the characters (with or without sex) were the most important factor. This is not to say that some fanfic writers didn't want, and produce, "more of" stories, which could have been episodes of the originals. But the "more from" brigade were, and still are, exploiting their freedom from TV's demands for 30 or 50 minutes of prime-time action by writing stories where there is quite frequently no "action", as such, at all, but a great deal of interaction and reflection. PWP (Plot? What plot?) means what it says: it consists of characters doing nothing but interact, in any way from talking to sleeping together. A later variant of this is the Japanese YAOI, acronymic for "**YA**ma nashi, **O**chi nashi, **I**mi nashi" – no plot, no point, no meaning[7]. But these latter seem to be invariably sexual, which not all PWPs were. Nowadays the designation PWP does imply a sex scene, but I have read several stories so defined where things didn't get that explicit.

A story may be defined as "angst", in which case the point is not what happens to the heroes but how they cope with it (or, quite often, don't cope). Angst stories are often written around canon episodes or as sequels to them. Many from the *Hornblower* universe focus on the aftermath of 'Retribution', when Hornblower has to come to terms with the fact that Archie sacrificed his posthumous good name for him. In writing these the fanfic writers can, among other things, rectify what some of them saw as Hornblower's unduly unemotional (or at least not obviously emotional) reaction to Archie's death in the episode itself. Rose's 'Regrets'[8] is a sequel to an episode of *The Bill* in which the station was petrol-bombed and several officers died. In 'Regrets' a surviving officer, Mickey Webb, sits at his desk grieving over their deaths. Other officers, on the periphery of his vision, react in ways typical of them. The most that actually happens is that he cries, and another officer consoles him.

This latter gives the story an element of hurt/comfort, a genre in which a character is systematically taken to bits emotionally (and sometimes physically too) before being consoled and sometimes rehabilitated by another character. This tends to happen most in fanfic to those canon characters who seem the most self-controlled and reticent about showing their feelings – Spock of *Star Trek*, Avon of *B7*, Illya of *The Man from UNCLE*, either of *The Professionals*, the buttoned-up Horatio Hornblower with his overriding sense of duty. With these "iron men" of canon who generally get the h/c treatment, the challenge of hurt/comfort for the writer is to make the loss of self-control seem still in character. The more inward and contained the character, and the harder his outer shell, the more she needs to do to him to achieve that, which is why some h/c segues into BUAR (beat up and rape).

But both the hurt/comfort and angst treatments can also be a reaction to perceived vulnerability in a character. The screen hobbits, particularly the fragile-looking Frodo as portrayed by Elijah Wood, are current favourites and Archie Kennedy of the *Hornblower* universe, with his low sense of self-worth, apparently tortured past and occasional epileptic fits, was a prime candidate from the nineties. 'Archieology 101', a *Hornblower* fan site focusing on Kennedy, even has an "Index of Archie Tortures"[9], detailing alphabetically the various things writers have done to him from "abdomen, abscessed/lacerated/impaled" to "vampirism". As the site author (Catherine the Terrible) remarks, "At first it may seem odd that it is often his most devoted fans who send Archie to the sick berth in their stories – not once but multiple times. However, one must understand that this is all in the spirit of "kiss it and make it better."

Arguably it is the "make it better" part of h/c that matters more: the infliction of pain and grief tends to be a means to an end. I have seen fans of h/c explain in mailing list debates that they write and read it as a kind of respite from the real-life pain they constantly see around them in the news and on the street, and which they can't kiss and make better. Signing petitions and putting money in boxes is all very well, but there comes a point when you realise you cannot save every suffering child/dolphin/political prisoner on the planet, and in that mood it can be consoling to minister to the grief or pain of a fictional character, particularly if he has become very real to you.

The petrol-bombing of *The Bill's* Sun Hill station, referred to above, was canonically the fault of a policeman, Des Taviner. At the time (mid-2003) when Kel's fic 'Suburban Wing'[10] was written, nobody knew that but him and his fellow-officer Reg Hollis, who for reasons not then specified in the canon was telling nobody. It had by no means been made clear by the canon writers why Reg, normally a conscientious officer, was acting that way. Either he didn't believe Des's confession, which was convincing enough, or his friendship with Des, the only friendship either man had, was too valuable to him. Kel's fic assumes, as do many, that the two are in a relationship, but this cannot assuage the gnawing guilt which is so often the stuff of angst. In the fic Reg, who does tend to be a bit of an anorak, has counted the holes in the polystyrene tiles on Des's bedroom ceiling. Worrell and Harker were officers who died in the fire. This fic, in third-person intimate, takes the point of view of Des, outwardly a hard man with a very vulnerable hidden core and therefore prime angst and hurt/comfort material:

> Three thousand, four hundred and ninety-two small black holes, all staring down out of the night like little wells, little *caves,* with little cavemen thugs lurking in them, just out of sight. Probably beating the bejesus out of each other with big sharp rocks. With big sharp rocks around a blazing big fi–
>
> Des closes his aching eyes, wishing the night and everything in it would go to hell. Wishing the whole bloody lot would just come down and be done with it.
>
> Three thousand, four hundred and ninety-two. That's a lot of holes, in a lot of tiles, and a lot of bedroom ceiling to house them.
>
> Not that he's counting, oh no. That'd be sad-fuck behaviour, that would. That'd be last bus to Twatsville, don't bother to write.
>
> And he doesn't have to count. Reg did it for him, bless his little trainspotter heart. Just calculated away, and dropped the figure into the conversation at breakfast refs. As you do. Just threw it out there, in front of everyone, threw it out and lured a cold and silent Des back

> from that magical, faraway place where Worrell still wiggles her stupid doris arse. Where Sam Harker's body is warm, and whole.
>
> His eyes hurt. Good.
>
> With effort, he turns away, turns inside; runs it all forward to a soft grey gaze and smile, masking the barest touch. Everyone looking, no-one to see in the too-light, too-bright canteen, with its smells and noise, its white and closing walls.
>
> "'Ere, Des, you'll never get this..."
>
> It had turned into a contest, of sorts; a desperately brittle guessing game. He's not the only one who needs something else to think about. He shouldn't have to be reminded.
>
> "Stupid prick" he whispers, savagely, and stares even harder at the ceiling, stares until it recedes to a safe distance. Until the holes merge, and dull, and disappear.

Angst in the Discworld quite often centres on the relationship between officers of the City Watch Carrot (a six-foot human brought up as a dwarf) and Angua, a werewolf. In the canon, Carrot is eager to settle down with Angua but she is dubious because of her mixed nature, worried as to what their offspring might be like and frequently on the point of Leaving Him For His Own Good. Pratchett, who doesn't come over as the emotional type, seldom dwells on the soppy bits of this or any other relationship. Hence, in fanfic, it becomes 'shipper territory ('shippers being fans who cannot get enough of the soppy bits). Vetinari, a very introverted character who tantalisingly lacks much in the way of canonical attachments or back-story, is also relatively good angst material in an otherwise not very angst-friendly universe. By and large, people and other species in the Discworld find practical ways around their problems, such as magic or violence, rather than agonising over them.

B7 is an angst-ridden canon universe in itself. A lot of the angst in its fanfic centres on the edgy, ambiguous and canonically never fully explored relationship between Blake and Avon, but this PGP fic by AstroGirl, 'Until It's Gone',[11] is about another crew member, Vila, self-confessed coward and butt of a lot of jokes. He's also a survivor and this one has him living on as a prisoner after the massacre on Gauda Prime, recalling his time on board the rebels' first space-ship, *Liberator*, and their second, *Scorpio*:

> In his dreams, he was always on the *Liberator*. Sometimes they were bad dreams. Hairy aliens had boarded the ship and were chasing him through endless corridors, but when he called for help the aliens were

nowhere to be seen, and his shipmates stood there, laughing at his fear, until the creatures dropped from the ceiling and devoured them as Vila watched in helpless terror. Or the one where he was alone on the ship, looking for something. He never knew just what it was, only that if he didn't find it, the others would never, ever come back, and that he never seemed to find it, no matter how hard and how desperately he looked.

Often, though – surprisingly often – they were happy. He would be sprawled on the flight deck couch, a glass of soma in his hand, and all the others would be there with him: Blake, Jenna, Cally, Gan, a much younger and happier-looking Avon. He would just sit there, listening to Blake talk. He could never remember about what, afterwards, but it hardly mattered. Just the sound of Blake's voice made him feel oddly safe and secure and... hopeful. Then Vila would say something clever and witty, and the others would laugh – *with* him – and Avon would say something affectionately insulting, and he would be suffused in a wonderful warm glow that felt like it could go on forever.

Those were always the worst. He'd wake from them afterward and stare at the blank, undecorated walls of his cabin on Xenon, or at the dull gray bleakness of *Scorpio* with the lights turned down for the sleep shift, and muse bitterly on the cruelty of Fate. Who would have ever thought that he would someday look back on those dangerous, fear-filled, frustrating times as the good days? *You never know what you've got until it's gone*, someone had told him once, and that sentence would echo around and around in his head until he wanted to rip it out of his mind with his fingernails.

As time went on and things got worse the happy dreams, perversely, grew more frequent, until he was almost afraid to go to sleep, knowing that eventually he'd have to wake up.

Then came Gauda Prime, and a sleep he thought he never would awaken from. But wake he did, at least a little. And in those however many drug- and pain- and sleep-filled days after, his dreams were all of goo oozing from walls, and of Servalan, and of snow.

Eventually they deemed him healed enough for interrogation. That first night, after a day of humiliation and pain, he fell into exhausted sleep in his tiny, dirty, new cell, and for the first time in many months, he did not dream of *Liberator*. He dreamed instead of the flight deck of *Scorpio*, of Tarrant's flashing grin, of Dayna's youthful laugh, of Avon's rare and precious genuine smile, of a happy homeward flight to Xenon.

And he woke with tears in his eyes and wondered how bad things would be when he finally began to dream of his cell.

Interestingly enough, some *B7* fanfic readers don't much like Vila being a target for angst and hurt/comfort scenarios, because he is seen as too vulnerable. Canonically he is easily hurt both physically and emotionally; he has no pain threshold to speak of and is often lonely, the butt of jokes from the others. (So is Reg of *The Bill*, but he is better at ignoring them.) Female characters are relatively immune from being used in this type of story, partly because it makes the readers feel uncomfortable, and in this respect Vila seems to be an honorary woman.

The fact that fanfic writers expand or play variations on episodes does not always mean they wanted the original scriptwriters to do so. Stories like 'Suburban Wing' or 'Until It's Gone' could never make a 30-minute episode of viewing and fanfic writers know that, though some would appreciate the odd few moments' reflection along the canonical way. Some, though, are happy for the scriptwriters to leave emotion- and relationship-shaped gaps for them to fill in. Indeed if the scriptwriters do not leave *some* such gaps, there may be nowhere for fanfic to happen. The shift in *The Bill* to showing characters' personal lives left some contributors to its fan forum feeling that there was no point in writing about that side of the characters because it had been or would be explored, though it did not stop other writers from doing so.

Similarly Austen's readers are not suggesting that *Emma,* for instance, is incomplete without Mr Knightley's private reflections; merely that they existed and that it might be interesting to explore them. As previously indicated, the men in the Austen universe are especially likely to be explored in this way, because we know less about their emotional life than about that of the female characters through whose eyes Austen chooses to look. Minor characters – Charlotte Lucas, Mrs Weston (formerly Taylor) – are popular as triggers for alternative viewpoint stories like Aja's 'So Much of Gratitude' at the Derbyshire Writers Guild[12], which takes Charlotte's viewpoint on the marriage market. They may even trigger spin-off universes, like Skylar's 'An Unlikely Missionary'[13]. This does not essentially differ from the process at work in literary fiction, in George Macdonald Fraser's *Flashman* series, and some of these spin-off universes are novella or novel-length (eg 'An Unlikely Missionary').

Minor characters can often be used to convey something of the author. In the past, many "plain" girls, or girls who worried that they were plain, must have identified with Charlotte Lucas. Or a minor character who was little fleshed out in canon can be expanded into what amounts to an original character (OC). In Kel's fic 'They Also Serve', referred to above, Paul and Joe Riley, though canonical, were so little used in the canon that here, in a fic which centres on them and gives them a back-story, they are effectively OCs. It is going one step further to invent your own original characters and mix them with those of the fanfic universe. This happens in all fandoms. In *B7*, Manna has invented the chilling federation "psychomanipulator" Toreth; in *The Bill*, BH invented the Australian probationer Rhianna Gillespie[14]. The hero of 'An Unlikely Missionary' is neither the Rev Collins nor Charlotte but a fellow-missionary who is an OC (and sounds suspiciously as if he must be St John Rivers' father, whom we never see in *Jane Eyre*).

OCs can often be fascinating characters. Many fanfic readers are prepared to accept them as such, especially if they seem to fit well into the universe being written about. Some fans still don't. Some are in love with their particular fanfic universe; others with a character or characters within it, and full-blown "character junkies" sometimes don't like any non-canon characters being a main focus in the story (as we saw, the Republic of Pemberley's guidelines frowned on this). In much the same way, some readers do not like the narrative voice to change. Even a TV series has a narrative voice of sorts, which in its own way is a character in the story, and a story which departs noticeably from this voice may not be universally thought of as fanfic.

A *B7* story in point is Penny Dreadful's 'The Killer of Dole Nu Lin'[15]. This concerns a mutoid (a human being who has been modified as a punitive measure, canonical in the source). The mutation needs certain conditions to persist; this particular mutoid, due to changing circumstances, begins to revert to humanity. Since she has at first no memories of her former state (which is why she refers to herself as "this object"), the process is one of slow, painful revelation of what it means to be human:

> Object drinks water. More of it lately than should be required, considering levels of exertion.
>
> If ordered to, object prepares rations: combine concentrate and water in the appropriate container. Heat. Bring the end product to the Commander, in the cockpit or his cabin. Smells good. But mutoids don't need to eat, any more than they need to sleep.
>
> The second attack of REM is far more serious than the first. Object has spent forty-four consecutive days away from Space

> Command when the incident occurs. It is awakened at its station by a light blow to the side of the head.
>
> My head snaps up. I am wide awake, Commander, I object this object was never asleep. Dreams like colourful film still crawling on the corneas of my open eyes. Call me liar. Translucent but true. [...]
>
> "Sleeping on duty," the Commander says.
>
> I blink.
>
> "Do you know the punishment for that?" He spits the words. A drop of saliva hits my cheek.
>
> This object spins its seat halfway around and smiles up at its Commander. Looks him straight in the angry well-rested eye. "Court martial?" it asks. Smiling.
>
> He strikes this object's face. Only with the open palm of his softer and weaker right hand, but still sufficient force such that the inside of the object's cheek breaks open on the sharp edge of a tooth.
>
> This object keeps smiling as it swallows the blood. Its own, but sweet as fresh water all the same.
>
> "There's something wrong with you," the Commander says.

Una McCormack, reviewing the story on *ttba's* web site[16], expressed the view:

> It is a story of the resilience of humanity, and its emergence in unexpected places; it exploits canon yet is scrupulously attentive to its detail; it is pure *B7*, yet something absolutely novel from a gifted writer.... it is putting aside simplistic divides and concentrating on creating bloody good fiction that allows such writing to emerge.

Many agreed. But though few would dissent from the praise of the writing, there are those who feel the "divide" McCormack mentions still exists and that for them, 'KDNL' falls on the non-fanfic side of it – not because the characters are OCs; they are in fact canon characters, though this does not immediately become clear. Rather it is that the narrative voice itself is arguably uncanonical: literary, experimental, darker than the canon source (which takes some doing). I have heard it suggested that this fic could easily be adapted to appeal to a general audience with no knowledge of the canon, by the process known in fanfic writing as "filing off the serial numbers". This means making a piece of fan fiction suitable for more mainstream publication by removing specific references to the fan universe. Quite a few fan fiction writers who are also profic writers do this from time to time. But for some, without a strong connection to the orignal canon, a story may work as fiction but it is no longer fanfic.

One might, in the same fandom, compare this with another fic, Susan Cutter's prequel 'Privilege'[17]. Like 'KDNL', it uses the personal as a metaphor for the political. It is canonical that the Federation is a stratified society, with classes that go at least from Alpha to Delta, and it is clearly difficult to move between classes, though not necessarily impossible. In the fic, a naïve young Alpha (who is a canon character, though he wouldn't need to be) is brutally beaten up and raped by two Delta mechanics. It is made clear that this is an act of class hatred: the Deltas are embittered and poisoned by the rigid system that gives them so little status and their victim so much. He is rescued by an army officer who is himself not an Alpha and has accomplished the rare feat of moving out of his class. However his success does not reconcile the officer to the system; he knows how much harder it has been for him and that he is not truly accepted by his Alpha colleagues. Up to this point, the story could indeed be "mainstream SF" making a general point about how social injustice can corrupt individuals like the mechanics and make them act in a way they might not otherwise have done. It is the identity of the army officer that gives it its fanfic dimension: he is Travis, who in this prequel fic still has a remnant of decency but who in the series will become a warped genocidal killer. One could, quite easily, file the serial numbers off this and make it mainstream fiction, but to anyone with the shared knowledge of this canon it also offers a "new twist" on how Travis got to be the way he is.

'KDNL' also gives the reader a new sidelight on Travis, and on another canon character. The difference between the two fics is the narrative voice, which in 'Privilege' is much more recognisably *B7*. As quoted above, some find 'KDNL' "pure *B7*". I would be among them, and its narrative voice, though more literary and modernist than that of most fanfic, does not strike me as being at odds with the actual "canon voice" in so far as there was one. But then, as we saw earlier, there is always room for disagreement on characters and in many ways the narrative voice is a character – so much so that I could not relate to Discworld fics that didn't include the Pratchett voice. Yet I hope this is because I hadn't found the right ones, or even because no-one had yet written them, rather than because the thing couldn't be successfully done.

I would not like to think that without mimetic reproduction of the canon's narrative voice a story was no longer fanfic, firstly because such a definition would exclude some of my favourite stories (and writers) in the genre and secondly because in some canons, Austen and Tolkien particularly, I think the mimetic tendency has limited the achievement of writers. It is, in the end, possible to be faithful to the canon characters (which is of the essence in fanfic) without simultaneously imitating the narrative voice of the original author. If the characters are "real" enough, and have been well enough understood and visualised, they can live in someone else's voice as well as in that of their creator. But this is straying into the territory of chapter 9, in which I want to discuss the development of individual voice in fanfic writers.

One worry for anyone writing an original character is that of creating, or being accused of creating, a Mary Sue. This name, used now in all fandoms, seems to have been coined in 1974 in the context of *Star Trek* fan fiction, in a satirical story by Paula Smith which lampooned the worst excesses of such characters. The term describes a character who is basically an idealised version of the author (and was, therefore, at least in the early days, generally young, female and beautiful). This character will go into the fanfic universe, save its characters, sort out all their problems, probably earn their undying love and often die an heroic death at the end. These characters are not unknown in litfic – back in 1856 George Eliot was fulminating in the Westminster Review about the typical heroine of what she described as "silly novels by lady novelists".

> Her eyes and her wit are both dazzling; her nose and her morals are alike free from any tendency to irregularity; she has a superb contralto and a superb intellect; she is perfectly well-dressed and perfectly religious; she dances like a sylph, and reads the Bible in the original tongues.

There have been similar comments by modern literary novelists like Beryl Bainbridge and Pat Barker about the "chick lit" genre, where the typical heroine is a young metropolitan woman shopping, hanging out with friends, looking for and eventually finding Mr Right. Criticism of the genre has focused not only on its fluffiness but on the fact that it acts as a mirror rather than a window, reflecting the lives of its readers and writers rather than showing them other lives. Pat Barker suggests that it is a phase readers grow out of:

> "I think young people, because they have an insecure sense of their own identity, love reading books which confirm that identity, which

> mirror their lifestyle choices back to them and I think as people get older they need that from their reading less and less"[18]

Chick lit came into fashion only in the 1990s; Mary Sues had become anathema in fanfic decades earlier. For one thing, the "character junkies" among fanfic readers saw them as an insult to the regular characters. Could they not sort their own lives out without the intervention of these "SuperSues saving the day, with everyone falling in love with them while they solve every relationship difficulty on the show before being swept off into the sunset by the object of the author's adoration" (Ika, echoing Eliot on an unarchived mailing list). Put like this, a "Mary Sue" character is obviously a bit of a risible cliché and it is understandable that fanfic writers did not want to be seen writing them. But it is possible to create a character partly based on oneself without going down this embarrassing road and profic authors do it all the time, without exciting the distrust and sometimes scorn that fanfic writers get from readers to whom any female OC equals a possible Mary Sue. (Not that male Mary Sues are impossible. Indeed the character of Wesley Crusher from *Star Trek: The Next Generation* was loathed partly because he was widely thought to be the personal Mary Sue of Gene Wesley Roddenberry.)

The fear of committing a Mary Sue, and consequent avoidance of writing oneself into a story except with obvious ironic intent, seems to have gone very deep in fanfic. I have seen it suggested on mailing lists that early fanfic writers, mainly women, had enough scorn to put up with from mundanes simply for taking fan universes seriously enough to write about, and wanted to avoid being seen as soppy "romantic" writers into the bargain.

For a long time, articles on this genre tended to have titles like 'Why Mary Sue Must Die'[19] or 'Why Mary Sue Needs to Die'[20] and tended to advise writers to avoid creating any character who might be interpreted in that way. The impassioned tone of the Liquid Crystal rant (the author's word) is revealing. It begins with an assertion I should have thought flawed in the extreme:

> Many experienced writers point out that Mary Sue-ism is the "baby stage" of writing. Writing yourself into a story is easier than creating a well-rounded and quality character that can exist on its own merit.

One could well argue that when you write yourself you are creating a character, just as much as if you drew a portrait of a friend or assembled a character from different sources. The character you invent out of "yourself" may be well rounded or otherwise; that will depend far more on the quality of the writer than on where her materials came from. A character who is wholly or partly an avatar of the author as she might like to see herself may end up being a vapid "chick lit" heroine – or she may be Maggie Tulliver. Indeed the rant seems to admit this, when it goes on to identify one of its author's main grudges against Mary Sues:

> This also creates another problem that hits me close to home – you see, every now and then I want to create original characters of my own. Unlike Mary Sues, my characters would be designed well. They wouldn't be special or wonderful or perfect, they would simply be ordinary but interesting people who have something to offer the story and its canon characters. But I can't write them, because other rightfully disgusted cynics such as myself will assume they're Mary Sues.

Ah. Another irregular verb. I create interesting original characters, you use original characters as avatars of yourself, she commits Mary Sues (this irregular verb or one very like it was originally coined by Una McCormack). It cannot be denied that some personal avatar characters are embarrassingly idealised – demi-goddesses, in Kirk's words – but that last assertion, that one cannot write OCs because readers will assume them to be so without, presumably, having checked, shows a writer putting defeatist and unnecessary limits on himself or herself.

Lately there has been a softening of tone in at least some quarters and a recognition that the fact that a thing has been done badly in the past does not mean it cannot possibly be done well. In 'Flies in Amber' (unarchived), a *B7* fic, Jennifer J McGee uses a child to narrate a ghost story. The child, living on Gauda Prime, hears the ghost-voices of the slaughtered crew and is eventually able to help them find rest. The "hearing voices" plot was partly based on the author's own childhood experience of having imaginary friends, and when first posting the story to an unarchived mailing list she felt obliged to apologise in case this was seen as a Mary Sue scenario. That she felt the need to do this is significant and shows how influential this critical taboo has been. More significant though was the response, which was uniformly positive. It would seem that on this list at least, fanfic readers these days are prepared to judge an OC on the basis of whether he or she works as a character, autobiographical or not. An example of the more open-minded attitude to OCs these days is the article 'Who's Afraid of the Mary Sue?' by Tavia[21]. This article also lists stories from several fandoms containing OCs which still manage to be worth reading.

One fanfic universe which seems always to have accommodated OCs more happily than most, and without even worrying unduly about Mary Sue-ism, is the Discworld, and this is for canonical reasons. A favourite Pratchett narrative opening is to introduce a new character, often a young ingénu (or ingénue) into the existing mix. This character may exist only for the length of the novel (like Buddy from *Soul Music*) but it is equally likely that he or she will join the huge and ever-expanding cast of regulars. Captain Carrot, Susan Sto Helit and several other major characters were introduced this way. This being so, the involvement of young, naïve OCs who in any other fandom might be seen as Mary Sues is practically canonical, and sure enough many plots of *Discworld* fics begin with a "young man" or "young girl", who is not a canon character, in some situation or other. In Libwolf's 'The Witches' Apprentice'[22], the narrative voice is recognisably *Discworld* and so is the situation: a young would-be witch who wants Granny Weatherwax to take her as a student:

> It was just before dawn. Granny woke, stretched and walked over to the window. The trees were green, the herbs were mugging passing birds. There was a young woman sitting in the middle of the lawn, right outside her back door. Muttering to herself, Granny wrapped a shawl around her and stamped down the stairs. Opening the door, she snapped.
>
> "And what do you want?"
>
> The girl blinked at her.
>
> "I want to be a witch, Mistress Weatherwax." she said calmly. Her accent was that of Ankh-Morpork.
>
> Granny studied her.
>
> She was about 16, with brown hair and eyes. Wearing her ankle length plain black dress, she didn't look like one of the normal girls that came around wanting to be a witch. However Granny couldn't be having with any of that at her time of life. She already had one student.
>
> "Go home to your mother, child!" she snapped, and slammed the door.
>
> She expected to hear sobbing, or at least the girl getting up and leaving. She didn't hear anything. She went through her normal morning routine, although she washed her face in the scullery, as she didn't want to go outside yet. Fishing the newts out of the kettle, she

sat down for a cuppa.

The girl was still outside. Just sitting there, watching the cottage.

Though, as it happens, Libwolf is one of the minority of male fanfic writers, this young girl, who could have stepped out of many a Pratchett novel, may very well have elements of what the author is or would like to be. In this fandom, at least, it doesn't matter. And since the story convinces as a *Discworld* fic, there is no reason why it should.

NOTES

1. BBC, 1980s
2. in a fanzine review on http://www.hermit.org/Blakes7/index.html 6.9.02
3. fanfiction.net http://www.fanfiction.net/s/854817/1 04.01.05
4. fanfiction.net http://www.fanfiction.net/s/849464/1/ 17.11.02
5. http://www.tilneysandtrapdoors.com/ff/acctc.html 17.03.03
6. http://www.goldweb.com.au/~bessie/ , 06.01.02
7. Mark McLelland, in his article in the online journal Intensities, "Why Are Japanese Girls' Comics Full of Boys Bonking?, http://www.cult-media.com
8. http://web.archive.org/web/20030630021752/212.67.202.77/~tbff/regrets.html 2.11.02
9. http://members.tripod.com/archieology101/tortures.htm 22.11.02
10. Arjuna, http://www.goldweb.com.au/~bessie/ 15.12.02
11. http://www.fanfiction.net/s/1205520/1 04.01.05
12. http://thedwg.com/derby/oldc/aja4.htm 05.01.05
13. http://www.literatureclassics.com/ancientpaths/jane3.html 04.01.05
14. see "Early Shift", at http://www.tbfanfic.com 23.04.03
15. in the *B7* fanzine *ttba* and online at http://www.viragene.com/ttba.htm 10.04.03
16. http://www.viragene.com/ttba.htm 6 November 2002
17. *ttba*
18. from an interview in the *Today* programme, BBC Radio 4, 22.8.01
19. http://www.tbns.net/mathinus 4.11.02
20. Kirk, on Liquid Crystal, http://rinpu.com/storypages/mary_sue_rant.html 8.11.02
21. on her website at http://www.viragene.com/OCs.htm 14.11.02
22. http://www.fanfiction.net/s/298038/1/ 04.01.05

5. Male Sorting

Slash

In the TV science fiction and police shows of the 1960s and 70s, which sparked renewed interest in creating fanfic, sex seldom featured. They generally ran too early in the evening, for one thing. But it would also have got in the way of the action and tied down the heroes too much, making them unavailable for future entanglements and, perhaps, for the romantic dreams of the fans. If some woman attracted the amorous attention of *Star Trek's* Captain Kirk, not only would matters get no further than a kiss, you could be reasonably sure she would be dead by the end of the episode.

Sex was similarly absent from the earliest 70s fanfic based on these shows. The term for fanfic with no overt sexual content is "gen" – i.e. suitable for a general audience – and at first it all was. Indeed gen is still by far the largest category of fanfic. For some fanfic writers this may have been a matter of moral preferences but as often as not it was due to the same respect for canon that made some unwilling to accept AU stories. Those fanfic writers and readers who do not like altering their canon will usually accept relationships, including sexual relationships, that are canonical. I am not sure any such onscreen relationship was unequivocally canonical in the original *Star Trek*, but in *B7* it was made clear in canon that one of the crew had had a sexual encounter with the chief villainess, while another had slept with a one-off guest character. (It is also probable from the situation shown in 'Rumours of Death', though not beyond doubt, that Avon has slept with Anna.) *Starsky & Hutch* showed its two male leads in situations with young women where it was unlikely that they had been playing Scrabble (though the young women still had a tendency to end up dead). But even if fans of these and other programmes of that time accepted the relationships as canon, they did not at first write explicitly about them. There was a great deal of emotion in some gen fanfic, but things did not become physical.

It did not, however, take long for the first "adult" *Star Trek* fanzine to appear (*Grup*, 1972), and in fandoms that began in the 70s, like *B7* and *Starsky & Hutch*, the first genzines were very closely followed by more adult ones. "Adult", at that time, meant explicit and heterosexual – there was nothing else, at least in published fanfic, for it to mean.

But in 1974 something else happened: a published *Star Trek* story which, albeit in a coded way, made Kirk and Spock lovers (Diane Marchant's 'A Fragment Out Of Time', published in the fanzine *Grup#3*). It was sometimes the practice, when describing a story for the benefit of potential readers, to list the main characters by name or initial. If these names or initials were joined by a hyphen it indicated a gen story, if by a forward slash, an adult one. Thus K-U would merely have indicated a story where Kirk and Uhura were the main characters, but K/U would mean they had a sexual relationship (which might be of varying degrees of explicitness). Stories linking Kirk and Spock romantically were therefore K/S stories, and before long the forward slash between them came to mean specifically stories which focused on m/m relationships. "Slash" became the name for such fiction and "adult" meant specifically heterosexual. This can be confusing for new readers and some now prefer "het" as the term for adult heterosexual fiction.

Slash – at least published slash – developed slowly and was at first confined to K/S. Zines published over the next few years contained some K/S slash and an all-slash *Star Trek* zine called Thrust was published in 1978. When, in the late 70s, fanfic spread to other fictional universes (notably *Star Wars*, *Blakes 7*, *The Professionals*, *The Man from UNCLE* and *Starsky & Hutch*) slash spread with it – see K S Boyd's 'History of Slash'[1]. There are now all-slash printzines in many fandoms, and many slashfic sites on the Net. Nonetheless, slash is still a very small part of fanfic. There is more het than slash and a great deal more gen than either. Slash, however, attracts more notice and comment from outside the fanfic writing and reading community than any other form of fanfic.

In part, this is for reasons that the community itself finds tiresome. Anti-slashers within fan fiction, of whom there are many, hate it when slash is seen as typical of, or synonymous with, fanfic. Slash readers and writers in their turn become impatient with the endless puzzlement of interviewers and commentators as to the motives which lead straight women to write and read m/m love scenes. (Most fanfic writers are women and nearly all slash writers are.) Mark McLelland, in his article on slash manga in the internet journal *Intensities* (Spring/Summer 2001), 'Why Are Japanese Girls' Comics

Full of Boys Bonking?"[2] raised a cheer from many slash fans when he answered his own question:

> Why *shouldn't* Japanese women's comics be full of boys bonking? [...] In Japan, as elsewhere, men seem to be granted greater license to experiment with sexuality than do women. Why should men's interest in 'lesbianism' be taken for granted whereas women's interest in male homosexuality somehow be in need of interpretation?

There is a lot of sense in this viewpoint, and certainly it would have saved Donald Symons and Catherine Salmon the trouble of conducting a survey to determine whether slash fans had "some sort of psycho-sexual quirk"[3]. Nonetheless, pertinent and refreshingly honest as McLelland's point is, things aren't quite as simple as that. I do not want to go into "motives" with the thoroughness of cultural and media studies like *Enterprising Women* and *Textual Poachers* (which is a good place to start if you do want to pursue this topic). But the original motives for writing slash are relevant to how it was and is written, how it has developed and why many things about it, including its definition, are still controversial even among fans of slash reading and writing, let alone the wider fan fiction community. And one good literary reason for paying slash a degree of attention disproportionate to its volume is that, certainly in its original form, it was something new, a genre which fanfic evolved to suit its own needs. Mary Sue-ing, writing oneself into a fictional universe, could have been such another genre, if fanfic writers hadn't let themselves be intimidated out of it, and at least one of the motives behind that kind of writing may also have contributed to the development of slash.

Fanfic happens in the gaps between canon, the unexplored or insufficiently explored territory. For that to happen, the gaps must be left, and the territory must exist – i.e. the canon writers must not spell too much out, but there must be somewhere to start from and something to build on. The fact that slash began with K/S may well baffle those who find it hard to see the wooden Kirk of the original *Star Trek* as any kind of a sexual being. (I accept that the writers meant us to see him as irresistible to women, but the willing suspension of disbelief does have its limits.) In truth the biggest canonical gap in that series was any kind of character or relationship development at all. The films, years later, did not share that flaw, since the official writers were finally, well after the fanfic writers, catching up with the zeitgeist. But you could have watched the episodes of the *Star Trek* TV series completely out of order and made very little difference to the experience. The nearest thing it had to an evolving character was Spock, being gradually influenced by the humans around him, and the nearest thing to a relationship which could be developed was his with Kirk.

The preceding chapter stressed the importance to fanfic readers and writers of reproducing the characters faithfully. Fanfic writers can change events, timelines, almost anything they want, but the characters must remain recognisable. This made it remarkably hard to write interesting female characters in most of the 70s fandoms, because by and large there weren't any in canon. Police shows, like *The Professionals* and *Starsky & Hutch*, had no regular female characters. *Star Trek* had Uhura, who had no character to speak of, and Nurse Chapel, who was a vapid over-emotional nitwit. They presented gaps all right, but no real territory to start from. If one wrote an interesting Uhura or a strong Chapel they wouldn't be themselves any more and the story, however it worked on its own terms, would not work as fanfic.

This left fanfic writers with two choices. They could invent their own original female characters, and many did, until the dread of Mary Sue-ism intervened. In a debate on an unarchived mailing list, someone asked why it was that some slash writers positively disliked het and wouldn't read it. A reply suggested that it had less to do with who slept with whom than with how it was written:

> A lot of older het stories were, I gather, gooey sweet Mary Sues, very different in tone from most slash stories. After all, in a fandom with few or no ongoing female characters, het would pretty much have to be with original female characters, who are all too likely to slide into Mary Sue-hood.
>
> – ST

Alternatively the writers could concentrate on the more developed male characters and the emotional relationships between them. And over and over in the 70s, this meant concentrating on a central male duo – the dyad, as Bacon Smith characterises it – on which any potential development and emotion is centred. Kirk and Spock, Bodie and Doyle, Starsky and Hutch, Solo and Illya, Blake and Avon were the couples of the late 60s, 70s and early 80s and it was the gaps in their territory which were explored by early slash writers. Their aim, as much as anything, was to ratchet up the emotional charge of the canon and to make their heroes more interesting by increasing their vulnerability and opening them to their own, often very closed-off, feelings. In a debate of 2002 on an unarchived mailing list, writers and readers discussed what exactly slash was in their minds, for by now it had developed way beyond its original remit:

> I know it's an oxymoron but I've always felt that you can have something like "het slash" in situations where both characters are highly walled off and afraid of being vulnerable. "Slashy" to me has always implied more an emotional style of genre than the actual mechanics of getting two guys into bed. So, for example, Aeryn and John on *Farscape* or Miss Parker and Jared on *The Pretender* have much more "slashy" relationships than, say, Obi-Wan and Qui-Gon (*Star Wars*) who seem to have very few issues with vulnerability and emotion. Usually, of course, women aren't the ones with the intimacy issues, which is what makes it more fun to get guys to fall for each other.
>
> – J J McGee

This viewpoint sees slash as a development of hurt/comfort or angst rather than something specifically sexual. If the idea is to open men up to emotion and explore male vulnerability, this is one of the most effective ways to do it. It would also explain why canons which did have stronger female characters still found their male characters slashed. *B7*, for one, did have more assertive, interesting female characters – not fully developed, but with enough character and back-story for fanfic writers to work on. Yet in this fandom as in others, fanfic writers, even gen ones, always paid far more attention to the male characters. There certainly were het adult stories from early on (the 'Alternative Seven' series began in 1978 while the show was still airing). But as early as 1979 the story 'Mindfire' by EPS, which had been posted to friends but not intended for publication, was circulating unauthorised (it was finally published as a stand-alone fanzine in 1998). It was mainly het but also implied a Blake/Avon relationship. Most early *B7* slash focused either on this pairing or on Avon/Vila and one reason would seem to be that Avon, to quote J J McGee above, definitely had "issues with vulnerability and emotion". Also the A/B onscreen relationship is charged with emotional tension; they quarrel often and Avon constantly undermines Blake's leadership verbally, yet in action he almost inevitably backs him up and his body language towards him is frequently at odds with his words. This is the sort of gap into which fanfic writers happily go exploring.

There were and are undoubtedly other motives for writing slash. McLelland is right enough to point out, for instance, that the idea of two good-looking men getting it on appeals to some women just as the reverse scenario does to some men. Executrix (via email) suggests another explanation resisted by some but recognised by others – "I think that at least some slash writers are unwilling to "see" some brazen hussy in bed with their fictional loves [...] they don't mind as much if it's another bloke".

It's also true that with some pairings, fans simply saw an unexplored gay subtext in the writing, which "official" series writers back in the seventies were never going to develop fully. Some slash writers who were themselves gay may have wanted to explore this territory partly for ideological reasons, but many fanfic writers, both gay and straight, just followed their insatiable curiosity about alternative scenarios. *Starsky & Hutch* was from early on a prime candidate for slashing, though this particular dyad had absolutely no trouble being vulnerable and emotional, either in words or body language. In this case what seems to have happened is that the official writers were themselves going so close to the boundary between "buddy" and "homoerotic" (but always shying away at the last moment) that the slash writers could not resist going one step further and crossing the boundary. Many *S & H* slashfics, in fact, focus on the effect that crossing this boundary, or becoming aware that they might want to, would have on the duo's habits of unembarrassed physical closeness. Would they be able to touch so casually, if they considered where it might lead or what it said about their desires?

But without denying these motives, I would contend that the link from the angst and hurt/comfort genres to slash is also important and shows in the kind of characters who are liable to be the subjects of both. It isn't just good-looking male characters who get slashed, though of course that helps. But if it were purely (or impurely) happening because female writers were turned on by the idea of pairing two attractive men, then Des and Reg would never have become a popular pairing in *The Bill*. Neither man is the stuff of sexual fantasy. But Des is a hard man hiding an inner vulnerability and Reg is openly vulnerable. They thus represent the two kinds of characters who were most likely to be put through the emotional wringer of angst and hurt/comfort.

It is this link, to my mind, which is ignored in Donald Symons' view of slash as a sort of sub-genre of mainstream romance[4]. Slash just didn't start from there. I would also argue that some of the "parallels" he identifies with mainstream romance can be differently interpreted, notably the "first time" slash scenario which he equates with the heroine in mainstream romance giving her virginity to the hero. For one thing, in a "first time" slash scenario both protagonists are quite likely to be contemplating the activity in question for the first time, which is seldom the case with heroes of mainstream romance. For another, in mainstream romance there is an inevitability about the eventual surrender of virginity, generally in the context of marriage: even if it happens offstage it is the natural end of the story and we and the heroine both know it. There is no inevitability about the "first time" slash scenario, which traditionally involved a man who had never had occasion to think of himself as other than straight and who now had to rethink himself and his relationships. Far from being the "natural" (in narrative terms) end to the man's story, it was an alternative path down which that story might go, if he were adventurous enough to recognise other possibilities in himself and open up to them. In this it reflected fanfic writers' interest in all varieties of AU and I think that is an important reason the scenario became and remained so popular.

Warrior Lovers also identifies a similarity between the artwork of slash fanzines and mainstream romance – "the artwork that illustrates many slash stories is unabashedly romantic and highly reminiscent of romance-novel cover art; it may portray nudity but it almost never portrays penetration"[5]. Two points arise here, if the verb is not inapposite. Firstly, penetration may be key for romance writers, since it inevitably goes with marriage and the surrender of virginity. But it is not the be-all and end-all of sex, as the gay men who speak at slash conventions sometimes point out to their audience. Slash writers are always looking to vary the scenario, for realism and because there are only so many ways you can fit tab A into slot B without boring your readers – sound literary reasons both. For similarly literary reasons, many slash writers are as interested in the preliminaries as in the main event, or more so. To quote the slash writer Elvichar (in private email), "there are only so many ways to write sex; there are thousands of ways to write people into the situation where they are likely to have sex".

Secondly, Symons and I may have been reading different fanzines but I have seen some extremely explicit illos (fanspeak for illustrations) in slash zines, as well as the "romantic" kind mentioned above. On covers, indeed, the artwork tends to be mild, for reasons of discretion; inside is another matter. In the *B7* slash zine *Fire and Ice 7*[6] the illos included two depictions of bondage and four erect penises, which I have yet to see in a Mills & Boon.

Slash was originally also essentially about men and their emotions, though since it was written by women the male characters they wrote inevitably partook of their own character, experiences and wishes. *Warrior Lovers* is puzzled as to why women readers would "identify" with a male character in this situation. I am puzzled by its assumption, firstly that this would be any harder than, say, identifying with one of Shakespeare's kings or Richard Adams's rabbits, and secondly that in order to enjoy a story a reader must necessarily "identify" with one of the main characters at all. (Surely it is possible to enjoy *Wuthering Heights* without either seeing oneself as Cathy or sharing her feelings for Heathcliff?). I have seen the question "which character do you identify with" asked on a slash mailing list, and from most readers the answer was "neither"; they were watching from outside, keenly interested in how the author would help her characters sort out their intimacy issues. In fact some slash stories provide the reader with a voyeur-figure, deliberately or accidentally watching the protagonists. At the end of Kel's *The Bill* fic 'Somewhere Within'[7], Jim Carver finds himself in this position and several *B7* slashfics cast Vila as voyeur.

Once slash took off, it found a place in almost every screen fandom, even those which did not fit the original pattern. The successors to *Star Trek* featured stronger female characters and more sensitive male ones, but fan writers could still find slash subtexts in them, as they could in shows like The *X-Files* which centred on a male/female duo. (At the same time it should be noted that by far the greater part of adult *X-Files* fanfic centres on the m/f duo of Mulder and Scully.) Slash writers, by the way, are often accused by anti-slashers of not so much making gay subtexts visible as inventing them where they never were. But they are sometimes vindicated from unexpected quarters. In an interview in *The Guardian*[8], Simon Nye, writer and creator of the sitcom *Men Behaving Badly* (ITV/ BBC 1992-98), casually remarked: "Nobody ever picked up on it, but Men Behaving Badly was about a same-sex relationship. Everyone latched on to the lad thing, but to me there was always a significant homoerotic content in the relationship between Gary and Tony. You always got the impression that they'd rather be left alone together, but that was something that they could never admit to themselves". He was wrong, of course, about nobody having picked up on it. There is not much *Men Behaving Badly* slash online, but it does exist – Elvichar's 'Postman's Knock'[9] is one example.

Slash could once be fairly easily defined as homoerotic relationships between male characters which did not happen on screen but might, given certain circumstances, have done. Nowadays there is frequent debate within the writing community about two more recent developments and whether they "count" as slash: (i) is "slash" purely m/m or can an f/f story also be so described? (ii) do stories about characters who are canonically gay count as slash?

The first question would seem odd – if a relationship can be postulated between two male characters, why not between two females – if it were not for the oft-cited motive of opening characters up to their emotions. As J J McGee notes, women aren't generally the ones with the intimacy issues. Nor did they generally feature in the angst and hurt/comfort scenarios from which I have suggested that slash developed. Partly again this was because they didn't need opening up to their emotions and partly because putting female characters through the physical and emotional wringer was more problematic for the writers and readers, most of whom after all were female themselves.

By McGee's definition, which (probably unusually) is wide enough to allow for "het slash", what matters is not so much the gender of the characters as the nature of the relationship and the effect it has on them. If two female characters were very closed-off to their emotions, then a story which changed that by putting them in a relationship would be slash. If they *didn't* have "issues with vulnerability and emotion" it presumably wouldn't be, and neither would it if it involved two male characters for whom falling for each other was no great matter.

Hence the problem of canonically gay characters. There were very few, in the 70s, who were unequivocally so, and certainly no hero-figures that I recall. Now there are. *The Bill* introduced a canonically gay male sergeant, Craig Gilmore, in 2001, and his passionate onscreen kiss with PC Luke Ashton (in 2002) was canon too. Fanfic stories exploring the future possibilities of this plotline started appearing soon after it aired, and in fact triggered an exponential increase in the amount of *Bill* slash fanfic being written. There is a website dedicated to the Gilmore character at "savegilmore"[10], (a name which has since changed, see Appendix 2) which, when I last looked, contained several novel-length fics and was still expanding daily. The slash writer Sioux has remarked on an unarchived mailing list that she cannot recall any British TV series ever generating fiction in these quantities in such a short time before. There is also a small but thriving fanfic universe based around the Channel 4 TV series *Queer As Folk* (1999-2000). The question is, are such stories slash or simply gayfic?

Again for many writers it seems to come back to the purpose of fanfic as a whole, and slash writers by their nature fall into the "more from" rather than "more of" category. To return to the mailing list debate:

> For me, fanfic is largely interesting in the way it explores things that weren't and wouldn't have been portrayed on screen. I'm not all that interested in most "could have been an episode" type stories. [...] a lot of the fic I enjoy reading are things that for various reasons simply weren't possible on the original show. – J J McGee

> There has been debate about whether you could slash QAF's characters, who were gay to start with. My own view was that you could with the original series, because though Stuart would shag anything male that moved, he did not get emotionally involved, i.e. fall in love. I see slashing someone as opening them up to their emotions, far more than making them try something physical they hadn't done before. So a story that made Stuart fall in love would, for me, have slashed him. After the follow-up, where he does admit his feelings, I didn't see the point. (H)

> I only really like slashing a pairing which is both visible and withheld [...] if they're snogging on-screen they don't need me to restore the relationship.
>
> – Ika

Some feel slash as it was has a limited life, with the advent of stronger female roles and overtly gay characters (though both still have a long way to go). This generates mixed feelings among people who, being habitually liberal-minded, are glad to see both developments but who miss the participatory triumph of being able to extend the canon, not to mention the sense of transgressiveness in doing so this way:

> Slash as I like to read and write it comes from a dying kind of canon, the central m/m pairing which is happening less and less as female actors get more respect. Which is a good thing but it means there's far more m/f central pairings and ensemble shows. A lot of the more recent slash I've seen seems to be almost for the sake of it [...] it's becoming something more imposed on a canon than organically growing out of it or being deduced from it. – Ika

> I feel as though I should want more explicit gay characters on prime time TV but in practice I prefer the gaps and the transgressiveness of slashing latency.
>
> – Nova

This is not a universal attitude, and the proof of it is in the unstoppable expansion of the slash fanfic website savegilmore (http://www.savegilmore.co.uk/ which held over a million words in late 2003). Not a lot was eventually withheld on this storyline, though what happened the night before they woke up in bed together was, unsurprisingly, a missing scene. But this filling in of gaps has not stopped fans from filling them in otherwise and making the story go on as they want it to.

The two themes that seem to emerge over and over when slash writers discuss slash are the importance of extending the canon, of exploring what was "visible but withheld", and the extent to which, however physically explicit slash may get, its core is emotion. The Gilmore/Ashton stories written by *The Bill's* slash writers have so far focused on the fact that while Gilmore is gay and relaxed about it, Ashton is very uncertain of his sexuality. (Or, as Claire's fic 'Did It Again',[11] put it, so far into the closet he's looking at real estate prices in Narnia). At the time some of these stories were written (late 2002) he had sought refuge in a relationship with a girlfriend, Kerry, but was still vacillating. With a fine disregard for the fact that the storyline was still open and might be taken any which way by the official writers, the fanfic writers began to explore what he might do next. Sioux's 'Unconditional'[12] assumes that Luke carries on with both clandestinely for a while until Kerry becomes pregnant. He marries her but hankers for the other side of his life. Since Gilmore will no longer have anything to do with him he seeks solace at a gay pick-up joint and gets beaten up. Gilmore rescues him, and he and his new partner Phil let Luke spend the night in their spare bedroom.

What is "visible but withheld" about this scenario is that it is told from Luke's viewpoint and we are allowed inside his head, which at the time this story was written had not happened in the canon. The Gilmore/Ashton encounter had been seen very much through Gilmore's eyes: Luke kisses him but then backs off and gets aggressive and Gilmore, like the viewers, has no idea what is really going on in Luke's mind. Luke had first told him that he did it out of curiosity and then that it was a wind-up, either of which, for all we or Gilmore knew, might have been true. In the fanfic story we are from the start inside the mind of a man who does not know for sure what he wants but has a fair idea of what it might be and is afraid to confront it. It is a situation with promising angst potential, especially when, in Craig's house, Luke watches him with his new lover Phil and finally knows what he wants:

> Craig noticed Luke eating very little.
>
> "Luke, if you want to go to bed just go. Don't feel you have to sit up with us."
>
> "Thanks. I think I will turn in. I'm a bit sore."
>
> "Do you want any painkillers," Phil offered, immediately.
>
> "No, it's alright thanks."
>
> Did the man have to be so nice? he thought to himself as he made his way upstairs.
>
> He lay awake for a little while listening to Phil and Craig still talking in the kitchen, then their voices moved to the lounge area. Eventually he dozed off only to be wakened a couple of hours later by the gentle sound of Craig and Phil making love. He lay listening to them until the soft sounds drifted into silence.

In its way, this is quite a nostalgic fic: slash as it used to be, involving at least one character who had never contemplated the possibility of such a relationship and had a hard time coming to terms with it and opening up to his feelings – what was sometimes called the "first time" scenario. This is undoubtedly how slash started off – to quote Executrix in the mailing list debate: "A not-uncommon theory is that properly speaking slash is about heterosexual males having sex with each other, so by definition they don't come out to themselves, much less other people". In one aspect it was the ultimate way of expressing physically the "comfort" side of hurt/comfort: a character who might otherwise have put his arm round another would make love to him. In the *Hornblower* fan fiction universe there are a great many very angsty Horatio-Archie hurt/comfort stories which remain gen, and an equal number which turn slashy, and there is very little to stop any one story going either way. In fact often the only reason I can see why one turns slashy and the other doesn't is that one website is slash-friendly and another isn't.

Slash in this context was the ultimate way of making a man, especially a hard man, face up to "issues with vulnerability and emotion" (while remaining a man, for it is important, as ever, to remain true to the characters and most fanfic readers loathe stories which feminise male characters. "Mpreg", where a male character becomes pregnant, seems to be especially hated even in SF universes where it would be theoretically possible.)

This view of slash as physicalising emotion would also explain why slash writers sometimes find themselves at odds with male readers (not that there are many) who object that sex just isn't like that for men – gay, straight or undecided; they don't talk or emote about it so much. Slash writers know that: in a way, it is part of the point. A slashed hero has more to do with what the writers wish men were like than with what they know men are like. It can also, as Nova points out, have something to do with what women are like. If someone is a writer, whatever she says about their characters will also say something about herself and the kind of relationships she wants. Though slash writers are very concerned to get physical details right, as we shall see in a later chapter, and though slash can involve very explicit sex, it is about far more than that. Usually the effect on the emotional and power dynamic within the pairing matters far more than anything that actually gets done in bed. To quote from list discussion again:

> In effect: the sex is actually a minor part of slash (I'm not knocking it – I love joyously bawdy, endlessly inventive sex – but it only works because I believe in the more important mental and emotional coupling rather than the anatomical attachments).
>
> – SM

Halimede echoes Nova's view about slash and female perspectives in an interesting analysis of why slash appeals more than het to some female readers:

> People being true to themselves is incredibly sexy. In slash, for the romance to occur the two (or more) characters usually have to leave the beaten path. The love is not expected the same way it is in mainstream-het, it's not the default option. As a result there is more individuation in the same sex set-up as the characters come to terms with this, whereas in mainstream-het romance the opposite occurs, with characters being subsumed by their partner or the relationship. I'd say this is true even in Romeo & Juliet type scenarios, where their het-love is stronger than the characters and (even if it destroys them) inevitable, while in the equal but opposite same sex scenario the peril comes from the fact that the love is precious but *not* inevitable.
>
> The difference in flavor between slash and mainstream-het then, for

> me, is that even in the context of romance the individuality of the characters is a stronger story element.
>
> Maybe that is also why a lot of slash feels feminist even when no women feature in it: It's (mostly) women imagining romances where the individuality of the partners is of as much value as the romantic relationship. I've always been puzzled why even the most soppy, twu wuv slash fic can have this feel for me. I think this might be why.[13]

So far in this chapter I have concentrated on TV texts, because this is where published slash began – and given the legal situation, it could hardly have begun much earlier. But at least some slash writers claim to have been mentally slashing their favourite books – not for publication obviously – a lot earlier. Nova, who actually started her writing career as a profic writer and later took up fanfic, states "I was a slasher at 12, matchmaking Georgette Heyer heroes". Other writers have mentioned doing the same for Antonio and Bassanio (I should have said that was canonical myself, but no doubt some wouldn't) or David Balfour and Alan Breck from *Kidnapped.* The great male dyad in book-based fandom for this purpose is Holmes and Watson, and there are several fanzines in print dedicated purely to Holmes/Watson slash, quite apart from any number of web sites. Jeeves and Wooster score quite well too, but probably more because of the TV series than the books. (It is true that the Sherlock Holmes stories have also been often filmed and televised but in this canon the book still seems to rule.)

In the two book-based fandoms on which I have concentrated, slash is not common. In the Discworld what there is tends to focus on Vimes/Carrot, on the basis of a degree of canonical hero-worship on Carrot's part. But though Pratchett's fans, like the man himself, are not afraid of seriousness and even darkness, the Discworld universe was after all created for humorous purposes, which means there is a limit to the amount of both angst and romance it can accommodate. If it comes to that, Pratchett does not really write het love scenes either, and though the Discworld is a tolerant and open-minded place, the reaction of most of his characters, male and female, to the suggestion that they should advertise their vulnerability and their emotions doesn't bear thinking about. Vimes/Carrot, though, is a possible match and, if it could happen, would provide more angst than most, because both are essentially decent, honest people who would be betraying a wife and a more-or-less fianceé. Manx's 'Because Love Makes You Stupid'[14] focuses on this point, and makes it reasonably credible by catching their voices well.

> 'I have to go, Carrot' he said, 'Sybil is expecting me at home *some* time tonight' he managed a weak chuckle, 'can't have her come looking for me'
>
> Carrot didn't reply for a while. Then;
>
> 'Sir...?'
>
> 'Sam, Carrot'
>
> 'Sam... do you ever wish... I mean, isn't there some way things could be... different'
>
> *Every dammed day* Vimes thought, looking at Carrot's hopeful face, *every godsdammed day...* 'How would that work, then, Carrot? You tell Angua, I tell Sybil. We flip a coin for who tells the Patrician?'
>
> Wounded blue eyes looked at him.
>
> *Gods Carrot, please don't... don't make this any harder* 'Carrot, I'm just being realistic. I love you, but I can't....I can't leave Sybil. You can't leave Angua, you've said so yourself'
>
> 'But I don't love her!' There was panic in Carrot's voice now 'Not like I love you'
>
> Vimes relented. 'I know, I know. But we can't have any more than this, no matter how much we want it.'

I have found little slash in the Austen fanfic universe either, which some might say was hardly surprising. The problem is not the historical setting – the fact that something was illegal and carried heavy penalties has never actually stopped people doing it, and in fact from a slash writer's viewpoint the legal and social situation just adds to the potential angst quotient. There is plenty of slash in the Hornblower, Sharpe and Sherlock Holmes fanfic universes. But in the first two of those, the canon is a TV series, rather than the books on which it was based, and in the third, which is more book-based, the voice is that of a character, Watson. The specific problem with Austen is one of voice, or rather of the fact that most Austen fanfic writers feel obliged to approximate her voice, which to a great extent is also that of her characters. The mimetic difficulty of keeping up an Austen voice is enough in gen fanfic; considering how to phrase slash material in the said voice is daunting. Lizard's fic 'Two Sides of the Same Coin', archived at fanfiction.net[15] opts for a neutral authorial voice which sounds more or less possible for any period.

> When we are young and in love, we think we will be in love forever, and when we are older, we know this is never true. After a few weeks of seemingly blissful rendezvous in the woods, George became older.

The premise of this fic is credible enough – that Darcy and George Wickham, in their shared boyhood, become for a while more than friends and that this (in particular Darcy's embarrassment about it) accounts for some of the animosity between them. Darcy's conviction, in the novel, that Wickham is out for revenge on him does seem odd – Wickham is irresponsible and venal but it is hard to see him as actively ill-natured, and he hardly seems to have the energy to be revengeful. In most fanfic universes this "childhood friends turned enemies" scenario would have been comprehensively explored by slash writers; in fact very few have done so. Partly this may be because Austen fanfic writers, like many with a book-based domain, are more mimetic than innovative, but I think another reason is the difficulty of getting the character voices right. The problem lies in finding a credible way for Austen's people to speak of such a thing.

Writers in other historical universes like Hornblower and Sherlock Holmes are slightly better off in this regard. In the British navy of Hornblower's day there was at least a credible vocabulary for such material: as for Holmes writers, one of their heroes is fairly unconventional and the other is a doctor. Susannah Shepherd's "Hidden Depths", archived at Allaire Mikhail's site[16] presupposes two things, neither beyond belief, first that Holmes is homosexual, and second that Watson, who so obviously likes women, hasn't married because his war wound is more serious and extensive than he makes out. He has scar tissue in awkward places, which causes him pain on arousal and prevents him from climaxing by normal means. He is desperately embarrassed by his marred appearance and masculinity, which is one reason Holmes tells him his own secret in exchange. Though shocked, he is also grateful, needy and trusting enough to accept Holmes' offer of help (with the aid of a blindfold):

> "I swear to you, John, that I shall do nothing with you that a woman could not do, if she were sufficiently bold and imaginative and... loving." His fingers brushed against the corner of my moustache. "Please, let me do this for you."
>
> I did wonder whether Holmes was really offering to do this for me or for himself, but I put the thought aside as unworthy. That left the rather more difficult problem of whether I was willing to accept a man's intimate touch on my body. A large part of me screamed with revulsion, but another part craved what Holmes was offering, tenderness and arousal and satisfaction.

Holmes shows him how to climax via stimulation of the prostate (being a doctor, Watson is allowed to recognise what it is exactly that Holmes is stimulating, which wouldn't be possible with most "first time" slash scenarios). This is a "first and last", for next morning Watson finds a note from a remorseful Holmes:

> *I should, in all conscience, have given you this earlier this afternoon, but I fell prey to my own private weaknesses. I hope you can find it in your heart to forgive me for my selfish actions, although I shall understand if you cannot.*
>
> *You will find below the name and address of a young woman with whom I have been in contact in my professional capacity. She is a warm-hearted soul who specialises in, shall we say, comforting gentlemen with special needs such as your own. Her talents have been of assistance to at least one of my esteemed clients, and she comes highly recommended. I do hope that she may be able to demonstrate to you that at least some of your fears are unfounded, given proper encouragement and imagination.*
>
> *I am, as always, your very dear friend,*
>
> *Sherlock Holmes*

Watson, unsurprisingly, finds forgiveness easy. Shepherd describes this as a "hurt/comfort" fic, which of course it is. It is much less about sex than about tenderness, trust, mutual needs and an act of friendship. It doesn't turn Watson gay but it does make him realise he is capable of feelings he did not previously recognise and it gives their relationship a new dimension. In this it is classic slashfic.

Hornblower, with its setting and mainly male cast, was always going to be a candidate for slashing too, and again it is one where the link from angst and hurt/comfort to slash is very clear. Before the death of Archie (and after it, since death has no dominion for fanfic writers) he and Horatio were a popular pairing and many fics focused on the presumed abuse in Archie's past, his low self-esteem and emotional need, for all of which there was at least some canonical evidence. By this reckoning, his relationship with Horatio is redemptive, as in Madelyn Scott's 'Flying'[17].

> "Archie?" The breeze came cool off the water, and Horatio shivered in it, because for that little time, Archie had not been lying with him in the sunshine, but in a midshipman's berth where the shadows grew and lengthened, and the arms about him belonged to another, and when he looked at his friend's own arms under those fingers, they were bruised. Then there was a shifting sound as the layers of the world slid back into conjunction again, and Archie smiled.

In this excerpt from Green's 'Unacceptable'[18], a slashfic angsty even by Archie standards, Archie is explaining to Bush, as both lie wounded in the infirmary, why he is about to confess to a crime he didn't commit in order to save Hornblower at a court-martial. In an interesting twist it is told from the point of view of an uninvolved and definitely straight Bush, who is the ingénu here. His conversion, if not to sharing Archie's feelings, at least to finding them moving and noble, could be read partly as an agenda. Slash writers face hostility in this as in other fanfic universes and one thing of which anti-slashers accuse them is demeaning the nature of friendship by sexualising it.

> Kennedy looks at him in surprise, and well he should, given that a Second Lieutenant of His Majesty's Navy has just sanctioned the worst crime in the calendar, and one for which Kennedy could expect to be hung whether or not it led him to the noose to save his beloved. Bush himself cannot believe what he has just said, what he has just condoned, and he doesn't want to think about the 'details' of that behaviour at all. But he knows that love is good, and somehow he can't see all this any other way. [...]
>
> But the passion in Kennedy's eyes is still present, with that purpose, and anger and strength. Bush suddenly receives a flash of understanding. He can see why Hornblower can love this man, and how those eyes would be so beautiful on a woman, and why did they have to entangle themselves when they knew this could happen any day and why can something so unpleasant seem so wonderful to them and how can love be with them, for all it is denied to so many 'natural' couples?
>
> But none of the answers are for Bush and none of them are for that day, or that time.

The reason there is so much debate on various mailing lists about the nature of slash is that, like most genres that have been about for a while, it has developed. Gay writers, or those concerned with gay issues, have used it to establish a gay presence in a straight universe, often in a way the scriptwriters were not allowed to do. AP, writing in the mailing list debate, records the effect of a change of producer on *The Bill*:

> Yes, I was at a lecture by a woman who was a writer for *The Bill* when this happened. The Executive Producer up to that time had been a very conservative person and she had been trying to sneak in various elements, such as a gay character, and got blocked at every turn. [...] She went on to write for *Casualty* (Saturday evening pre-watershed

> soap) and managed to get in a gay male character in a central role and achieved her career ambition when she managed to get a series to end with a gay wedding. It is interesting to me that the ambitions of the screenwriters are very often the same as the ambitions of the fanfic writers, but that they are fighting against a restrictive system. Seriously. They say things like "I wanted to get them to kiss but we were given a list of allowed body contact." In the case of *Casualty* these guys were getting *married*, for goodness sake, and they were allowed to "ruffle hair" as long as their bodies didn't come into contact.

Some slash fanfic writers have used their immunity from such constraints to do what this scriptwriter was trying to do, so that slash becomes as much political as personal. Inevitably, then, it goes beyond "first time" self-realisation and indeed beyond men. The 2002 *B7* fanzine 'Sleer as Folk' was all f/f slash, a first for the fandom. In an online review[19] Nova comments on how "deviant" sexuality in the zine constantly becomes a metaphor for political deviancy – or even a means of expressing it:

> Ika's 'Future Perfect' combines the personal and the political more optimistically, tracking the progress of Della, an OC in the Federation's itinerant labour pool, from a bitter acceptance of her temporary life to understanding and resistance – a progression that is embodied in the story's shift from the vivid or historic present to the narrative perfect , with occasional glimpses of the future perfect [...] It's an amazing juggling act, creating and then dissecting the Federation's methods of social control, while simultaneously showing us how the basic organising principles of a society affect the construction of sexuality and critiquing any form of resistance that concentrates on class to the exclusion of gender and sexual preference.

In an interview on 'Arts Today', an Australian radio programme (Radio National), Ika, the author referred to above, speaks of the kind of slash that develops relationships out of hints and possibilities in canon ("making gay subtexts visible" as BC puts it). Ika places it in both a literary context of "filling in the gaps" and a socio-political one of changing the reader's perceptions not just of the fanfic universe but of the one she lives in.

> I think the pleasure of it for me is that that interaction between them marks out a space, which for me is a very erotic space, but then doesn't fill it, so that you're free to kind of imagine – any sort of relationship, without having to subject it to your sort of men-act-this-

> way, women-act-that-way heterosexual kind of grid. You're much freer to imagine a space of eroticizing equality, which used to be one of the old feminist goals.

There is much more f/f slash (femslash) about now than there used to be, and while one reason for that is the advent of more interesting female canon characters, (eg in the Buffyverse) it certainly has a socio-political agenda as well. Some female femslash writers are themselves gay or bisexual and are marking out a territory. Nova, who writes both slash and femslash but no het, once said not entirely flippantly in private email that the world was het-biased enough already. Other writers, Executrix among them, feel uneasy at the lack of attention given to female canon characters in the past by fanfic writers, themselves largely female, and want to rectify that. They are setting out to write about the female characters; if the writing happens to turn slashy that is, quite often, incidental to their main purpose of marking out more female territory.

Executrix, having posed the question of whether slash can be about characters who identify as gay, states her position; "my own definition is that a fic involving same-sex relationships is slash, even if the character is canonically gay". This doesn't agree with definitions that involve making subtexts visible and filling in gaps, and it is probable that the genre has gone beyond the point where people can agree on exactly what constitutes it. In some ways this is exactly what pleases writers and readers who, by definition, like to push boundaries:

> One of the things about the dynamic of showing-and-withholding a relationship that inspires me to write slash is that it's an opportunity to explore a form of queer intimacy which is not bound by the conventions for representing gay relationships which have already come into being. I have no interest in accurately representing the anatomy, sex lives, emotional attachments and lifestyles of gay men: they can do that themselves. I have no interest in accurately representing my *own* anatomy, sex life, emotional attachments and lifestyle either, except maybe in very fragmented and metaphorized bits. The stuff that matters to me, that I want to get across in fiction, is not about "being" a woman, or "being" queer, or "being" anything else. I like writing slash because it precisely **resists** attributing identity categories – gay, straight, male, female – which then determine how a character acts or is represented. It's all about making up new ways of understanding the relationship between sex, gender and experience.
>
> – Ika: unarchived mailing list

It might, however, be useful to bear in mind that most slash is still written and read by a female audience and whatever other political or literary goals it may have, it is a genre which aims to do something in a way that pleases women. In this it differs from fiction aimed at gay men, being generally far more character-driven and circumstantial (though it still, in my view, has far more in common with such fiction than it does with the Mills & Boon "romance" genre).

What constitutes good and bad writing within slash might, possibly, be easier to secure some agreement on. In this world of shared writers' resources there are convenient online lists of "slash clichés" to be avoided, and a general consensus about certain pitfalls. Feminising the characters in any way is, as previously indicated, deeply deplored, both because fanfic readers feel it to be untrue to the characters and, I think, for political reasons. One thing some slash readers and writers like about slash as opposed to het is the "eroticizing equality" mentioned earlier by Ika. It is difficult, in any sex scene involving penetration, to make the two participants completely equal and avoid any hint of dominance. In a slash partnership you can, which is one reason many slash writers try not to get into the habit of letting one partner be permanently on top, either physically or emotionally. Either the characters will make love in ways other than penetrative or alternate the roles.

"ATG" (Any Two Guys") is a dismissive term for slash writing in which the sex rather than the characters is the focus, to the extent that it could be anyone doing it and it wouldn't make a difference. It is not unexpected that this would be disapproved of, in a genre where characters matter so much. Many would echo the view expressed (on an unarchived list) by Ika:

> I guess for me, the most satisfying, rigorous, sexy and significant slash is about the shape and dynamic of a particular relationship, which recapitulates and/or changes the shape and dynamic of the universe in which the relationship is set. And that's usually OTP slash.

OTP stands for One True Pairing. Those who believe two characters were made for each other sometimes do not want to read or write about them with anyone else. Some fandoms lend themselves to this (*The Man from UNCLE*, *Starsky & Hutch*). Others do not. I have seen Horatio Hornblower paired with Archie, Bush, Pellew, Edrington and too many women to recall: I am assured, though I have not seen it, that at least one fic exists where he is paired with a mermaid. But there are OTP believers in all fandoms, and some pairings, like the original K/S, became almost sub-genres in themselves: "Sparrington" (Captain Jack Sparrow and Commodore Norrington from *Pirates of the Caribbean*) looks like becoming another. Some of the fan resistance to the turns taken by the canonical Gilmore-Ashton storyline in *The Bill* came about because fans were convinced that the two were an OTP and therefore destined to end up together. Certainly this is what generally happens in the fiction on the savegilmore website. (OTP belief is not confined to slash fans either. Many *Bill* fans are convinced that Jim Carver and June Ackland are a het OTP, and object when the scriptwriters threaten to pair them with anyone else.)

But the disapproval of sex-focused (as opposed to character-focused) stories may also reflect the worry of some slash writers and readers about their motives. By no means all slash fans believe in an OTP: in fact their tendency to be curious about alternatives usually leads them to consider many. This probably does not bother most slash fans, but as McLelland points out, there is still a residual feeling that women aren't *meant* to enjoy that sort of thing, and need some other reason to like the writing. I have seen a mailing list discuss the question "are those of us who like our pairings to come in as many flavours as possible less likely to be monogamous?" Not many respondents thought so, or were judgmental about monogamy or the lack of it. Nonetheless it is telling that the question was raised, and a fictional preference associated with personal behaviour.

Recognised pitfalls in slash writing, whether OTP or not, are the over-physical approach, sometimes known as "fit tab A into slot B", which can become very mechanical and repetitive, and the over-emotional, which can soon degenerate into sentimental mush. Having said this, slash, with its interest in opening up emotions, naturally contains some of the most heightened writing in fanfic. This is a brief slash scene from a much longer (as yet unpublished) *B7* PGP fic, 'The Only Engine of Survival', by that rarest of creatures, a male m/m slash writer, Dan G. The reference to the "interplanetary banking system" is one of those pieces of shared canon information; Avon had committed a computer fraud aimed at robbing it of millions.

> Insanity comes and goes with the weather; I knew you well, you knew me even better. You shot the stars right out of the sky, From the sky Special One, Ultra Vivid Scene Inalienable law of human nature. Sit down with a stylus and a tarriel cell. Place B in A, fold tab C. Type in any combination of names you want – vidcast hosts, academics,

subversives, members of the High Council. Add the word "fucking". Simmer. Within the week, no matter how absurd and unlikely the combination, you will find that adolescent fingers have been trying to tickle more details from your stylus databank. X fucking Y. Y fucking X. It's the ineluctable power of the search engine guide to human sexuality. Blake fucking Avon. Avon fucking Blake. Blake fucking Avon. Which is curious, in a way. Blake and Avon have had something which could be identified by the referent "sex" maybe somewhere between three and four hundred times. Of those times, the majority had nothing much to do with putting things in other things. Too tired, too busy, too short of time, too taken up with reading a chart or monitoring a transmission. So we're actually probably talking perhaps 50 or 60 actual incidences of fucking itself. All of which Avon has run through, synthesized, distilled and started again. It's been a running motif. He hasn't touched on random moments of tenderness, affectionate hair-ruffling, momentary touches of upturned hand and downcurved fingers. For the last two days, when he hasn't been sleeping fitfully or idly flicking through Carnell's restricted files, idly wondering why he had the security camera footage destroyed, the ballistics reports fudged and the danger of a swift and unambiguous end in front of a firing squad of heroes deferred, Avon has foregone every other possible, painless expression of whatever it was they needed to express. Just Blake fucking Avon. Avon fucking Blake. Blake inside Avon, putting one hand behind his head and pulling his mouth to his nipple, grinding into a taut bow, telling him what a good, good soldier he is because, no matter the pain, no matter the provocation, he never bites down hard. Avon inside Blake, running hands down flanks, across his back, dragging neat-cut fingernails either side of his spine. Down to his chest, tangling in the surprisingly light dusting of hair, down further to his belly, playing the very tips of his fingers across his balls, waiting, waiting until Blake gave that tiny grunt, surrender, frustration, relief and propped his weight on one shoulder, muscles tensed as one arm formed a triangle against the bed, fingers digging into the sheet as the other shot with a homing instinct to his cock. The tremors as he pumped it hard, mercilessly, and Avon enjoying the tension in his own face made by his own infuriating smile. Blake doing that incredible thing, arching his entire body upwards from Avon's, the strength that showed he'd been fighting one way or another for fifteen years, maybe, and even as a spoilt, cleansed citizen never missed an appointment at the Alpha Gymnasium, bracing himself on drawn-up knees as he reached down for Avon, one finger of the other hand tracing the base of his own cock, deep, so deep. Avon the prisoner, Blake the guard. Blake the rebellion, Avon the Federation. Blake the

> punishment, Avon the penitent. Avon Avon, Blake the entire interplanetary banking system. Blake Blake, Avon Avon. Blake fucking Avon. Avon fucking Blake.

Seeing that we are here in the point of view of someone recalling sex with someone he's not long ago shot, the emotional charge is not surprising. But even when slash stories aren't actually describing sex their emotional and angst-quotient tends to be high. In this excerpt from Kel's 'Somewhere Within', referred to earlier in this chapter, PC Jim Carver of *The Bill* (many years ago, before he was middle-aged and stout) is recalling how he became infatuated with his colleague Loxton.

> It began in the breaking of silence, the silence of tired, bored colleagues following a tired, boring routine. See this: a drugs obbo on the Jasmine Allen, a long, flat day, cramped together in an abandoned caretaker's office, vandalised, smelling of dust and old sandwiches. His long, lean frame arced in interest over the video camera, glad to be out of uniform, off the street. No fuss, no spark. Colleagues, drinking companions, friends in that vague and undefined way that has nothing to do with commonalty of interest or mutual knowledge but rests rather on professional trust and the semi-formulaic camaraderie of the canteen and the bar and the job well done.
>
> As colleagues do, we said little, shared a joke, a curse, nothing of import. He kept busy, enjoyed the work. I enjoyed the company. And the view. How much more compelling is the hidden, the denied, the wanted. Doubly sweet, when the wanting itself is hidden. I know every inch of his body now, have seen him pale, flushed, heated, chafed, chilled, naked, open... and I'd roll it all back if I could, know nothing but that wish-list vision of leather and denim and unguessable softness beneath the seams. Maybe.

The affair is not in fact giving poor Jim any happiness, since Loxton's arrogance and self-sufficiency ensure that it is conducted entirely on his terms. Nonetheless Carver seems to accept that he has chosen to be where he is and would not really "roll it all back" to get off his rollercoaster angst ride. There is a subtext in this as in so much slash, that feeling something – almost anything – is better than feeling nothing, or being unaware or afraid of one's feelings. In the beginning the idea of the genre was precisely to unlock closed, inhibited male characters into what the fanfic writers felt they had it in them to be. Now that TV canons are catching up with them in that respect, the writers have gone on to use it for other purposes, notably reclaiming some territory for diversity and demonstrating that the world is more various than TV producers think.

It will be a while before the "official" canons catch up with this one. The gay wedding on *Casualty* referred to earlier earned the BBC a bomb threat. The producer on *The Bill* who thought audiences would not want to see a gay policeman was wrong: the development was popular with more viewers than disliked it. But the Gilmore/Ashton kiss still generated over 300 complaints. And on *The Bill's* fan forum,[20] which unlike the fiction is not female-dominated, it seems more often than not to be the male fans who complain of the show's new relationship-dominated ethos and want it to focus entirely on the characters' working lives. They state, among other things, that they want pure police drama (car chases being specifically mentioned) and that they want to see "no sex" between characters, gay or straight. They suggest that it is unrealistic to include love lives in a work-based show because people do not take their love lives into the office (at which point one longs to ask which planet their offices are on). They contend that it is not the business of a police drama to portray its characters fully, suggesting that this is the province of soaps and straight drama. And while it is sometimes female fans who take this line, it does seem more commonly to be men

It will take some time yet before male issues of vulnerability and emotion are sorted.

NOTES

1. http://www.sfu.ca/~ksboyd/history.html 12.11.02
2. http://www.cult-media.com/issue1/CMRmcle.htm 15.10.02
3. *Warrior Lovers*, Weidenfeld & Nicolson 2001
4. *Warrior Lovers*, chapters 7 and 8
5. *Warrior Lovers*, p83
6. ed Kathleen Resch 2002
7. http://www.goldweb.com.au/~bessie/ 5.7.04
8. *The Guardian*, 21.10.02
9. archived at http://www.geocities.com/elvichar/slasharama.html 17.11.02
10. http://www.savegilmore.co.uk 13.03.03
11. http://www.goldweb.com.au/~bessie/ 7.12.02
12. http://www.savegilmore.co.uk 3.3.03
13. http://www.livejournal.com/users/halimede/99142.html?view=326982#t326982 23.09.04

14. fanfiction.net http://www.fanfiction.net/s/854189/1/ 04.01.05
15. http://www.fanfiction.net/s/971580/1 04.01.05
16. http://www.skeeter63.org/allaire/FavStories.htm 13.11.02
17. http://www.frolixers.com/flying.html 24.08.04
18. http://www.fanfiction.net/s/1009249/1/ 5.12.02
19. http://www.hermit.org/blakes7
20. http://forum.billfans.net/DCForumID2/1723.html 1.12.02

6. The Communal Online Sandpit

Collaboration and Support

On *The Bill's* gen fanfic website Wolfie, the site owner, gives the following advice to writers submitting stories:

> I will accept unformatted/incorrect work from new writers up until around their third story (depending on the length of story) and will correct it myself, whilst emailing the appropriate advice to the writer. However, if the work continues to be submitted with the same errors, I will be forced to return it to the writer and let them correct it. By the time of the third story (depending on length), I would have given you enough hints, tips, guidelines, and most likely one-on-one advice (via e-mail, ICQ, AOL Messenger or a chat room) for you to have taken notice of what I've said.[1]

I have been writing and publishing poems and novels, in magazines and in book form, for nearly 30 years, and I have never come across a profic editor who gave feedback like that. I also teach creative writing to students, and try to help them improve the technical aspects of their work in the way Wolfie outlines above, but if there were very many editors like her (and if writers always listened properly to them) I would probably be out of a job.

Despite the name, "fandom", though vast, is less a kingdom than a bunch of independent federated republics that do not necessarily have much in common. Writers of *Buffy* fan fiction may be working in the same genre as writers of *X-Files* fan fiction, but they do not necessarily have any interest in each other's fandom; indeed they may despise it. And that means they do not read each other's work. Some writers do write in more than one fan universe but it would be rare to write in more than two or three, and many are faithful to one only (though with some this is serial monogamy in that they might move out of one fandom into another). Most fanfic writers, except those in really large fandoms, are writing for a fairly small community.

Fortunately for them, it is also a very supportive one. Before the modern explosion of the genre, book-based fan fiction had occasionally been printed and distributed in magazines by science fiction fans[2]. When the fandoms of the late sixties and seventies started producing their own fanfic, they had both a global audience and a problem accessing it – there was TV, syndicating the source material worldwide, but neither email nor the Net to do the like for fanfic. Fans could keep in touch via fan clubs and conventions, they could set up writers' groups and buy and read fanzines and letterzines (comments on various issues by the members of the letterzine, collated and sent out by a central editor). An APA (amateur press association) worked like a letterzine except that each member would write a fixed number of pages, make photocopies and send them to the person acting as editor, who would then collate and distribute them. They had a long history in fan culture; they had begun in the nineteenth century as journalistic enterprises but back in 1937 Donald A. Wollheim founded the Fantasy Amateur Press Association (FAPA), which was the first national APA that consisted entirely of fans and admirers of speculative fiction.

By this means feedback could be received on fiction, as it could via the culture in some fandoms of LOC (letters of comment) on fanzine stories. At conventions there could be events and discussion centred on fanfic writing.

But all this took time and effort, and the feedback was necessarily a long time in coming. Nor could everyone find the time and money to attend conventions, which might be a long way from home, indeed on a different continent. One writer comments on her own experience before going online: "I had a few pen-pals but we didn't discuss stories in progress because of the time-lag. A few editors commented on stories, but mostly I wrote in a vacuum." (Willa, on an unarchived mailing list). It is amazing there was anything like the association that existed, and still exists, for APAs continue, even now that writers can post stories to message boards and mailing lists and receive feedback from them. Some APAs have updated to the internet age, with editors accepting email contributions and all members paying their share of the costs.

The degree of association and interaction is a testament to the sense of community among fans, possibly not unconnected to their sense of isolation from mundanes. A lot of fans prickle with awareness of baffled disapproval from those outside their own community. I once asked on an unarchived list why the plural of "fan" within the fandom world is not "fans" but "fen", and I got two answers, both of which I suspect are true. One was that it derived from a mistype at a convention, which caught on because of its analogy with the plurals of "man" and "woman". This may very well have happened – it certainly did in the case of "filk", a song on a fandom theme written to an existing tune, which began life as a mistype for "folk". But that doesn't explain why "fen" was widely adopted – if that happened to every mistype, the language would soon be unrecognisable. The reason I have heard suggested is "to differentiate it from the mainstream world's derogatory use of the term. 'Fans', to rhyme with 'sad and/or mad geeks'" (Leia Fee). Fanfic writers get this in spades, particularly if they happen also to be profic writers or academics, because of the disdain of many writers and readers for those who choose not to use "original characters" and the low value set by academics and critics on genre fiction of any kind. It is not uncommon for a slash writer to observe wryly that though her colleagues at the university or wherever would be unfazed by the news that she wrote explicit m/m love scenes, they would be horrified to learn that these were set in an SF or fantasy universe.

Communities which feel beleaguered or misunderstood are generally close-knit. But as Willa's comment above shows, there were real problems. To join lists, contribute to zines and attend conventions you had to be aware that they existed, and many were not, particularly if they had not come to fandom at a young age. "Fan clubs", to many, were something adolescents joined; if you were older you indulged your fantasies in private without ever supposing others out there might be doing the same. What changed all this, of course, was the advent of the web and of email. Suddenly you could type the title of a film, book or TV series into a search engine and come up with the web addresses of news groups, mailing lists, message boards, information sites and, above all, fan fiction based on the source material. The community had always been worldwide, but now that was clear to those who had never suspected it and nobody, any longer, had to work in a vacuum.

This did not happen all at once. Usenet groups for particular fandoms, to which fans could post fiction, began to be set up in the eighties. Fanfic archives for several fandoms were set up in the nineties, and information sites on the source material were expanding throughout this period, often including fanfic resources like transcripts and encyclopaedia information (even the well informed can forget in which street of Sun Hill a pub stands or whether Hutch had a moustache in

Season 3). As individual web skills became more widespread, writers could set up their own sites as a home for their fiction, and solicit immediate feedback via email. Web rings, search engines and umbrella sites with lots of links made it easier to collate and find not only material for individual fandoms but resources that were relevant to all, like articles on common writing pitfalls. Mailing lists could act like online writing groups, providing not only feedback but ideas and potential collaborators.

All this was not an unmixed blessing. As one writer of both profic and fanfic observes, "90% of anything is dreck" (Alicia Ann Fox), and the exponential increase in Net fanfic, much of it posted without the intervention of an editor, ensures there is plenty of dreck to be found. And the availability of free netfic has inevitably meant fewer fanzines, which do have an editorial process to maintain some kind of standard (though those that are left, having more good quality material to choose from, are arguably better). But nobody any longer is writing in a vacuum; they have an audience to consider, who can and sometimes do tell them if they don't like what they are reading, and they have fellow-writers to learn from. Two quotes from authors on an unarchived list:

> This list and others like it have themselves propelled improvement in writing skills. Writers get much quicker feedback and from more sources. [...] compare this to waiting 2 years for a zine to come out, then another 2 years to see if anyone wrote a LOC [...] the influence of other fan writers on us is vastly sped up.
>
> – Alicia Ann Fox

> By the time I wrote and posted my own first story here I'd read a fair amount of mediocre fanfic and had a pretty good idea of what to avoid. [...] What's more, being part of this list and posting stories to it has made me very conscious of the fact that I have an audience. And it's not some faceless mass of unknown people either. I'm writing for people I like and whose opinions I value, which gives me a good reason to want the fiction I'm putting out to represent me well".
>
> – Belatrix Carter

Fanfic writers who also write profic, and are used to the depressing lack of reviews and feedback from the readers, if any, frequently value the far greater feedback and more supportive culture they find in fanfic. Of course, "writing for people you like" does have its dangers. You may be tempted to give them what they like, rather than what you feel the story needs – eg ratcheting up the suffering quotient for angst fans when the story might be better with less. Also the people you like may like you, in which case they may be hesitant to criticise properly, certainly on-list. As one would expect, lists vary greatly in this respect, but on some mailing lists and message boards the comments do often look uncritical. It must be borne in mind, though, that many list members or site readers who did wish to send adverse comments would send them back-channel to the author alone, as a matter of courtesy. In general the distance of email is more conducive to honest criticism than, say, the situation that prevails in many writing groups where one may well be face to face with the author in her own living room.

And there is another device for obtaining honest comment: the beta-reader. This is a friend, usually a fellow-writer, who will read a fic in detail and comment, also in detail, before it is sent anywhere or shown to anyone else – "beta testers" check computer software for bugs before its release. Often two fanfic writers will beta-read for each other. They may know each other in real life, or they may live on different continents and come together in this way because their methods or aims are similar and modern technology allows it. And in this relationship the gloves are off: a beta-reader will try to be constructive, and will generally be in sympathy with the work she has agreed to consider, but she will read critically and let nothing go by. A good beta doesn't miss a comma out of place or a two-word slippage in point of view.

The editors of printed fanzines are generally rigorous too, reading in detail and working on the text with the author. Their technical competence is high; little in the spelling and punctuation line gets past them and they have of necessity a sharp ear for inconsistencies of voice. They take an active line on editing, seeing their job as far more than the uncritical collating of material. Naturally, writers do not always agree with their interventions. Executrix, in a caustic mood, remarked that they were well capable of "finding Rome a city of marble and leaving it one of brick" (a private email, which would seem to indicate that the relationship between writers and editors is much the same even when money doesn't come into it). Printed fan fiction has its own literary awards, the FanQs (plus a parallel set, the SCREWZ, specifically for slash). There are also some fandom-specific awards like the 5033s, instigated by *The Bill's* slash writers. As you might expect, all these awards are voted on by the reading and writing community itself.

Online zines are more variable in quality than printzines, and usually less rigorously edited, probably because of the amount of material submitted. Sites like the Republic of Pemberley, the Derbyshire Writers' Guild[3] and Wolfie's *The Bill* site all contain writers' guides on technical matters like grammar and punctuation, and on the facts of the source material. Some also contain advice on style and structure and some offer specialised help. The Sharpetorium[4], devoted to the TV series *Sharpe*, about a soldier in Napoleonic times (ITV 1993-97, based on the books by Bernard Cornwell), contains an invaluable set of links to factual sites on life in the 18th century, to help writers get their historical references right. This is very important to fan writers in an historical canon: *Sharpe* fanfic writers need to become expert on conditions and practices in the British army at the time, because many of their potential readers will be. The same goes for *Hornblower* writers who need to do their research on naval life of their period – see Kathy Kirchner's fic 'The Ties That Bind'[5], where at one point Archie is taking his lieutenant's exam and the author's note explains:

> Archie's answers to Captain Pellew's questions are taken from "Examination of a young officer, The New Practical Navigator"(1814).

But, like the Bennet girls, writers are not obliged to profit from the educational opportunities surrounding them: those who choose to be idle still may, and not all Net archives edit for technical competence or literary merit. Despite Wolfie's best editorial efforts, *The Bill's* gen fanfic site still contains examples of poor spelling and grammar. So do most online fanfic archives, though you would not find many in the Republic of Pemberley and the Derbyshire Guild of Writers. The archive sites for *B7* at the Hermit Library[6] and Liberated[7], Sarah B's *Hornblower* archive[8] and Henneth Annun, a site for book-based Tolkien fan fiction[9] are also more literate than the average.

Henneth Annun, in fact, is an exception to the general rule that online sites tend to be less rigorously edited. On this site fiction is admitted via a review process set up by members of the site, who vote on whether a story meets the standards of the archive. This, of course, raises the "Clinton question" of chapter 2 again: it depends what you mean by standards. It is not only a matter of literary quality but of canon, as in the Republic of Pemberley. Sites which exist to promote and preserve book-based fan fiction in its original form tend to be extremely protective in this way, and Henneth Annun, up against the immense pull of the films, may be more so than most. Tolkien uses poetry in the books, so there can be no doubt that fics in poetic form are compatible with canon. But when members submitted poems in forms Tolkien had not used, like the sonnet and villanelle, it sparked a debate as to whether they should be allowed into the archive. This was essentially the "more from" versus "more of" question, and as usual it was a thornier issue in a book-based fandom, where loyalty to and admiration of a single author can come into conflict with the desire of some fanfic writers to develop the material further or try things another way.

Kristi Lee Brobeck has recently conducted an interesting survey of the way the members of this particular online fan community regard its workings, and has kindly allowed me to reproduce her findings in an appendix. Naturally enough, opinions vary according to the degree to which the individual respondents feel they and their fiction are accepted by the community. One thing that became clear was that, as in most communities, the degree of democracy depends a lot on the extent of voluntary participation:

> There are 243 reviewers eligible to submit reviews. However, only 174 of them have done a single review since July 2003. Of the 174 that remain, fewer than 50 have reviewed 20 or more submissions.
>
> – Appendix 3: Under the Waterfall

Another thing this study illustrates is, to quote one of the respondents, "a profound tension in the site between the attempt to be inclusive in the members' area and the need to be exclusive in the archive". Any fan fiction site which operates a selection process (as opposed to the fanfiction.net model where anyone may post unedited), is going to come up against a body of opinion that feels this process is in a way incompatible with the basic premise of fan fiction, namely that anyone can be an author. Not everyone does feel this as a contradiction any more, and plenty of respondents reflect the more confident mindset of today's fan fiction writers who do not feel that "amateur" in the sense of "unpaid" has to be "amateur" in the sense of "not very good at it". Many respondents clearly see themselves as writers who want to improve, and regard honest criticism and peer review as a means to that end. But even profic writers who say they welcome criticism sometimes disagree with and resent it. Fan fiction writers are perhaps even likelier to defend their own take on their writing against anyone else's, and to resent any attempt by a committee to control or amend it.

The same body of opinion sometimes resists any form of critical judgement as somehow detracting from the "fun" and self-expression elements of fanfic. The Mithril Awards, Tolkien-specific literary awards decided by a judging panel that, though not the same entity as Henneth Annun's reviewing panel, does have personnel in common with it, have over the past two years caused similar controversy in the fandom. Some dissenters, again, see this judging process as elitist and opposed to the very nature of fanfic. The judging panel therefore suggested there should be a list of authors who did not wish their stories to be nominated. You might think this would have solved the problem, but it has not. The debate is not easy to follow, because it is being conducted in several different online spaces at once and some individual stances do not appear to be consistent. But as far as I can see, some authors feel such awards should be voted on by the community as a whole, while others want no such awards at all. Some of those who do approve of the awards have, not surprisingly, suggested there is an element of sour grapes in some of those who do not, and that it is their personal lack of success in this forum that bothers them.

This whole argument is not unknown in litfic, where again attitudes to awards differ and the selection process is often called into question. A few years ago, a member of poetry's Forward Prize judging panel resigned because of suggestions that he was too closely connected with the publisher of one of the entrants. Litfic, like fanfic, is a fairly hermetic world where cliques are often suspected of operating. But I have never seen this debate become as bitter and personal in a litfic context as it seems to have done in Henneth Annun. Most genres eventually evolve their own critical apparatus. Various fanfic domains have posted reviews of zines for many years now, and literary debates on mailing lists are common. But the selection and awards process on Henneth Annun goes further than most in establishing perceived criteria and standards, and the controversy it has aroused is an interesting pointer to what might happen if more fanfic writers decide they want this kind of validation as well as the individual response of their fellow writers and readers. Some will; others, I suspect, will always find it inimical to the very nature of the genre.

Sites where individual writers display their own unedited fiction vary wildly in quality, as might be expected. Some of these writers will be reading widely, learning from feedback on earlier work, checking their source references with videos, transcripts or fellow fans, eliminating technical errors with the help of writing guides and beta-readers and generally taking advantage of a supportive writing community. Others will be doing none of that, and you can usually tell one set from the other. One writer's comment, from an unarchived list:

> With paper zines, the necessity for editing imposed some degree of quality checking. The net allows anyone to write and toss it up with very little trouble. [...] I've been on a few Buffy fanfic lists and the dross that is generally posted came as a shock. There is not the pressure on writers to make the effort to improve their writing so that [it] can be published.
>
> – Meg

Four of the fandoms on which I have concentrated have dedicated web sites where advice specifically aimed at fan fiction writers can be sought. The exception is *Discworld*, and that is because of the special problem of living book authors. The attitude of TV writers and producers to fanfic often depends on whether it can do them any good. Terry Nation, who as a science fiction writer had to contend with the basic disdain of the BBC for his genre, welcomed fanfic (gen at least) as evidence of public support. Others, notably those who controlled *Star Wars*, tried to come to an accommodation with what they realised they could not prevent. The Lucas empire sent out guidelines in 1981 expressing support for fan publications provided they stuck to gen fiction[10]. But writers of books have to take into account the fear of litigation generated by the "Marion Zimmer Bradley incident" of 1992. The late Bradley, an American writer whose *Darkover* books had generated a lot of fan fiction since 1977, was supportive of it and even contributed material to the fanzines, until she was unfortunate enough to run across an unreasonable fan who accused her of plagiarism and threatened to sue. Ever since, writers and more especially their lawyers have worried about this possibility and even those who are tolerant of fanfic understandably make a point of stressing in public that they never read it, lest this accusation be made against them. There is at least one brave, or possibly reckless, exception. JK Rowling has said in more than one interview that she reads it and finds it flattering:

> I only recently found the web pages devoted to Harry, and it was like Christmas – Christmas in August.[11]

> Hello, I would like to know if you ever read any Harry Potter fan fiction on the Web.
>
> I have read some, and I've been very flattered to see how absorbed people are in the world.[12]

Her literary agent (Christopher Little) has since been quoted on the subject, giving her blessing to non-adult, non-profit fan fiction:

> JK Rowling's reaction is that she is very flattered by the fact there is such great interest in her Harry Potter series and that people take the time to write their own stories. Her concern would be to make sure that it remains a non-commercial activity to ensure fans are not exploited and it is not being published in the strict sense of traditional print publishing.
>
> He said writers had to ensure that the stories were not obscene and were credited to the author and not to JK Rowling.[13]

One sincerely hopes that this time it doesn't go wrong, and continues to be the happy story of mutual respect and association which *Darkover* should have remained. But most writers understandably won't risk it. This is Pratchett's position, as set out in the Discworld newsletter, *Discworld Monthly*:

> If [fan fiction] is done for fun and not for money and not presented as if it's some canonical work by the original author, then it comes under the heading of what the Hell. I'd prefer it kept off Web pages and not put where I can stumble over it, just in case some joker decides to claim that I've "stolen their idea".

His attitude to fanfic is much more pragmatic than that of some; he sees no reason either to become upset or to spend his royalties on lawyers. (Indeed in a talk at the 2003 Hay Festival, he claimed to have once written a *Lord of the Rings/Pride and Prejudice* crossover in which orcs attack Hunsford Parsonage.) But he interacts a great deal with his fans via his website and the mailing list alt.fan.pratchett, and for his own protection he must ensure that fanfic is not posted to those places. So it isn't, because his fans value his interaction with them too much to jeopardise it, and its existence is not acknowledged on the official site. It lives on individual sites and umbrella sites like fanfiction.net, where it can also receive feedback via readers' comments posted either on the site or back-channel to an email address. (There was also a mailing list set up specifically for fiction, but when I tried to contact it, its address no longer seemed to be working.)

Mailing lists and message boards are not only useful to writers who want an audience to try out their stories on. The discussion they generate on the source material, on individual fics and fiction in general and sometimes on completely off-topic matters can often throw up ideas for stories. Sometimes the list moderator or members will suggest projects like story challenges – write a story about this or that character, or in the second person, or with a certain theme or setting. The "All About" stories and the "Replies" in the *Hornblower* fan fiction archive[14] were generated in this way. A writer who is uncertain of some technical or factual detail in a story she is working on can get advice from others, for there is generally a wide range of expertise in the community. Points of English usage, the behaviour of viruses or transporter beams, the web address of some style guide or precedent story can all be quickly resolved.

These environments also provide opportunities for collaboration. This does not only involve two writers working on the same story, though that often happens, generally with each playing to her particular strengths, e.g. one taking care of the plot while the other writes the dialogue. Just as important, though, is the kind of serial collaboration that results in feeding off each other's ideas and styles. Fanfic writers use each other's writing in the same way that they use the canon. If someone writes a story from the point of view of character A, another writer is liable to want to tell it from B's viewpoint. Or a writer may want to write a sequel to a recently posted story, and whole mailing-list sagas can start this way – see, for example, the 'Atonement Cycle', a series of seven stories from three authors, in the *B7* zine *Tales from Space City 4*[15]. A writer who invents an interesting OC may find others wanting to use him, and maybe team him up with an OC of their own in a spin-off universe.

Writers who want to do such a thing will almost invariably ask permission of the fanfic writer whose work they want to use as a jumping-off point – a common way of phrasing it is "can I play in your sandpit?" – and if the other writer were unwilling they probably would not do it. This is thought of as normal courtesy, a desire not to offend. Yet in one way it is also deeply illogical, given what fanfic is all about. *All* fanfic writers are playing in someone else's sandpit, with other people's characters and universes, and nobody is asking permission of the original creators, who in some cases would rather they didn't play there. Myself I am on the side of fanfic writers in this: if you create a character who comes alive for readers I think you must accept their feeling that they co-own him and can continue his story. But the same must then surely apply to the characters and universes created by fanfic writers themselves.

Some, while admitting there is little logic to their stance, explain their greater reluctance to offend their fellow fanfic writers on the grounds that they don't know the original canon writers, whereas they do know, if only in a virtual sense, the people on their mailing list. One can go along with the urge toward courtesy on their part, especially in an online environment where, without the benefit of facial and body language, it is easy for offence to be taken and flame wars to be started. Harder to understand is the attitude of those fanfic writers who *are* proprietary about their sandpit. From my experience they are very much in a minority, but it puzzles me that they exist at all. Nearly all fanfics carry a disclaimer, on the lines of "I don't own the characters. So-and-so does". Occasionally it is "I don't own the characters, except for X and Y", and every now and then one will continue "if you want to use X and Y, please ask me". To me at least, this seems totally unreasonable in the context, and I suppose it only shows that the powerful proprietary feelings of authors for their creations sometimes triumph over any sense of logic.

Most fanfic writers do let people play in their sandpit: in fact they are flattered by the request. If they were not natural collaborators in the first place, they often become so via the exercise of their craft in a like-minded community. They become used to seeking and sharing not only factual information but ideas on narrative strategies – how can I get this information across to the reader unobtrusively; what would make this rather taciturn character open up? Often someone will collate suggestions that have emerged from such a discussion and put them online as a resource available to all. It might be a guide to handling original characters without being accused of Mary Sue-ing, or an outline of how TV scriptwriters structure a script to maintain momentum and tension[16]. There is even '50+ Ways To Strip Your Lover'[17], a list of relatively innocent plot devices for getting a character's clothes off – tongue in cheek but quite useful to anyone trying to plot a convincing "first time" slashfic.

These online resources go beyond individual fandoms and word of them passes around via people on more than one mailing list, also among participants at multi-fandom conventions like Eclecticon, thereby to some extent counteracting the isolation of one fandom from another. There are also mailing lists that go beyond specific fandoms, like the Fan Fiction Writers' Support Group[18] and BritSlash[19]. At any one time, discussion on these will tend to be dominated by fans in the current most popular fandom, but on all mailing lists there are many "lurkers" who do not post often but have specific interests and areas of expertise which they will share on request.

Conventions too, whether dedicated to one fandom or more general, are places for discussing writing and holding workshops, challenges and competitions. The kind of writers' resources available can also be more esoteric: it became common at conventions to invite gay men along to speak on the mechanics of m/m sex to slash writers who were anxious not to get their facts wrong. In fact slash writers may be more likely than most to seek a sense of community in cross-fandom groupings, though that doesn't necessarily mean they read and write in other fandoms. Rather it is because slash is still controversial in most fandoms; it can take no more than a mention on a mailing list to spark a flame war and some fandoms avoid that by separating such discussions off from the main list. The multi-fandom slash convention Red Rose was advertised with extreme discretion; slash fans were specifcally advised "The convention has not been advertised directly in the fannish press, and we ask you to pass this flyer only to like-minded friends"[20]. The cross-fandom group crack_van, within the livejournal blogging community, exists for fans to recommend, via brief reviews with hyperlinks, stories in their fandom which those in other fandoms might not otherwise encounter. It is open to all kinds of fic, but slash does seem to be heavily represented, possibly because slash fans are more used to this kind of interactivity than others.

A fanfic writer on a supportive mailing list is in effect a member of a global online workshop in which she can get feedback, ideas and criticism from like-minded readers and writers all over the world. She can be rigorously edited for free by her beta-readers, while if she performs the same service for them she can greatly improve her own editing and critical skills. She has a far larger audience than would be the case in a real-life workshop – even a small mailing list may have 40 or 50 members. Not all will be writers, but all will be readers and many will volunteer feedback. Like any writer working in a group, she is likely to have a strong sense of audience; if she posts a story to a mailing list she knows there are people out there reading it and has an incentive to please them. The fanfic writers I know insist that they basically write for themselves but admit that this consciousness of audience influences them, causing them to hone and develop their work in ways that might not otherwise happen.

One aspect of the fanfic community's concern for its readers can, I think, sometimes work against its writing, and this is the habit of classifying and defining fiction into various pigeonholes. In many online fanfic libraries authors will be asked, for the convenience of the readers, to define all sorts of things about their fic. Is it gen, het or slash; if it has adult content, how adult? Is there a sad or a happy ending, any character death, humour or angst? Which characters are involved; is it a sequel or prequel fic, or an AU? Many of these questions can be hard to answer: some of the best fics are on borderlines and unclassifiable and these can sometimes have a harder job finding a home. The profic writer in me also protests at a policy that helps readers to stick with what they know and are comfortable with, rather than encouraging them to try something they might be surprised to like. But in this environment the reader is the writer's equal and partner, and writers have to live with it. As someone who is both writer and reader said on an unarchived list, "You write what you want to, and the reader reads what they want to". (SA) Some, like Executrix, take it as a challenge – in the essay "Reading between the Loins", published here as Appendix 4, she says, "I've been known to cackle "Classify THIS!" as I finish a story".

Of course this reader tendency to want more of the same exists in profic too, though arguably fanfic's system of classification panders to it more. I have already indicated how, on a mailing list devoted to literary fiction, I found the same prejudice against first person narration that exists in fanfic. And Nova, referring to reviews of her profic writing, complains:

> I hate it when someone says they don't like one of my books because they don't like that kind of character or setting or plot line, rejecting the entire story out of hand, rather than giving me a chance to convince them through craft.

And in fanfic, as in profic, it is undoubtedly, and reassuringly, possible for an individual writer's skill to overcome fixed ideas and spur her readers into new territory. A character junkie may go beyond her favourite characters; a believer in an OTP (One True Pairing) may consider the possibility of others, if the writing is persuasive enough. Readers may follow a favourite writer into profic, if they know her profic identity as well as her fanfic pseud: I have myself, as a reader, followed writers not only into profic but into unfamiliar genres of it, when I knew who they were. In that case the writing has transcended its genre, and that happens to the best fanfic writers as it does in any other genre fiction. To quote from an unarchived list:

> I've quite recently realised that I'm not so interested in fandoms as writers. [...] In fact, not knowing/liking the fandom almost helps in some cases.
>
> – AS

> I'll often follow a writer whose work I enjoy into other fandoms – even fandoms I know nothing about! [...] I have learned never to say never, the most improbable pairings *work* in the right author's hands. Perhaps there is a difference between a) appreciating fanfic [...] for the fannish joy in a particular pairing, and b) appreciating it for the writing. I have drifted from a to b over the course of my reading.
>
> – Sulis

What sort of people does this writing and reading community consist of? Two decades ago Camille Bacon Smith, in *Enterprising Women*, asked this question about slash fans. Using a sample of attenders at an American slash convention, she concluded that they were mainly female, white, middle class, university educated, single and heterosexual. The age range was wide but most were in their thirties. These were, however, specifically slash fans and not necessarily writers either. And they had the time and money to attend conventions, which is not true of all fans or all writers. In addition Net access has widened considerably since then and may have changed the profile.

The profile of writers would vary from one fandom to another, and since my interest is not primarily sociological I am not about to conduct an exhaustive survey. But I thought it might be instructive at least to look at the profiles of the writers in one fanzine. *TTBA*, edited by Tavia, was a *B7* zine published in 2001. It was mixed, containing both gen and adult material – of 29 stories, I would classify 14 as gen. The remainder had some het or slash element but in some cases this was very slight and reflected the zine's aim to be "addressing adult issues but not an 'adult' zine" (Editorial). Of the 15 containing adult content, 9 had some element of slash. The zine featured both established and new writers and aimed for a mix of stories "with a particular focus on those that cross boundaries of genre or category"[21], which is why I thought it would be more widely representative than some. Also it included some details about its authors, which many of them kindly supplemented.

But I am not suggesting it was in any way a "typical" zine. I am not sure such a beast exists, but actually *ttba* was unusual in having mixed gen and adult content. Also many of its stories were effectively commissioned from writers known to the editor, which is not the norm, and the editor's rejection rate (around 50%) was regarded by fellow-editors as higher than normal. (A profic editor might regard it as low, but then few profic editors would have been prepared to edit contributions as actively as Tavia did.)

There were 16 writers in the zine, and all were female. This is not unusual, though not inevitable either. There are male fanfic writers, but it would be rare to find more than one or two in a zine, always excepting the male-dominated *Doctor Who* fandom. There are more male writers in the *Discworld* universe than in most, but they don't produce fiction printzines.

At least 15 were university graduates, in a variety of disciplines including law, the sciences, social and political sciences and humanities. Seven were either postgraduate students or employed in further education institutions in some capacity – in two cases, that of librarian. Other occupations included a writer on law, an historian, a virologist, a businesswoman, a zine publisher and distributor working from home and a full-time profic writer. One was from Canada, one from Australia, four from the USA and ten from the UK, reflecting the fact that this is in origin a British fandom.

Whether a TV-based fandom has members in a particular country usually depends on whether it ever aired there, though not always – some people become fans, and even fanfic writers, via videos. *The Bill* airs in Australia as well as Britain and its fan base seems to be wholly British-Australian. *B7*, in its time, was broadcast in a lot more countries, including the USA and Eastern Europe, and the fan base still reflects that (as does the fiction, with some writers working in what for them is a second language). Book-based fanfic can go beyond language as long as the original has been translated. *Discworld* fan fiction exists in French[22] and in German[23]. Oddly enough, though there is great interest in Austen in both countries, I have found little actual Austen fan fiction in those languages. By and large, and this also applies to film and TV-based fandoms, nationality of fandom overrides nationality of fanfic author, and authors seem to want to write in the language of the original if at all possible. Perhaps this has to do with wanting a sense of belonging to a community: the main fanfic reading and writing community in these fandoms is inevitably English-speaking.

Most of the *ttba* writers were either married or living with a partner, and most were straight, though at least four defined themselves as something other. The average age would have been older than Bacon Smith's group: more like late 30s. This is a fandom based around a programme that was never aimed at teenage fans (the average audience age when it aired was mid-20s). Writers in the *Buffy/Angel* universe would undoubtedly have a younger average age. And the number of writers with a scientific background may reflect the futuristic, science fiction element in the source material. The proportion of adult (particularly slash) to gen material in *ttba* was slightly higher than I expected to find. This might reflect a growing willingness in fanfic to engage with more "adult issues" but it could equally be that some gen writers prefer their work not to appear in zines with mixed content and choose instead to submit it to purely gen zines. There are certainly still more gen than adult zines published, in this as in most fandoms.

Their reading preferences ranged very widely, from classics through contemporary literary fiction to genre writers in horror and SF, not forgetting non-fiction. They were all avid readers, often describing themselves as having been bookworms from childhood. Many are also fond of other art forms like film and song, and cite them as inspirations – songfics, inspired by a song title or lyric, are a recognised sub-genre in fanfic.

They are fond of role-play games, from *Sealed Knot*-type battle re-enactments to *The Sims*, the Maxis computer game in which you create virtual people and control their lives. (Many fanfic writers have created "sims" of their favourite characters.) They are in short unusually zealous consumers of fiction, as well as producers of it. It has already been noted how many fanfic titles are themselves quotes, and how readily fanfic writers use references from the fiction in which they are steeped. In Charley Hart's Hornblower slashfic 'Educating Horatio'[24] Major Edrington uses a homoerotic sonnet, 'Sighing and sadly sitting by my love', by the sixteenth-century poet Richard Barnfield, as a chat-up line. In the sequel fic 'Stalemate', Archie Kennedy expresses his feelings via the words of Gaveston in Marlowe's *Edward II*. True to the collaborative nature of fanfic, a friend of the author's came up with the title 'Educating Horatio', which she felt might have been a subconscious memory of the film *Educating Rita*, based on the play by Willy Russell. Ironically enough, neither the author nor her friend was aware of the probable source of Russell's title, the unlikely radio ventriloquist act Peter Brough and his 1950s series on the BBC, *Educating Archie*.

For what it is worth, the characteristic that most strikes me in the fanfic writers (and readers) I know is a highly developed imagination. Though they live and work, often very successfully, in the "real" world, they cannot get enough of imagined worlds, fantasy worlds, and even within the fantasy they are always looking for alternative possibilities, other ways the story might have gone.

I think this is one reason several of the *ttba* writers defined their sexuality as open to suggestion. They tend to be adventurous by nature, at least in theory, and, as writers, not to reject anything out of hand (with two exceptions: anti-slashers are usually unpersuadable about slash, though often not for literary reasons, and fanfic writers in general have a hard time liberating themselves from the taboo on Mary Sues). They are also very apt to see possible connections between different fantasy worlds, or between a fantasy world and the real world. "Plot bunnies" in fanfic terms are ideas that get into your head and force you to write about them, and quite often they come from a chance connection like this. It might be verbal – the *Hamlet*/Dr Seuss crossover fic 'Green Eggs and Hamlet' (see chapter 3) obviously started from a play on words. Or it might be some visual trigger – Executrix's *B7*/*Cabaret* crossover fic 'Wanderjahr'[25] was inspired by the fact that Servalan's hairstyle in *B7* reminded her of Sally Bowles' in *Cabaret*. These connection triggers can get quite complicated. Executrix's 'Ask-Tell-Pursue'[26] is an echo of the syntax of a *B7* episode title, 'Seek-Locate-Destroy' but also of the then policy on homosexuality in the US armed forces – "don't ask, don't tell, don't pursue".

What qualities do fanfic writers aim for and value in their own writing, and are these any different from those a "profic" writer aims for? Some of them *are* also profic writers: are they conscious of a difference in their method?

One quality on which they clearly do not put the same value as Anne Rice did on her website is "originality", at least in the sense in which she uses the word. They are following the advice to write "your own original stories" but not with "your own characters". In fact this advice misses the point. People write (and read) fan fiction because they want more of *these* characters, and not any others. It does not follow that they do not want to write and read about anyone else ever: the eclectic and voracious nature of their reading shows that, as do the excursions of some into profic. But when writers write fanfic they are using the talent they have for a specific purpose, namely to extend, both in time and scope, a universe and characters they did not want to come to an end. For them, these characters have become archetypes, part of a myth-kitty on which they draw as writers have for centuries on myth, legend and folk tale. If that makes them "less original" writers it is only in the same sense that Robert Henryson was, when he chose to use the characters Chaucer had already taken from Greek myth, or, in another poem sequence, the characters and plots of Aesop's fables. It was still perfectly possible for him to do his own thing with them, to make them speak to his time and his concerns, as none can doubt who read the peroration to his version of the fable of the wolf and the lamb:

> Oh thou great lord, that riches has and rent,
> Be not a wolf, thus to devour the poor.
> Think how nothing cruel or violent
> May in this world perpetually endure...[27]

When I try to decide what qualities *are* important specifically to these writers I come back again and again to point of view. Fanfic writers are intensely interested in replaying the same scene from different viewpoints and in different voices, and in articulating points of view that were never heard in the source at all. For this purpose they need to be very secure in point of view and it is one of the skills the best of them have developed over the years. One example of this development can be seen in the use of personal pronouns. When writing in the third person with a number of characters of the same sex, as fanfic writers often are, one soon runs into the problem of who is meant by "he", "him" and "his". It is a particular problem for slash writers, as might be imagined. In early fics, you frequently find two methods of solving this, neither ideal. Some writers would use proper names much more often than usual, in fact whenever there was any risk of confusion. This was awkward and interrupted the narrative flow, but was still not as bad as the second strategy, which was to use what might be termed kennings when the writer got bored with names, or feared that the reader might. Spock, for example, often became "the Vulcan" or "the science officer", even in situations where nobody would be thinking of him as such.

It was not long before writers and readers realised that this would not do: kennings became one of the staples of fanfic cliché and were anathematised in writers' guides. These days they are very much the sign of a new writer, and more experienced fanfic writers have found better strategies. One is their increasing readiness to use first person, which avoids the problem from the start by turning "he" and "him" into "I" and "him". Another is learning to trust the reader more, rather than rushing to explain each possible ambiguous use. The use of dialogue can help a lot too. Above all, the better writers simply realised that if they were secure enough in character X's point of view, X would become the default setting for "he" and "him" and should seldom need his name mentioned at all. One of the faults editors most look out for, and writers most want their beta-readers to look out for, is the slightest wavering in the point of view. Many "story challenges" and exercises on mailing lists involve point of view and one of the likeliest ways for one story to spin off another is by changing the viewpoint

Along with this fascination with point of view goes an extensive use of dialogue. Though this makes a lot of sense in the case of TV and film-based fanfic, where voices are heard all the time, like the use of first person it took time to develop, because it was risky: if you got the character voice wrong you would immediately alienate many readers. So a writer had to be very sure in the voice. These days, far more of them are. They also make much use of interior monologue. This is another aspect of their interest in voice, but is also connected with their fascination with motivation and what goes on inside people's heads, particularly where there is some discrepancy between the inner voice and the outer. In a very brief example, Executrix, in her *B7* fic 'Portrait of a Pair Bond'[28] cuts between outer and inner voice in the same sentence by using italics:

> *His hair's too damn long* Blake thought. *I'd like to get my hands into – on – it.* He envisioned a warm tress yielding *to my hands* to a pair of scissors, scattering *across a pillow* to the floor.

But for all their interest in voice, fanfic writers are also very interested in "nonverbals", exploring character and motivation through body language and actions. With writers in TV and film canons, this presumably derives from how much of this they see on screen – and can see, and interpret, again and again thanks to the VCR. Among the more useful online resources are collections of "frame grabs", freeze-frame shots which fix an evanescent expression or gesture. Apparent discrepancies between words and nonverbals are especially fruitful territory when looking for subtexts, and slash writers are especially liable to pick up on these. In the Gilmore/Ashton storyline from *The Bill*, discussed in the previous chapter, Ashton's body language with his fiancée Kerry is frequently at odds with his words. At one point, having been suspicious of his relationship with Gilmore, she tells him she is now reassured and happy with their engagement. His face, seen over her shoulder as they embrace, is not rapturous, and by the next morning fans on the Britslash mailing list had picked this up and were discussing it. Similarly in the *B7* episode 'Redemption', Avon is engaged in a bitter, barbed debate with Blake when suddenly the ship is attacked. Both fall to the deck, but Avon falls with his arm stretched out across Blake as if to protect him. In many fandoms' online resources for writers, there are records of how and under what circumstances various characters touch each other in the canon.

One slash writer (from an unarchived list, again) identifies the kind of story in which she is more likely to use first person:

> I noticed that my PWPs are all first person – much easier on the pronouns and at the same time much easier to blend the emotional and physical aspects. Not that the blend can't be achieved in third person – it can and is – but first person gives instant access. And focusing on the character's individual voice is a useful antidote to clichés.
>
> – Nova

PWPs are "Plot? What plot?" stories, generally focusing on love scenes/sexual encounters. Some fanfic writers attribute their liking for allusion and literary analogy partly to the depth it can give but also to an inability to plot:

> One motivation is that rewriting works that are likely to be known to the audience can add depth from the parallels with the other work. It also saves one from having to come up with a plot.
>
> – Tavia

> I do a lot of pastiches not only because I can't plot [...] but for the reciprocal light characters in one property can shine on those in another.
>
> – Executrix

Actually both the writers quoted can plot well enough if they have to, but it may well be true that for many fanfic writers, it isn't the thing they most enjoy doing. They are much less interested in how two characters got from X to Y than in what they said to each other along the way and how they felt about each other when they got there. Ika, speaking of her attitude to plot on an unarchived mailing list, cites a *B7* episode, 'Pressure Point', in which plot details have been criticised:

> I dislike plot (when I put it in, it's only in order to set up the concepts which I'm going to need for metaphors). I tend to translate plot into "They all ran round and it worked out in the end". (This may stand for anything up to several chapters of a novel, or sometimes entire films.) I also worked out recently that this is one of the reasons I don't object to the flaws in Pressure Point as much as some other people do: because I translate all the scenes inside Central Control into "There were many obstacles to overcome and they overcame them", and am serenely indifferent to the fact that said obstacles are mostly, um, corridors, seeing as the only point of those scenes is to deliver us to the moment with Blake and Avon on the floor...

Generalisation is always dangerous: there are fanfic writers who are adept at complex, twisty plots (Manna in *B7*, Nat in *The Bill*, an unusual number in the *Discworld*). But E M Forster's regretful "oh dear yes, the novel tells a story" would probably strike more of a chord with most fanfic writers than Sheridan's remark in *The Critic*: "I think it wants incident". (Generalising again, I have to say that though Manna and Nat, named above, are female, in the main it is the few male fanfic writers I know who value plot more.)

In particular the adherents of "more from" rather than "more of" would far rather spend time on one incident, investigating why it happened, what it says about the characters and how it looked from all possible points of view, than invent more incidents. Where there is "incident" it will not usually be there for its own sake. If its purpose is to move the plot along, it is liable to be skated over at speed, and if what is wanted is to create tension, then for most fanfic writers – 'shippers in particular – tension equals people and their relationships. In Victoria Bitter's 'Salus'[29], one of the many *Hornblower* "missing scene" fics from the episode 'Retribution', the core of the action is that Bush, having realised that the dying Archie intends to go and testify at Hornblower's court-martial, helps him get dressed. The detailed description of this extends over eight paragraphs, at once lyrical and harrowing: both men are wounded and tired and one is near death:

Bush stood, steadying himself for a moment on the wall before moving as quickly as he could over to the other cot. Kennedy was still sitting upright [...] His tangled hair tumbled discordantly over his shoulders, and Bush gathered it up in his hand, yanking the ribbon from his own hair and wrapping it around the queue to secure it. The result wasn't pretty, but it was neat. He took two more steps to the foot of the bed and picked up the kerchief, turning to face Kennedy, who stared at him in stunned disbelief. "What are you doing?"

The wounds were burning badly now. He needed to move quickly before he tore them open again. [...] "I heard stories about you, Mr. Kennedy...[...]" He looped the black fabric around Kennedy's neck. The other man brought his hands up slowly, tying the knot himself as Bush reached back to the pile and fetched out the vest. "That you were broken in a Spanish prison. That you tried to die. I didn't think I could respect a man who'd had his spirit broken. I thought such things were beyond mending, and I had... concerns about serving with you." Kennedy made a sound that seemed half a laugh, half a choking bleat of pain, and he continued quickly. "But my fears were ill-founded."

"Spirits are like bones, Mr. Bush." A thin smile appeared on Kennedy's lips as he gingerly slipped his arms through the holes of the vest, gasping in pain when Bush pulled it together to button the brightly polished buttons. A red stain appeared on the white fabric of the vest, and he averted his eyes. He didn't want to think about it. "Badly healed, they're never the same. Well attended, I like to believe they mend stronger than before."

Bush lifted the dark blue Lieutenant's jacket, not so much as the next piece of the uniform, but to hide the blood spreading scarlet on the white. "Yours was clearly attended by an expert, sir."

He could see Kennedy's arm trembling as he lifted it towards the sleeve, and he took the wrist in his hand, supporting and guiding it. The pulse fluttered under his fingers, and he looked into Kennedy's face again, expecting to see him on the verge of collapse. Instead, his expression seemed calm [...]. Only the tension at the edges of the eyes and the sweat running rivulets down the flushed skin spoke of pain or exertion. "The son of a doctor, I'm told."

"Is that why you..." He took the other hand, guiding it around to the second sleeve while trying to avoid brushing the bright stain that marked Kennedy's wound.

"No." [...] "It has to be done."

He finished dressing Kennedy in silence. Jacket. Stockings. Breeches. Belt. Shoes. They both needed to conserve their strength for what lay ahead, and by the time Bush had buckled the silver buckles on the shoes, both men were clearly feeling the strain.

Plot, in the sense of what people do and what is done to them, is mostly there for the same purpose as what people say – to show them to us, other characters and themselves as they are. In *B7* PGP fics, a fairly often-used plot device is to render Avon mute from the trauma of having shot Blake. In part this demonstrates the depth of his feelings but it is also done because, like PC Ashton, he tends in canon to say many things he does not mean and to fail to say what he does mean. His sarcasm and verbal hostility are often at odds with his actions and body language; by depriving him of speech the writer also deprives him of his mask.

Plot detail, like dialogue and place description, may of course also be there to establish the kind of universe we are in. Writers in some fandoms – notably those set in other times or fantasy worlds – have a particular need to establish a sense of place and time. It might be life in the British navy at the time of the Anglo-French wars (*Hornblower*) or in a futuristic totalitarian state (*B7*). But even writers in fandoms set in a version of the current everyday world need to pay particular attention to place, since it is to this version of the world that their readers wish to go.

This is the start of a *Bill* fic by Kel, 'Sins of Omission'[30], an angsty PWP in which the place details, like everything else, are chosen to focus on the character and mood of the protagonist, DS Alistair Greig. Greig is a conscientious enough officer but he is introspective, doesn't socialise much and some suspect him of being far more interested in the clarinet he plays in his spare time. The fic opens just after an episode in which he has failed to gain promotion:

> He loves this, the eternal nightscape, never quite dark, never quite silent. The reflected glow of eight million souls honeying the underside of thick night clouds, dissipating through the winter air.
>
> Coming up here reminds him of what it's all about, of why he bothers.
>
> He imagines the strains of old, familiar songs floating over the silhouettes, mingling with the cadence of shouts from the night markets and the ever-present rumbling of the traffic. Symphony for horns and clarinet.
>
> The noise reaches a particularly dissonant peak, somewhere to his left, a few blocks away. He listens. Waits. Hears the quiet, rusty complaint of the outer roof door under the cacophony, and quiet footsteps, close, behind him.
>
> "That'll be those bloody traffic lights down the High Street."
>
> "Again? They were working this morning."

> "Aye. For all of five minutes."
> Quiet laughter.
> He moves over, a little, bunches up against the rusting handrail of the fire escape. His eyes never leave the streams of red and white lights weaving in and out between the darkened city blocks.

When fanfic writers are rendering character or dialogue the mimetic tendency kicks in; their writing is rooted in the reality of the characters. But working against this tendency is the "what if" factor. Fanfic writers are used to speculating on alternatives; this happened, but what if that had instead? It is this that makes them, sometimes, willing to depart from the demands of "realism" down a path that looks more interesting; it is why slash writers, for example, don't mind being accused of creating unrealistically emotional men or supposing improbable relationships. They are as interested in what *might* happen as in what probably did, and they see AUs where less speculative writers might not. X and Y are probably not in love, but what if they were? Character Z does not normally spill his heart to others, but what if something made him do so? It is no surprise that when fanfic writers are asked to name litfic favourites, magic realists figure heavily. When I first began reading fanfic, I was puzzled that individual writers could see their fanfic universe in more than one way. A writer would make character X in love with Y in one fic and Z in another; she might invent totally different back-stories for him. Even when a writer does have a personal vision of a character's background and preferences she will happily imagine and write them different just to see if it works that way.

One other characteristic of fanfic writing may be relevant. An unusual number of fanfic stories strike me as being in one way or another mirrors for the process of writing. Sometimes this can be obvious at first sight. Fanfic, like profic, has its own metafiction, such as the *Discworld* metafic 'Wroundworld' by Owen Burgoyne[31]. This plays with the idea that the inhabitants of the Discworld might want to read about us as we do about them, and would see our world as equally fantastic. The Discworld wannabe writer trying to create the stories is, despite superficial similarities (of names and a slight lisp), not a Pratchett but a would-be Pratchett, a vicious parody of a bad fanfic writer. He hasn't done his proof-reading or his homework on the canon, and the magician Rincewind, in the role of editor, is unsympathetic:

> "So," started Rincewind, noting the appalling spelling, "you say you're from the Writers' Guild?"
>
> "Mm-hmm," nodded Mr Pritchard.
>
> "Been there long?"
>
> "Not wreally."
>
> "I didn't think so," said Rincewind. "Well, I really have to, er, be getting on with ... something. Yes. I definitely have something to do. Somewhere else."

A lot of *Discworld* fics, perhaps inspired by the central role of Pratchett's own authorial voice, are fascinated both by the figure of "the writer" and by the power he wields. In most fandoms, one of the few acceptable ways to Mary-Sue is as "The Writer" in a metafic, ironically and consciously writing herself into her creation and interacting with the characters. Sophist's 'Of Things to Come'[32] has the author interviewing Vimes (the "interview" technique of narration had a spell of popularity in fanfic, perhaps because of Anne Rice's *Interview with the Vampire*). In this case the author is ascertaining what kind of fic Vimes wants written for him (specifically, whom he wants a relationship with), and trying to oblige. The same writer, in 'When the Smoke Clears',[33] chats to Vimes in an epilogue to a fic, asking in essence how it was for him. In this case the interaction of writer and character is perhaps also an extension of the reality and centrality of favourite characters to fanfic writers, particularly 'shippers (see chapter 4)

Sometimes the link with writing is more buried. In Pat Jacquerie's *B7* slash novella 'Duty'[34], two male crew members are stranded on an apparently male-dominated planet called Fargone (they meet only men and assume the women are secluded). The planet also has odd social customs, as planets in slash SF tend to do, and they find themselves having to sleep with each other, exploring the nature of their relationship in the process. Only near the end of their stay and the story do they discover that this has been on the orders not of the men but of the ruling and hitherto unseen women, who have been controlling, observing and recording their actions throughout. For the reader, this discovery inevitably brings Fargone rather closer to home: in effect these shadowy women are fanfic writers and readers, and the whole situation can be read as a metaphor for what they do.

NOTES

1. http://web.archive.org/web/*/http://www.tbfanfic.com/ 15.11.02
2. see K S Boyd, http://www.sfu.ca/~ksboyd/history.html 6.9.02
3. http://www.austen.com/derby 17.11.02
4. http://members.ozemail.com.au/~jriddler/dick.html 17.11.02
5. http://www.fanfiction.net/s/1174176/1/ 04.01.05
6. http://www.hermit.org/blakes7/Library/SrchReq.cgi 04.03.03
7. http://www.liberated.org.uk 04.03.03
8. at http://members.tripod.com/SarahB1/hharchive.html 04.03.03
9. at http://www.henneth-annun.net/index.cfm 25.04.03
10 see "A History of Fan Fiction", http://writersu.s5.com/history/history01.html 23.11.02
11. Interview on Barnes & Noble's website, 8.9.99, quoted on the Writers' University site, http://www.writersu.net/?link=authpolicy&id=107 20.11.02
12. Barnes & Noble 20.10.2000, quoted on Writers' University, 20.11.02
13. quoted on the BBC website http://news.bbc.co.uk/1/hi/entertainment/arts/3753001.stm 28.5.04
14. http://members.tripod.com/SarahB1/hharchive.html 02.02.03
15. ed Helen Patrick, 2002
16. see Wolfie's advice on http://web.archive.org/web/*/www.tbfanfic.com/ 19.1102
17. at http://homepage.mac.com/shelobmarian/handmade/innocent_reasons_to_strip.html 19.11.02
18. http://hometown.aol.com/CheleSedai 21.6.02
19. http://www.britslash.co.uk 20.11.02
20. see the notice on Judth Proctor's website, http://www.hermit.org/blakes7/Convention/RedRose.html
21. Tavia, http://www.viragene.com/ttba.htm 20.11.02
22. see http://perso.club-internet.fr/jmlsimon/pratchett/fan.htm 21.11.02
23. see the web ring http://www.pratchett-fanclub.de/webring/webring/index.php 21.11.020
24. archived at http://www.frolixers.com/parlour/index.html 6.12.02
25. http://www.liberated.org.uk 31.12.02
26. http://www.hermit.org/blakes7/Library 31.12.02
27. *Poems*, p 83. I have modernised the spelling
28. archived at 'Remember Us' http://teland.com/remember/B7portrait.html
29. http://members.tripod.com/SarahB1/salus.html 03.01.05
30. Jasmine Alley http://www.wcs.net.au/~bessie/sunhill/index.html 24.11.02
31. http://www.fanfiction.net/s/769073/1/ 24.11.02
32. http://discsophist.com 27.05.05
33. archived at http://www.geocities.com/sophistry_for_hire/whenthesmokeclears.html 10.01.03
34. http://tarrantnostra.com/pat/fargone/duty.htm 24.11.02

7. Across the Borderline

Fanfic and Profic

As mentioned in the previous chapter, some fanfic writers also write profic (i.e. published and paid fiction). Sometimes this is in a genre related to their particular fanfic universe – e.g. fantasy, horror or science fiction; sometimes it is in a different genre altogether (I know of one who publishes mediaeval murder mysteries in her native language while writing futuristic fanfic in English). It can be literary fiction, as in the case of Nova, an Australian *B7* fanfic writer who also wins awards for litfic (or indeed Paul Magrs and Russell T Davies, if one counts as paid fanfic the official *Doctor Who* novels which both authors used to write).

Some writers who work on both sides of the borderline make a conscious difference between them. Nova sometimes uses the same themes in her litfic and fanfic, though she identifies different influences:

> I read TS Eliot's *Tradition and the Individual Talent* at an impressionable age, so I always see my writing as part of a dialogue with the area I'm writing in. In fanfic, my strongest influences are [names long list of fanfic authors]. I'm also influenced by the whole gestalt of fanfic, its implicit rules and regulations, its fanon, its forbidden zones. My profic works exactly the same way, except that the names are different.[1]

Nova was writing litfic before she began writing fanfic – although, like many who later become fanfic writers, she was continuing her favourite stories in her head as a child. Some go the other way, writing a fanfic story and then "filing off the serial numbers", i.e. changing obviously fan-based references like names, and marketing the story as profic.

There are also what are known as "avatars", characters in profic novels who are widely believed to be partly based on popular fanfic characters. These usually involve genre fiction, often SF, fantasy or horror. The profic fantasy writer Tanith Lee, who wrote two episodes for the third and fourth seasons of *B7*, subsequently published a novel, *Kill the Dead*, two of whose protagonists were avatars of characters from the series. Erotica based on slash fanfic, with avatar characters, happens quite a lot. Wayward Books, a small press specialising in gay fiction, publishes some novels that first saw the light of day as slashfic in *The Professionals* fandom. The novel *White Rose of Night*[2] by Mel Keegan similarly developed from an Australian slash fanzine, *The White Rose of Night*[3], which was an AU based on the 1970s TV show *UFO*, but set in the twelfth century. And fanfic authors like Kitty Fisher have appeared in the Virgin Publishing series of "women's erotica", *Wicked Words*, again with the serial numbers filed off.

When I first began reading fanfic, it baffled and astounded me that many fanfic writers chose never to try the profic waters. I had been a profic writer for years, and for a lot of that time a freelance, earning what money I could at it. I was therefore imbued with the first law of the freelance writer: never write a word unless there's a good chance of getting paid for it. Now I was watching writers post hundreds of thousands of words on the web for nothing, or publish them in fanzines for no more than a contributor's copy. Because of the genre they were writing in, these stories never *would* be able to be published commercially, for legal reasons – it didn't matter how good they were. Of course, on the "90% of anything is dreck" principle, many fanfic authors don't write well enough to be published commercially. And one can understand that, for them, unpaid fanfic is a chance to be heard, just as self-publication is for some writers. As Executrix once said, in private email:

> In a sense, litfic is an elitist form and fanfic is a far more democratic form. The New York State Lottery slogan is "all it takes is a dollar and a dream" and fanfic really says all you need is an email account and a dream. I think this is an extremely positive development in social terms, although it does mean that a lot of perfectly terrible writers are writing and posting.

But what puzzled me were the ones who, far from being perfectly terrible, were eminently publishable, and apparently not bothered about trying. Executrix herself was one of them. She was alarmingly widely read, had a most urbane, witty, readable style and could hold zine and mailing list readers spellbound, yet she wrote no mainstream fiction. In response to my impertinent query as to why, she said she earned a living by writing books and articles about the law, and it was just not economically feasible for her to spend time writing uneconomic profics. This was, at least to a freelance writer, a very understandable reason, though it didn't explain why she did spend time writing fanfic which was absolutely certain not to be paid. That can, presumably, only be for personal entertainment or relaxation. And I have since encountered a number of fanfic writers in a similar employment position, doing jobs which demand a lot of technical, official, non-fictional writing in science departments, government libraries and the like. Some of them have told me that in their case fanfic, the polar opposite of such writing, is what they do for fun. Importing deadlines and publishers into it would turn it into work, which they are unwilling to do.

But another reason that is frequently given, and perhaps even more frequently withheld, is fear. A lot of fanfic writers have told me "oh, I don't think I'm good enough" or "I couldn't cope with all the rejection slips". This is of course a turn-off for many would-be writers. The difference with fanfic writers is that they can if they choose have at least part of the best of both worlds. They have a writing community, to whom they can post stories and who will give them feedback and support, without going near editors or publishers. True, if they want to be in fanzines they will have to encounter editors every bit as rigorous as those in the profic world, but they don't have to submit stories to zines; they can post them on mailing lists and web sites.

I must be careful here not to give the wrong impression. Kel, a slash writer in *The Bill* fandom, said in email correspondence with me:

> I get very cross when people dismiss fanfic as a substitute for originality, or a haven for people too scared to try "proper writing" – dear God you have to be original doing this... Especially in slash. Original, and disciplined. Isn't that the **heart** of fanfic? Creating something new within given boundaries? Okay, so I'm not entirely convinced I could create and sustain an original universe *yet*, if at all. But I'd like to prove myself wrong on that count one day, and intend to try. To that end, this isn't Claytons writing, it's practice. It's all part of the path...

I entirely agree that fanfic is not a substitute for originality (a wildly overrated characteristic anyway), nor do I think its practitioners are scared to try "proper writing" (what they do in fanfic *is* proper writing). I do however think that some are scared to try their writing in a profic writing universe that they see as far less supportive than the fanfic writing environment. It is a preference hard to argue with, for as a profic writer, I would have to say that their perception is not wrong. A writer, other than a very successful one, who publishes a litfic novel or collection of stories (supposing she can get any publisher to look at a collection of stories), may if she is lucky see a couple of reviews after many months. Or maybe not. She may get the odd comment from a reader, but probably the book, which may have occupied years of her life, will enter the pond causing hardly a ripple and sink out of print within a couple of years. And this is supposing she can get published in the first place. In a buyer's market where it is very difficult to interest an agent or publisher even in good work, other writers are more likely to be rivals and competitors than allies or supporters. Nor, in most cases, will writing actually earn her much, especially in proportion to the time spent on it.

Contrast this, as I often enviously have, with the lot of a good fanfic writer. In the first place she is not in competition with her fellow-writers. Mailing list audiences have an inexhaustible appetite for fiction, and if she wants a more permanent home for it, a good fic will always find a place in a fanzine or a web archive. In this situation fellow-writers can forget about eyeing each other sideways as rivals and enjoy each other's talent, learning from and helping each other, even collaborating with each other. Then she has a guaranteed audience of informed people who share her interests and are anxious to read whatever she has to entertain them with. If she posts fiction to them, she will get quick and detailed feedback. It may not be unreservedly favourable, but it will be supportive and, if they like the fic, decidedly encouraging. If she wants to improve her writing or is too uncertain to post it cold, she can ask someone to beta-read her work and help her polish it before launching it on her public. (And it can be someone she has never met and isn't likely to, which to an insecure writer can make a lot of difference.) To lose all this in exchange for a minuscule amount of money and an equally minuscule chance of fame isn't necessarily such a good bargain (even if it's still the path I, as an indoctrinated profic writer, would feel haplessly compelled to choose).

In her email Kel also remarks on the position in the *Doctor Who* fanfic universe, where not only did some writers of unpaid fanfic graduate to writing the official kind for the BBC, but some went on to write in quite other genres – or came the other way:

> This comes up occasionally in Doctor Who fandom – there are those who dismiss the Virgin/BBC novel ranges as "paid fanfic"... something which does a huge disservice to both the writers and fanfiction per se when meant derogatorily. Especially since those novels *are* Doctor Who to all intents and purposes and have been since 1991... On the other hand, "normal fans" who write fanfic tend to be inspired – and in turn aspire to quality – because the brightest stars among the novelists came from grass-roots level themselves. The beauty of it is that we're all fans... and if "fanfic" – "paid fanfic" results consistently in professional authors who can and do hold their own outside Who as well as within it, then there **is** no difference, surely?

What strikes me about the *Who* authors who went on to "hold their own outside it" is that they all seem, typically for that fandom though very atypically for fanfic as a whole, to be men. (There are women among the professional *Who* writers, but not many.) And I do wonder if the female writers in fandom are sometimes more diffident about their own talent, and more reliant on the security and supportiveness of their writing and reading community, than they need to be. Kel, a publishable writer if ever I read one, even while admitting her ambition to write professionally feels a need to downplay the possibility:

> I would of course dearly like to do this (fiction) professionally. However I tend to regard that as Mittyist in the extreme. Kel the Novelist ranks right up there with Kel the Replacement Bassist In Metallica <giggling> it just ain't gonna happen. Although that's no reason not to give it a shot, is it? I'm a much better writer than bassist... at least I know which way up the pen goes.

There could hardly be a greater contrast with the casual acceptance of Paul Magrs that this novel-writing was something he could do; yet he started off like many fanfic writers (not unlike Nova, slashing her Heyer heroes as a twelve-year-old, see chapter 5):

> *What made you first want to write a Doctor Who novel?*
> I was writing them when I was ten. There was a bit of a gap for a while, I wrote some other novels and published them.
>
> By then, Virgin and then the BBC were publishing original Doctor Who novels. I'd been at school with Mark Gatiss and did my MA in creative writing with Paul Cornell, so I thought, "Hang on – shouldn't I be writing one as well?" I knew it would be great fun.[4]

To expand on the references above, Paul Cornell wrote official *Who* novels and screenplays for programmes like Coronation Street, but in 2001 published his first "original" novel, the dystopian *Something More*[5]. He has since published a second with Gollancz, *British Summertime*[6]. Mark Gatiss also wrote *Who* novels, then starred in the comic team The League of Gentlemen and is now publishing a litfic novel. Meanwhile Russell Davies, of course, was becoming famous for *Queer as Folk* while Magrs himself was winning plaudits for his young-adult novel *Strange Boy*[7] and teaching creative writing at the University of East Anglia. All of these four are writers who essentially graduated from fandom writing to mainstream fiction, (if one takes into account Magrs' ten-year-old start) and they are all from the one major fandom where male fan fiction writers have always dominated.

I don't want to overplay this as a gender difference. I know many female fanfic writers who are strong, confident characters well able to cope with rejection slips (I'm sure Executrix, for one, doesn't write profic for exactly the reason she gave me and no other). But if there is a cultural expectation that women will be more diffident about their abilities than men, and less inclined to competition, then it would make sense that the collaborative, non-competitive environment of fanfic might give some female writers a confidence to write and share their writing that they would not have outside it. If that's so, then the alternative for these writers probably wouldn't be to write profic, even when they are capable of it, but not to write for an audience at all. The anonymity of pseudonyms and email works well for these writers, as I could see once I managed to look past the screaming ego of the profic writer and accept reluctantly that the vague chance of everlasting fame was not something all writers would pursue at any cost.

But there are more positive reasons for choosing to write in this genre rather than another, and to illustrate them I cannot do better than to quote Belatrix Carter (in private email) on the subject. She writes in SF domains (eg *B7* and *Farscape*) and is another eminently publishable writer:

> I can't speak for anybody else, but for my own part, well, I've not infrequently had the experience of reading a professionally published piece of fiction and thinking, "Hey, my writing is better than that!" There are, I think, basically, two reasons why I write fanfic but am not much interested in writing profic.
>
> Fanfic is what I get inspiration for. All my life, I've enjoyed writing.

I've liked the idea of being a writer (not in the "I'd like to pen a best-seller and go to cocktail parties" kind of way, but in a "I'd like to write and have people read it" way.) I have a good grasp of the English language, and, I like to think, a modicum of talent at stringing words together. But I never had any ideas, at least not any good ones. And, over and over, I'd heard professional writers being asked "where do you get your ideas?" and responding that ideas are the easy part. They just come to you. They visit you in the shower, they mug you on the streets. Ideas never did that to me. I had writing ability but nothing to write about, and I sadly concluded that I really just wasn't a writer by nature.

Then I got into fan fiction, and suddenly, whaddaya know, I was getting ideas! Ideas were coming to me, they were visiting me in the shower, in bed, they were mugging me on the street. They were lodging themselves in my brain and jumping up and down waving their arms at me until I had to write them down just to get them to shut up and leave me alone. But they were all ideas that were very specifically related to these existing TV characters, in these existing TV universes. Apparently, this is just how the creative part of my brain works. I didn't choose to write fanfic; in a sense, it chose me.

Fanfic is in many ways the best medium for doing the kinds of things that I want to do. I don't much like writing plot; I'm not very good at it and I don't find it interesting. I do like writing very short things, often just character vignettes, which are designed to have a very sharp emotional punch. I like playing around with this intertextuality stuff [...] too, experimenting with how much I have to actually put on the paper, and how much I can leave to happen in the reader's head. And I like taking familiar things and putting new twists on them, making the reader see them in new ways or completely reinterpret things that she thought she understood. [...] And all of those things are difficult-to-impossible to do in a profic story, where you have to invent everything from scratch. If all I want to write is, basically, the emotional-punch ending, I can do it in fanfic, because the beginning's already been written. If I were doing it in profic, I'd have to do umpteen zillion pages of set-up to get the reader emotionally invested in the characters and up to speed on the situation before I could hit them with the zinger ending. Not only is that a lot more work (and the kind of work that I find uninteresting), but it would badly dilute the effect I like to achieve (i.e. hit 'em before they know it's even coming!).

Now, it's possible to avoid that, and to have fun with intertextuality, and to do the new-twists-on-the-familiar thing and have it publishable as profic if you do it with source material that's a) public domain, and b) familiar to everybody, not just a small fannish subcul-

> ture. A lot of profic writers do that. I mean, I love re-interpretations of fairy tales, that sort of thing. And maybe I could write stuff like that. But myth and legend and fairy tales and folklore are sources that have already been very intensely mined by a great many writers, some of them far better than I'll ever hope to be [...] This makes it really, really hard to come up with a new twist, something that will truly take the reader by surprise, something that will provoke a real emotional impact, rather than a "seen it all before" yawn. Paradoxically, I find that in fanfic I have a lot more confidence in the thought that I'm doing something original.

This is pure genre choice, a sense that this is the field in which the writer can best play to both her writing strengths and preferences. Belatrix's recognition that "all I want to write is, basically, the emotional-punch ending" has lately led her to specialise in drabbles, the 100-word stories popular across many fandoms, and in even shorter forms. Fanfic, with its shared information, enables her to give these tiny stories the "emotional punch" she values, because her reader is already conversant with the back-story. Drabbles and similar forms of short-short fiction are widely used by fan fiction writers and the constraints they place on writing are peculiarly suited to this genre. In such condensed fiction one is always looking to be able to leave things out, to convey narrative with the briefest of references, and with such a complicit audience this is unusually possible.

It's true that even here, when discussing literature that mines the traditional myth-kitties, there is an implied deference to earlier writers. But this is no more than the deference to "worthie Chaucer glorious" displayed by Henryson, which did not deter him from playing in the same sandpit. The difference here, I think, is that this particular sandpit has now been played in so much. Those writers who like to work with myth and folklore are finding they need to work with new forms of it in order to do anything original – with, for instance, the modern avatars of Robin Hood rather than the figure himself.

Jane Mortimer, in her very interesting online essay 'The Advantages of Fan Fiction as an Art Form'[8], makes some of the same points, and also warns against the fallacy of supposing that activities which do not happen to earn money cannot be worthy of serious consideration:

> There was a time when "amateur" was a compliment. Pursuing something for love was admired, while doing it for filthy lucre was

> despised. We live in a harsher age, when values have turned around, and if there's no immediate money from a project, writers are urged to abandon it. I find it reassuring to know the artistic impulse remains this strong, that people will still invest in something for sheer pleasure in its creation, and the hell with what the rest of the world may say.

Indeed there was once a time when gentlemen amateurs were not expected even to sign their work, much to the frustration of later scholars trying to determine whether Sir Walter Raleigh, for instance, did or did not write a certain poem. In the next chapter I am going on to discuss some individual fics which made a particular impression on me. One of them was called 'Make With Your Hands', and when I first found it on fanfiction.net I thought I would not be able to assign an individual author to it, even by fanfic pseud. On this site one can generally click on an author's pseud to find out more about them. But this one was signed "Team Bonet", which the click revealed was a seven-member team of writers (some from the same family, hence the name) working mainly in the anime and manga fields. I couldn't resist emailing them, not only because I liked the fic but because it was so plainly *not* a team effort: it had one person's individual style stamped all over it and I wanted to know how this one person could resist trumpeting her authorship, and why. I was lucky: the actual author read my email and responded:

> Team Bonet built their homepage together but each individual member wrote his or her own stories. [...] The reason was twofold. One, I am somewhat paranoid about the Internet and everybody knowing my name. Second, I truly, honest-to-goodness did not mind in the slightest that my writing went under Team Bonet. We seven were great friends [...] it was supposed to be fun, after all.

Rather movingly, the credits at the end of the fic include:

> The characters Athos, Aramis, Porthos, Milady de Winter, Raoul, and Philippe are © 1840 Alexandre Dumas and all of those who helped him.

This alludes to the fact that Dumas, too, worked with collaborators. In his case they were rather like the pupils in an artist's studio; who filled in the boring plot outlines and background bits while the master did the big set-piece scenes. The most important of Dumas' collaborators, Auguste Maquet, was a history teacher who assembled the historical backgrounds, characters and incidents Dumas turned into fiction. But Dumas' collaborators are not credited by name on the books, nor is their part in his success widely acknowledged or known to the general reader. Fanfic writers by contrast tend to credit their beta-readers, any fic, writer, film or song that may have influenced them and anyone else who might have had some small part in what they made. I don't think most fanfic writers really believe in the notion of the single-authored book.

It is easy to identify literary and other influences on fanfic from the quotations and references so prevalent in stories and from the names mentioned in forum and mailing list discussions. Not surprisingly, Barthes is important to writers whose work derives from their readings of others and who frequently have to defend their readings to those who think only the author's has any validity. He sometimes gets cited as a sort of academic justification by fanfic writers defending their practice to non-believers – as here, by Ika on an unarchived list:

> [...] fanfic is practising what a lot of academics theorise. [...] what Barthes was originally trying to do in a lot of his work was to explain how it *felt* to read, and to come up with an explanation of how meaning gets produced in a sort of three-way interaction between reader, writer and text – and those are the the sorts of interaction that happen in fanfic. Even if fan writers aren't deliberately killing the author, their practice shrieks that they don't believe interpretations of canon are nothing more than attempts to retrieve what the canonical writers intended.

It is harder to identify influences going the other way, and this is not necessarily because there aren't any. Not many litfic writers will cheerfully admit, as Magrs does, to having written Doctor Who novels, nor even to having read fan fiction. In the case of fiction based on their own work, as indicated in the last chapter, this is partly for legal reasons, to avoid plagiarism accusations – though in the interview mentioned above Magrs, like Rowling, expresses his pleasure in fan fiction centred on his own original character Iris Wildthyme, who began life as an OC in his Doctor Who novels:

> I like it when other people put her in things – her cameos in Lawrence and Lance's work, or in Steve Cole's forthcoming audio – or in the fan fiction on the net that's floating around out there.

But the stigma attaching in critical and academic circles to any genre fiction, much less a genre often seen as derivative and vaguely comical in such circles, means that few writers will admit publicly to having a foot in both camps. There are profic writers, particularly in certain genres, who are widely believed in fandom to have started out as fanfic writers, but since they would have been using different names there would be no way of proving that and very little point in asking them outright. And there are fanfic writers currently writing profic as well, but again they will not be using the same name for both, and again they will not generally admit to both except within the fan community.

It is more fruitful to identify parallels, trends which seem to have happened over the last few decades in both litfic and fanfic, but usually rather earlier in the latter. Fanfic writers, as I have indicated, are avid consumers of all sorts of fiction; the same is true of their readers, and what they enjoy writing and reading has a habit of turning up in the mainstream, once publishers have, often more belatedly, caught up with public taste. I have already (in chapter 1) alluded to how certain popular TV shows changed during the 1970s and 80s, becoming more sensitive and relationship-oriented, and how this paralleled the way in which fanfic writers had already been skewing the canons in question. An interesting later parallel might be identified between the fanfic AU scenario, which deliberately alters its canon, and the current fashion for "what if" histories which speculate on how events *might* have gone and how this would have changed the world we know.

Slash presents another such parallel. It has been around in fanfic since the mid-70s, growing in scope through the succeeding decades. At the time it started, this phenomenon – women writing about and exploring the emotions of men in homoerotic relationships – had few parallels in litfic. Iris Murdoch's *The Bell*[9] had a homosexual subplot but the only female writer who was making a speciality of this theme then was the novelist Mary Renault, who since the late 1950s had been writing books set in Ancient Greece and, usually, centring on just such relationships. She continued to do so through the 60s and 70s, concluding with *Funeral Games* in 1981, two years before her death. But she was pretty much a one-off. (When I first encountered slash fanfic, I assumed she must have been a major influence on its writers, but that does not seem to be the case: she is occasionally mentioned as an influence, but not by many.)

These days, if I wanted examples of women writing about men in intense and often erotic relationships, I should not have far to look, even if I limited myself to English-language fiction. Genre fiction, of course, would give me Anne Rice and Poppy Z Brite, but litfic would be even more fruitful. From the early 70s, when slash first took off, one could name, apart from Renault, Susan Hill's *Strange Meeting*[10], which described an intense friendship between First World War soldiers, Patricia Nell Warren's *The Front Runner*[11], Audrey Laski's *Night Music*[12] and Cecelia Holland's *City of God*[13]. By the time we get to the 90s, names occur far more easily. Pat Barker's *Regeneration* trilogy[14], Ruth Rendell's *No Night Is Too Long*[15], Cecelia Holland's *Jerusalem*[16], Beryl Bainbridge's *Master Georgie*[17], Anne Carson's *Autobiography of Red*[18] and Annie Proulx's 'Brokeback Mountain'[19]. In the current decade, we already have Maria McCann's *As Meat Loves Salt*[20] and Louise Welsh's *The Cutting Room*[21].

It is clear that, despite the bafflement of some commentators as to why female slash writers would want to do this, it is actually an interest that extends far beyond fanfic. Women writers generally are currently interested in exploring the emotions and potential vulnerability of men in this situation. The novelist and short story writer Catherine Merriman, in her collection of stories *Getting A Life*[22] has a story called 'The Pursuit of Beauty', in which a young man haunts the National Portrait Gallery in pursuit, he thinks, of a girl who spends time there. But what he ends up doing is having a sexual encounter with a security guard and though at first he persuades himself that it is happening against his will, in the end he has to recognise that it is not.

This is such a classic "first time" slash scenario – young man who assumes he's straight is enlightened by someone more experienced who knows otherwise – that when I read it I assumed the writer might be a slash fan. Taking advantage of the fact that I knew her, I risked the impertinence of asking (via email). In fact it turned out she had never heard of the existence of slash. In a way this makes it all the more interesting that her motives for choosing this theme paralleled so closely the sort of thing a slashfic writer might say:

> I am drawn to issues of sexuality at the moment and I have always been interested in male vulnerability. I suppose vulnerabilities are much more interesting than strengths in fiction (not, I think, necessarily in real life) and I also find something weirdly sexy about them when they concern men (again though, only in fiction and not in real life, where I much prefer strengths!). I don't know why there is a discrepancy between fictional/fantasy notions and real life ones.

The interest in male vulnerability, the perception of it as sexy in a fantasy context and the bemused realisation that one probably would not find it so in real life all crop up fairly regularly in forum and mailing list discussions between slash fans. That female litfic writers find the same issues engaging them makes it even less likely that slash fans are strange creatures with a psycho-sexual quirk (see the reference to *Warrior Lovers* in chapter 5). Rather they are in tune with an area of interest to contemporary women litfic writers, though fan fiction seems to have started exploring the territory a little earlier.

Indeed, how general this interest is becomes clear if we move beyond a Eurocentric view of literature. Mark McLelland's article 'Why Are Japanese Girls' Comics Full Of Boys Bonking?' in the internet journal *Intensities*[23] gives a fascinating account of how, independently but at the same time, Japanese women writers have been using this theme. It developed from the tradition of "shonen ai" ("boys' love") genre of women's comics of the early 70s, which were original works by professional women manga artists. In the late 70s some women began to parody boys' comics by imagining love scenes between the heroes. This paralleled the Western slash fanfic culture, but branched out, in YAOI (see chapter 5) into creating its own original characters. YAOI, written for and by women, is even a commercial proposition, as McLelland reports:

> Western slash fiction has never been taken up commercially, and most women's slash fanzines barely make enough to cover costs. But Japanese publishing companies with an eye for profit have picked up some of the brightest amateur YAOI artists of the early 80s and published their work. One of the earliest 'boy love' monthly magazines was June (pronounced ju-neh) first published in 1978. In 1995, June was still being published, now in a 300-page bimonthly format, and with a circulation of between 80,000 and 100,000 (Schodt 1996: 120). In contrast, G-Men, one of Japan's most popular gay magazines, sells only 20,000 copies per month.

But perhaps the most obvious litfic/fanfic parallel is the modern interest in fiction which takes existing texts as starting points. As I suggested in chapter 1, this is nothing new, but it does seem to be increasingly popular in our own day, and this trend in litfic gained momentum around the same time as the late 60s and early 70s explosion of fanfic, suggesting that the same needs drove them. Apart from the Jane Austen sequel industry mentioned in chapter 3 and involving such writers as Emma Tennant, there is George Macdonald Fraser, who has been constructing, from 1969 to the present, an entire sequel universe around Flashman, a minor character from *Tom Brown's Schooldays*. Flashman (Fraser's, not Hughes's) now attracts societies of devotees all over the world, rather like Sherlock Holmes. In more recent times John Sullivan has written the TV series *Micawber*[24], sequelizing Charles Dickens's character. Will Self has published *Dorian*[25], an updated version of Wilde's *The Picture of Dorian Gray*. Susan Hill, in 1993, broke a long silence by publishing *Mrs de Winter*[26], her response to du Maurier's *Rebecca*. Hill was a great admirer of Jean Rhys's *Wide Sargasso Sea* (1956), saying of it "It is not merely a gloss on *Jane Eyre*, it enhances, echoes and illuminates it, explains, qualifies and even changes it".[27]

This clearly goes beyond the need not to let a story end, but that is still part of it. It is hard, for instance, not to conclude from Macdonald Fraser's comprehensively researched familiarity with Victorian Britain and its empire that he'd actually quite like to have lived in the times he describes with such wistful gusto. The modern habit of sequelizing films, as in the *Rocky*, *Godfather*, *Jaws* and other serial universes, suggests that we are an audience unwilling to let one thing drop and move on to another – as does the outcry when almost any TV series is ended. In an article in the *Independent on Sunday*[28] Andrew Gumbel previewed some films due out in 2003. Not only would we see the third *Lord of the Rings* film and the next *Bridget Jones*, but also:

> *The Matrix: Reloaded* in the summer, followed six months later by *The Matrix Revolutions*, parts two and three of the futuristic blockbuster, [...] the second instalment of *X-Men*, a new *Terminator* movie, [...] a *Charlie's Angels* sequel, a Lara Croft *Tomb Raider* sequel and – if you can believe it – a *Friday the 13th* sequel combined with a *Nightmare on Elm Street* sequel entitled *Freddie versus Jason*.

That last would be a crossover, presumably. Of course anyone who has to do with publishers in any creative medium is aware of their liking for more of the same. Given the choice they (or their marketing men) will go for a repeat of whatever sold well last year rather than risk something new and untried. But unless the said marketing men are *totally* incompetent, they presumably do have some reason, in the form of market research, sales and audience figures, to suppose that "more of the same" is what a considerable part of their market wants.

It is tempting to associate this unwillingness to let things end with serialisation and TV schedules, which put us in the addictive habit of entering a particular universe at the same time each week (or sometimes day). Not that this is new. The readers of a Dickens novel would have encountered it as a serial in a magazine, and would have known that it must eventually end – though, of course, it was in this form that Conan Doyle sprang the death of Holmes on his audience, only to find that they had other ideas.

If I might be allowed to be fanciful for a moment, I think modern medicine might have something to do with it. Among the audiences we have been talking about, mainly in the USA, western Europe and Japan, most people these days expect to live a long time. Actual wars in these regions are rarer than they were; the effect of poverty on lifespan is less obvious and drastic, though it still exists, and when illness does arise, we expect doctors to be able to do something about it. In fact, if there proves not to be a miracle cure, our attitude is more likely to be indignation than the "oh well, I've had a good innings" fatalism of fifty or a hundred years ago. There is less fatalistic acceptance of death than there once was, and less familiarity with it: many people have never seen a dead person in real life. It is at least possible that this affects our expectations of fiction and makes unequivocal endings of any kind harder to deal with, in the same way that it drove some to have their corpses frozen and stored for possible future resuscitation, rather than accept that they were unequivocally dead. Perhaps I ought not, in chapter 3, to have been quite so puzzled about the fanfic taboo on character death.

But the quote from Susan Hill earlier also touches on intertextuality, on our voracious feeding off each other's various forms of fiction to create more fiction and alter what is already there to suit our own needs. Again this is not new: it is the stuff of storytelling and has always been (see the Introduction and chapter 1). But it did perhaps fade into the background for some generations with the rise of paid professional fiction-makers on a mass scale – not just authors but producers, directors, scriptwriters – whose audiences became not so much participatory as passive. There is an essay[29] by Michela Ecks, discussing the ethics of book-based fan fiction as opposed to the TV and film-based kind. In summarising the objections of some authors, it reflects attitudes to writer and reader that would have been fairly commonplace when I was growing up in the Fifties and Sixties. Now, post-Barthes, they look antediluvian:

> Another concern authors have is that fans will radically or intentionally misinterpret their stories. As such, the fan writer will compose a story with the author's characters in the author's universe that is radically different than the canonical versions of the characters and universe. The fan fiction writer creates his or her own original characters under the auspices of the original story. The characters help to push the fan fiction writer's own agenda, which may be at odds with the professional author's. They are not writing stories derived from the original because, in a book, there is only one correct version of the story: the author's.

Not any more... If people ever were happy to be such a passive audience for fiction they are not now. Children have interactive fantasy books, which allow them to partly determine the course of the narrative by making different choices: adults have to write these choices in to what they read or see.

Indeed many teenage writers with stories on the fanfiction.net website wrote them because they were actively encouraged so to do by their English Literature teachers, who set assignments which involve not just reading the book in question but interacting with it and writing one's own take on some scene from it. Time after time, the note to an Austen or Shakespeare fic reads "I wrote this as an assignment for English class".

Human beings have always had an inexhaustible need for fiction and while fictional characters cannot die, they can and do become less relevant. Robin Hood and his avatars will be with us as long as people object to oppressive or interfering governments and admire outlaws, but the great myth-kitties of Greece, Rome and the Bible are perhaps harder to use in the absence of both belief and widely shared knowledge of the canons. New characters and new canons shared by writers and readers must come from somewhere: one source is fiction itself in all its modern forms, and another is real life. The modern heroes of film, manga, anime and TV are the equivalent of the heroes of myth, and sometimes also their avatars. Blake of *B7* is a recognisable avatar of Robin Hood, the archetypal opponent of unjust governments, in fact Terry Nation, its creator, is said to have referred to *B7* as "Robin Hood in space". But real people are also potential material for a writer, and here a relatively recent development of fan fiction becomes relevant.

Characters, except in purely book-based fandoms, necessarily go about behind the faces of real people, actors. Descriptions of Frodo in many *Lord of the Rings* fics clearly owe more to the features and figure of Elijah Wood, who plays him in the Peter Jackson films, than to Tolkien's canonical concept of something tubby, short-legged and hairy. Illya's piercing blue eyes are also those of David McCallum; we all know this, even if we do not often think about it. But the relationship between actor and character has sometimes caused controversy, especially in the realms of adult fanfic. Actors have occasionally been unhappy about seeing "their" characters portrayed in ways they didn't agree with. But while understanding their viewpoint most fanfic writers have taken the view that the actor is not the character and that everybody concerned should understand this. In fact it is sometimes the actors who foster confusion, by identifying so closely with the characters they portray.

But fanzines, quite often, are illustrated, and sometimes explicitly. Even fans who have no qualms about het and slash fanfic sometimes cavil at nude or suggestive illustrations of people who may *be* the characters but inevitably have the faces and bodies of the actors. Some editors, reprinting zines which were first published in pre-Internet days, have omitted explicit illos from the new editions, on the ground that people outside fandom have occasionally got hold of such illos and put them online where all could see them. "Photomanips", i.e. photographs doctored to look like who they are not, are one step farther down the line. At one time, this meant heads grafted rather unsubtly on to the wrong bodies, but with internet tools like Photoshop they can be made far more convincing. And the next step happened when actors themselves began to be used in fanfic as their creations were.

"Real person" fanfic seems to have developed specifically from slash; indeed real person slash (RPS) makes up most of it. In this respect it might be seen as the Western equivalent of YAOI. The Japanese writers, when they had slashed all the fictional characters who interested them, took to inventing their own: Western writers seem to have turned instead to real people. It does seem to have started with actors, often those who played slashable characters: in the early days the favourite pairing was Ben Affleck and Matt Damon. (From all accounts they were hugely amused and took to playing up to the image in public in the hope of generating more fics.) Other actors succeeded them and ever since the first *Lord of the Rings* film (*Fellowship of the Ring*, Peter Jackson 2001), the LotR actors have generated almost as much fiction in this department as their characters have in conventional fanfic. Indeed the RPS pairing of Dominic Monaghan (Merry) and Elijah Wood (Frodo) has achieved the status of a small sub-genre with its own name, Domlijah.

The reason LotR is so popular as slash material may be sought in the canon: the books, published back in the Fifties, are as male-centric as any Seventies cop-show. The female love interest is shadowy. Arwen, Aragorn's betrothed, is conveniently absent for most of the time, Gimli's adoration of Galadriel is strictly chivalric and hands-off, and Eowyn, who has a crush on Aragorn, spends quite a lot of time disguised as a man. Meanwhile all the important and intimate relationships are m/m: Frodo and Sam form a classic central male dyad. The film-makers did go some way to increase the female presence; Arwen has more of a role than in the books. But the m/m relationships were still central, and casting a Frodo (Elijah Wood) who was arguably somewhat younger and prettier than the canon required was not something any slash writer was going to ignore.

In a fair few of these LotR "real person" fics, the setting is actually the film set of *Fellowship of the Ring*, as if to compound the actor/character confusion. Brenda, in 'Relax'[30], which pairs Sean Bean (Boromir) and Elijah Wood (Frodo), uses the actual words of the script (which are faithful to the book) but relates them to the actors speaking them as well as to the characters they are playing. Thus the words express something other than they meant onscreen. In the scene they are rehearsing, Boromir, who though basically a good man has been corrupted by the Ring's power, is trying to get Frodo to trust him enough to surrender it to him:

> Breathe, Sean, relax. It's only a scene. "Frodo?" he started, infusing the word with concern and the first beginnings of madness, and looked into Lij's eyes. "None of us should wander alone. You least of all. So much depends on you. Frodo?"
>
> And Lij simply stared at him, but it was through Frodo's eyes, Frodo's wary countenance.
>
> "I know why you seek solitude." Sean's voice dropped to a husky, intimate whisper. Yes, Boromir was friendly, non-threatening, an ally. "You suffer. I see it day by day. Be sure you do not suffer needlessly."
>
> And, with those soft words, something shifted, changed. No longer Boromir, no longer Frodo – but Sean and Elijah. And the words took on a whole new meaning as Sean lost himself inside blue eyes and a gentle soul.
>
> "There are other ways, Frodo. Other paths that we might take." Don't tempt me, Lij. We can still be just friends, still pretend.

> Lij continued to look straight at him, gaze never wavering. "I know what you would say. And it would seem like wisdom but for the warning in my heart."

I should point out, by the way, that this site, like all RPS sites, is liberally festooned with acknowledgements that None Of This Is True, and I can only repeat them. I have been trying to avoid quoting RPS fics for obvious legal reasons but this one goes to the heart of the deliberate blurring of actor/character, real/fictional boundaries that I am trying to illustrate.

But RPS is no longer confined to actors. The next departure was a lot of boy band slash, generally written by their fans, who are naturally very young, inexperienced writers. It tends therefore to be of a literary quality to make one despair. (To be fair, it is not that much worse than a lot of *Buffy* fanfic, written by a similar age group.) RPS continued to branch out and now involves, admittedly on a smaller scale than with actors and boy bands, all sorts of people – politicians, sportsmen (footballers, Formula One racing drivers, whose racing teams conveniently form male dyads) and almost anyone else with a degree of celebrity. The recent advent of the young, long-haired Paul Hunter has triggered a small outbreak of snooker slash; another sport whose gladiatorial nature and physical conditions are well suited to the genre.

It has gone beyond slash too; there are gen and het sites, like "Diana Lives On"[31], Japanese in origin, which exists to continue the story of Diana, Princess of Wales – it should by now be clear that, with the aid of prequels and AUs, that is quite easy.

Indeed the latest example was a profic one, published in 2004, *Balmoral*, by "Isabel Vane",[32] a pseudonym behind which the *Observer's* reviewer suspected Emma Tennant.[33] This is a sequel fic in which Diana survives. The reviewer, Jonathan Heawood, mentioned "literary pastiche", but of course Diana was not a fictional character and this is straight (albeit paid) RPF.

On the face of it, it would seem unlikely that this trend could be paralleled in profic, at least with reference to the living, since few publishers want to finish up on the wrong end of a libel suit. Like conventional fanfic based on the works of living book authors, it probably would never have taken off but for the anonymity of the Internet. It is for this reason that I have not generally been quoting from the examples I have cited, though personally I think the law and individuals should recognise that there is a difference between asserting that a person has actually done such-and-such and using him as material for a fictional character who does. If I read a story featuring a couple of named Formula One drivers, I do not come away with the conviction that the people whose names have been used are in fact at it like rabbits; merely that two characters who have been given their names and some of their traits are. But tempting as it is to argue the case for living people, like the dead, to be legitimate sources of material for a writer, the courts might prove an expensive place to do it. Nevertheless, the protection of clearly satirical intent means it can occasionally happen. A piece in the online satirical magazine *The Onion*[34] suggested a novel explanation for the animosity between Ariel Sharon and Yasser Arafat:

> JERUSALEM – The long-simmering sexual tension between Israeli Prime Minister Ariel Sharon and Palestinian leader Yasser Arafat finally reached a breaking point Monday, culminating in a passionate kiss before a shocked delegation of Mideast negotiators.
>
> "You always got the feeling that there was something more behind all the anger and tension," said European Union Foreign Policy Chief Javier Solana. "They wouldn't agree on anything, even though their people were dying, locked in this unending conflict. It never made sense – until now."
>
> Continued Solana: "All that repressed passion. And neither of them would admit it to the other... or to themselves."

At least, it would have been a novel explanation to anyone but a slash fan, to whom it would be a classic subtext reading. The fictional comments of the US envoy encapsulate years of slash theorising on male intimacy issues in cop and space shows:

> "If trapping Yasser in his Ramallah compound for months was Ariel's way of getting Yasser's attention, he should have tried a less antagonistic approach, like sending a card," Roed-Larsen said. "And Yasser is no better, trying to catch Ariel's eye with all those deadly suicide bombings. God, men can be so stupid and macho."

In true slash style, facing up to their emotions solves all the tensions and ends the war. If only... I don't know who wrote the *Onion* piece but it was seized on with delighted amusement by slash fans on lists across the Internet as the work of a kindred spirit. British slash fans were equally amused by the Valentine's Day 2003 cover of the *Daily Mirror*, referring to the preparations for war with Iraq, "Make

Love Not War", with its heart-framed photomanip of George Bush and Tony Blair appearing to kiss. The writer and director Attilio Magguilli also chose to satirise Blair's perceived sycophancy by putting a slash subtext in his play *George W Bush ou le triste cowboy de Dieu* (*George W Bush or God's sad cowboy*), staged at the Comédie Italienne in Paris in May 2003. It was not clear whether the unknown assailants who beat him up outside the theatre on 4 May were anti-slashers or just Bush fans in general.

The transgressive, subversive nature of slash, and the way it forces readers to re-examine texts and characters they thought they knew, has obvious applications in litfic satire about real people. If one test of a democratic society is its attitude to subversive literature, the new Russia's credentials did not look too healthy in the affair of Vladimir Sorokin's *Goluboe Salo*[35], which supposed a homosexual relationship between Stalin and Khruschev. A "loyalist youth group" destroyed copies in Moscow and the author was threatened with prosecution and accused of spreading pornography. Springing to his defence, the gay website Banana Guide[36] described him as a slash writer. I don't know whether he would endorse or even understand the description, but it is a fact that some Western slash writers wrote letters in support of him as a fellow-slasher in a censorious world.

In less prickly societies dead people, who cannot be libelled, have always been a legitimate source of material for writers, of course. What is perhaps new is the length of time which now has to elapse before they are fair game. RPS was around in the nineties but since the turn of the century there seems to have been a litfic explosion of "real person" fiction. Muriel Spark had waited twenty-six years from the disappearance of Lord Lucan to publish a fictionalised version of him in *Aiding and Abetting*[37] – and some reviews still queried the propriety of doing so while people affected by the real events were still alive. But some writers no longer acknowledge any such time constraint. Emma Tennant's *Sylvia and Ted*[38], billed as "a fictional re-creation of the turbulent courtship, marriage, and separation of poets Sylvia Plath and Ted Hughes", was published only three years after Hughes died. A review on the Literal Mind site[39] quoted this passage:

> The red cord on the floor makes a gash – like a smiling mouth in a perfect face, like a scar high on the cheek of a woman who lies where she has fallen – and she stays a while looking down on it.

The reviewer objects to the way this uses a detail that wouldn't mean much to readers who did not know the back-story of Plath's life:

> Only those familiar with Plath's full life will recognize the reference in the scar on the cheek to the scar on Plath's face, the result of a failed suicide attempt when she was a college student. To everybody else, it's an image that goes nowhere.

This objection surely fails to take account of the precise genre in which Tennant was working and consequently the audience at which she was aiming. Her name is one that crops up again and again in the context of paid fanfic – or to put it in litfic terms, writing which makes creative use of intertextuality – and if her Austen sequels equate to paid fanfic, *Sylvia and Ted* is the profic equivalent of real person het. She is, effectively, writing fan fiction, aimed at people who *do* know the canon of their heroine's life and will pick up on the reference automatically. The fact that she herself knew these people and was part of their life no more changes the genre than the fact that she was paid for it.

Tennant has always been interested in reinterpreting existing texts. Later she progressed to using the facts of her own life in a similar way, producing books which, to judge by the description on publisher Canongate's web site[40], they find hard to define:

> More recent work has seen Tennant turn to a creative reflection on her own life, starting with *Strangers: a family romance* (1998), much praised for its lyrical mixing of imagination and recollection as it engaged with the history of her talented and eccentric family and her own early years. *Girlitude*: a memoir of the 50s and 60s (1999) covers her experiences from 18 to 30, followed by *Burnt Diaries* (1999).

Strangers was in fact described by its publisher Cape as a "literary memoir", but the term "romance", not to mention the "lyrical mixing of imagination and reflection" mentioned above, suggest rather more of a fictional input – fictionalised autobiography, as *Sylvia and Ted* is fictionalised biography. If you run out of fictional texts that you feel an urge to reinterpret and interact with, you either – like the Japanese slash manga writers – invent more texts of your own, or – like RPS fans – turn to real life as fictional material. Blurring of genres is not new: there have long been novels in verse and works that inhabit a no-man's land between fiction and biography, but this blurring of boundaries does seem to be increasingly popular. Spark's

Aiding and Abetting used a real person as the basis for a fictional character in someone else's story. Fictionalised biography is not quite that – rather a step on the way to it – and there have been several recent examples like Kate Moses' *Wintering*[39], again about Sylvia Plath, Colum McCann's *Dancer*[42] about Rudolf Nureyev and Joyce Carol Oates' *Blonde*[43] about Marilyn Monroe. The latter was described by the author as being not a biography but a "radically distilled life in the form of fiction"[44], while Margaret Reynolds' review of *Dancer* in *The Sunday Times* interestingly highlighted critical unease about writing that resists being pigeonholed into genres:

> Novels based on real life can get confused about their own textuality. We are seeing a fashion for this, but the balance between fact and fiction has to be exactly right to avoid a genre crisis.

When I first read this, I misread "sexuality" for "textuality", and the implied objection to people trying to have it both ways strikes me as fundamentally the same. Crisis? What crisis? Obviously the thing must be labelled "novel" or "fictionalised life", or anything other than "biography", which might mislead those looking for undisputed facts (or, in most biographies, reasonably undisputed facts plus possibilities, opinions and theories). But if something is described as fiction, the admixture of fact is surely something the recipe has always accommodated.

The name Daniel Defoe comes immediately to mind. His *A Journal of the Plague Year* is the most realistic, gripping piece of apparent reportage that could (literally) be imagined. We could swear every word was personal recollection, if we didn't know for a fact that the author was aged five in the year he recalls so perfectly in the persona of an adult. He had done a great deal of research; his novel is amongst other things a repository of factual information on the plague year. But his narrator, an ordinary citizen with no literary pretensions and an apparently breathless, haphazard style of jotting down events and conversations, is a fictional construct, an invented OC added to an historical canon. As Anthony Burgess remarked in his introduction to the Penguin edition of 1966, the novel has "the truth of the conscientious and scrupulous historian but its deeper truth belongs to the creative imagination". Defoe, who hid behind so many pseudonyms and had a foot in so many literary camps – fiction, journalism, propaganda, history – was having genre crises before they became fashionable, though he saw them rather as opportunities.

BBC Films, with a number of partners, are currently (2003) producing a film about the marriage of Plath and Hughes, directed by Christine Jeffs, in which Gwyneth Paltrow and Daniel Craig will play the principals. When it comes out, Sylvia and Ted will undoubtedly become subjects for unpaid fan fiction as well as Tennant's kind. Historical characters have always been material for fiction. Usually, though, writers have let some time elapse before fictionalising such material, no doubt partly for reasons of their own safety. Shakespeare could hardly have taken his English history plays closer to his own day than *Henry VIII* without inviting trouble: as it was, Elizabeth I is said to have thought the situation of *Richard II* too close for comfort.

Perhaps, though, natural reticence also played a part. When one looks for examples from earlier times of people whose lives were fictionalised very soon after their death, they tend to be notorious rather than famous, e.g. *The Late Lancashire Witches* (Heywood and Brome 1634), based on a court case of the preceding year. In the case of more respectable folks it seems to have been thought proper to observe a decent interval, to avoid causing offence to their relatives or to give the writer greater distance from the material. Perhaps there was even still a residual feeling that being written about, unless you were a king or a hero, was more notoriety than fame, in the same way that it was once not thought altogether respectable to be mentioned, even favourably, in a newspaper.

These days, "fame" is fairly unreservedly regarded as a good thing. Even when it isn't, there are limits to what you can do about it. Frieda Hughes, daughter of Ted and Sylvia, refused to collaborate with the BBC film in any way and expressed hostility both to the film-makers and the presumed audience. The BBC's reaction was unruffled: "We are naturally concerned for the family's feelings but believe that we have approached making the film in a responsible and unsensational way"[45]. Whether they have or not is, arguably, irrelevant: this line of debate does not allow for the possibility that the family might not want the material dramatised *even* in a responsible way. Or rather, it recognises that they might not want it, but not that this view should prevail. What Frieda Hughes sees as a family matter they see as being in the public domain: a film, to quote Thompson again, about "two extraordinary geniuses" who belong to our shared history. These days, you do not have to be long dead to count as history, myth and/or fictional material, and if you are famous enough, you don't even have to wait to be dead.

NOTES

1. from an unarchived mailing list
2. Heretic Books, 1997
3. IIBFN Press, http://members.ozemail.com.au/~brussell/fanzines.htm 31.01.03
4. interview on BBC Online Cult: Dr Who, http://www.bbc.co.uk/cult/doctor who/books/telepress/magrs/page1.shtml 11.12.02
5. Gollancz
6. 2002
7. Simon & Schuster, 2002
8. http://members.aol.com/janemort/fanfic.html 08.03.03
9. Chatto & Windus 1958
10. Hamish Hamilton, 1971
11. William Morrow, 1974
12. Hutchinson, 1974
13. Random House, 1979
14. Penguin, 1991-5
15. as Barbara Vine, Viking, 1994
16. Forge, 1996
17. Duckworth, 1998
18. Cape, 1999
19. from *Close Range*, Fourth Estate 1999
20. Flamingo 2001
21. Canongate 2002
22. Honno, 2001
23. http://www.cult-media.com/issue1/CMRmcle.htm 13.12.02
24. 2001
25. Viking 2002
26. Sinclair Stevenson, 1993
27. *The Lighting of the Lamps*, Hamish Hamilton 1986
28. 29.12.02
29. on the website http://www.whoosh.org/issue62/ecks2.html 15.12.02
30. http://www.tandq.com/LOTR/index2 17.12.02
31. http://www.mmjp.or.jp/amlang.atc/diliveson/index.htm 14.12.02
32. Robson Books
33. *The Observer*, 25 April 2004
34. http://www.theonion.com/onion3820/sexual_tension.html 14.12.02
35. *Blue Bacon Fat*, 2002
36. http://www.bananaguide.com/bgwire76.htm#stalin 10.01.03
37. Doubleday 2000
38. Holt, 2001
39. http://literalmind.com/0107.html 15.12.02
40. http://www.canongate.net/people/pep.taf?_p=2215 15.12.02
41. Sceptre 2003

42. Weidenfeld, 2003
43. Ecco Press, 2000
44. *Blonde*, Author's Note
45. David Thompson, head of BBC Films, quoted in *The Guardian*, 03.02.03

8. Going There

Narrative Forms and Methods

Fan fiction can be defined as writing based on a canon invented by another writer or writers and shared by the intended audience. This is a definition based on subject matter, as one might say detective fiction was based on the solving of crime or romantic fiction on the resolving of a relationship. Genres can be based on something other than subject matter – urban fiction involves a certain kind of gritty setting, magic realism a certain attitude to reality – and they can overlap. Margaret Atwood's *The Handmaid's Tale*[1] may be found under "literary fiction" in the bookshop, but also under "futuristic" or "science fiction", while those looking for the novels of Lindsey Davis or David Wishart may have to search both "historical" and "crime", since both feature Ancient Roman detectives.

Actual writing *techniques* do not necessarily differ from genre to genre; there is no obvious reason why a futuristic novel, say, should handle characterisation or structure differently from an historical one. Indeed the better the writer, the more likely that he or she will transcend any perceived limitations of genre anyway and prove the adage that the only two genres that matter are good writing and bad.

Nevertheless it may be possible to identify elements that *tend* to be characteristic of a genre, while admitting that all generalisations are flawed and incomplete. In this chapter I am interested in investigating whether there are narrative forms and methods particularly typical of fanfic, or where fanfic might, perhaps, take a different approach from other genres (on the principle of the man asked for directions, who replies "If I were going there, I wouldn't start from here"). And the first instance I would like to look at is the use of two forms in fanfic and profic: the mini-story and the serial story.

Mini-stories have long had a place in profic; indeed the 100-word story is known as the drabble after its supposed inventor the writer Margaret Drabble. The website the-phone-book-com[2] archives many such stories from both new and established writers, collected and paid for by a digital publishing project with support from the Arts

Council of England. Categories include the mini-story (50-150 words), the micro (under 50 words) and the mini-micro (under 150 characters). The rise of text messaging sparked a new interest in very minimal writing, and *The Guardian* runs a competition for text message poetry[3].

A writer who has recently specialised in mini-stories is the novelist Dan Rhodes, whose first published work was *Anthropology*[4], a collection of 101 short stories, each of 101 words (because he did not want to write drabbles). All these little pieces were about love, which was generally, though not always, doomed and almost invariably obsessive. They were all narrated by a male voice which could not, in all the stories, be that of the same character, but was recognisably the same voice; he was an archetype of Man In Love, and because of this unifying narrative voice the stories had a cumulative as well as an individual effect.

Rhodes' observations on why he chose the form (from private email) are reproduced below:

> I really just stumbled into writing very short fiction. I had read about people writing stories to set numbers of words, 55 and 100 in particular, and decided to have a go at writing 100-worders myself. At first it was just a fun experiment. It wasn't until I had written a handful that I was unexpectedly happy with that I began to see it as a potentially publishable collection. When I found out that what I was writing were called Drabbles I added an extra word – I didn't want to write a thing called a Drabble, so I sensationally invented my own form. As I got into the swing of things I found that 101 words was the perfect amount for the ideas my brain was spewing out at the time. Oddly, it felt perfectly natural to write like that. I thought that what I was writing was the closest fiction had ever come to the pop song, and part of me (perhaps somewhat pompously) still thinks that.
>
> When I reached 101 stories that I was happy with (there were plenty of rejects), the part of my brain that created them imploded. I would occasionally try to write in the form, but it wouldn't be the same – either I would write unsatisfactory stories to 101 words, or I would take decent ideas and fail to get them to fit the shape.
>
> When the book was published I was very keen to counter any accusations of originality of form. Also, I asked my publisher not to mention the word count in their publicity for the book, for fear it would be dismissed as a gimmick. After all, they had accepted the manuscript before they knew the stories were all the same length. As it turned out they overplayed the form in publicity, as though it were

> the only interesting thing about the book. I thought, and still think, it was the least interesting thing about it – the form is unoriginal, but the voice and the stories were entirely my own. There were 101 word story competitions on Front Row and in the Daily Mail (of all places), the implication being that anyone can write a 101 word story. Of course anyone can, but as the winners of these competitions showed, it's really difficult to make those 101 words kick arse – ever since finishing Anthropology I've found it impossible.

Rhodes' comparison with pop songs echoes the description I have sometimes heard of short-short fic as being "prose haiku", except perhaps that haiku are meant to entice the reader's mind beyond the words on the page to implications and conclusions that are never spelled out. Rhodes' pieces did that too, in that they raised questions about the people, relationships and emotions into which they gave the curious reader only the briefest and most tantalising glimpse. The man in 'Real', so unsure of his happiness in love that he cannot believe he is awake, who progresses from pinching himself to carving chunks out of his flesh with a surgical saw; the girl so besotted she watches her boyfriend through night-vision goggles as he sleeps. Most of these vignettes do involve obsession, and because of the word limit it does not develop gradually, as it otherwise might; the reader is plunged into the most alarming manifestations of it and frequently obliged to think again about the more dangerous and disturbing side of concepts like love, exclusivity, protectiveness and fidelity.

His comments show some ambivalence about the form he chose. On the one hand, he resented the interest shown in the form as opposed to the content; on the other, he tacitly admits that the form had a lot to do with how the stories turned out. It also, I would contend, had a lot to do with how the voice sounded; Rhodes' voice in his full-length stories and novels since is recognisably the same writer, but there is a particular intensity about the voice in these tiny fictions. His comments also testify to the difficulty of condensing utterance so much, and this is evident in collections like those on the phone-book site. Some have the same condensed force and massive implied back-story as Rhodes' fictions, but many verge on the merely anecdotal.

But two of his most interesting observations concern the "gaps" where stories happen and the extent to which back-story can be left out:

> In Anthropology most of the action happens Off Camera. That's

> where the laughs are (I hope) and where the sadness lies. As I was writing it, I would often find a story came together when I struck out the joke. I like to think that the reader has fun filling in the gaps.
>
> Something that spurred me on when I was writing it was from Borges' introduction to Fictions: "The composition of vast books is a laborious and impoverishing experience. To go on for five hundred pages developing an idea whose perfect oral exposition is possible in a few minutes!"

Both these motives have parallels in fanfic, though the parallels are not exact. Rhodes' remarks recall those of Belatrix Carter, quoted in chapter 7, and it will be profitable to repeat them here by way of comparison. Fanfic comes in all lengths, including full-length novels, but there is no doubting the popularity, in most fandoms, of short-short forms like the drabble, the half-drabble, sometimes also known as the byatt, and mini-stories generally, often in multiples of 50 words up to 500. At first sight, that might seem surprising. Fanfic, after all, is about wanting more, rather than less, expanding an existing canon rather than condensing it.

But the remarks of Belatrix Carter both echo Rhodes' motives and give an insight into the specific fanfic popularity of this form:

> I do like writing very short things, often just character vignettes, which are designed to have a very sharp emotional punch. I like playing around with this intertextuality stuff [...] too, experimenting with how much I have to actually put on the paper, and how much I can leave to happen in the reader's head. And I like taking familiar things and putting new twists on them, making the reader see them in new ways or completely reinterpret things that she thought she understood. [...] And all of those things are difficult-to-impossible to do in a profic story, where you have to invent everything from scratch. If all I want to write is, basically, the emotional-punch ending, I can do it in fanfic, because the beginning's already been written. If I were doing it in profic, I'd have to do umpteen zillion pages of set-up to get the reader emotionally invested in the characters and up to speed on the situation before I could hit them with the zinger ending. Not only is that a lot more work (and the kind of work that I find uninteresting), but it would badly dilute the effect I like to achieve (i.e. hit 'em before they know it's even coming!).

Mini-stories may be used for all sorts of reasons in profic, but one overriding reason for their popularity among fanfic writers is their suitability for a shared canon. Because her audience already shares so much background information, it is possible for a fanfic writer to come in at the middle or end of a story and still take them with her. Exposition is largely irrelevant and information can be conveyed via very brief allusions which will mean more to the "canon" audience than they would to outsiders. Suppose, for instance, a *B7* mini-story had an unnamed woman address an unnamed man jocularly as "killer". This would immediately tell a fanfic audience that the man was Vila and the woman Kerril, a one-off guest character who had a brief liaison with him and gave him that nickname in irony (Vila is hopeless at killing). It wouldn't be necessary to describe or identify them in any other way.

Similarly beginnings can be invested with all the emotional charge of the consequences the audience knows about but the characters do not. A *Hornblower* mini-story focusing on the joy of a young midshipman called Wellard at his imminent posting to the *Renown* would quickly excite the sorrow and pity of readers who know he will suffer and die there. A *Bill* mini-story which had one officer address another as "Reggie-babe" would not only identify the pair at once as Des and Reg but foreshadow a time unknown to either when the originator of this affectionate nickname will, in the canon, try to kill the man for whom he invented it. Belatrix indicated how she would use the shared canon to dispense with beginnings which had "already been written" and go straight to the "emotional-punch ending", but it can work the other way too: the ending also has been written and can thus be powerfully evoked, simply by using a couple of highly charged words to allude to it.

Quite often, in fact, part of the fun of a fanfic mini-story for the reader is working out who is who and what is what from the minimal clues given, while for the writer the challenge lies in giving neither too little nor too much. In particular, character names may be avoided. This touches on fanfic authors' methods of characterisation, a topic I want to discuss more fully later in this chapter; it can be a matter of pride for a fanfic author not to have to name the character. But in the case of mini-stories it happens because, as Belatrix says, it is a way of "experimenting with how much I have to actually put on the paper, and how much I can leave to happen in the reader's head". Within the brief scope of a mini-story, the more that can be left to happen in the reader's head, the better, and these little stories tend to be very much a participant sport: they demand not only background knowledge but, often, a bit of deductive work from the reader. Many fanfic writers and readers feel they gain from this, and that the reader's emotional reaction is liable to be more intense if she has come at the facts in this interactive way rather than having them baldly spelled out.

Obviously these motives echo those of Rhodes, when he said he hoped the reader would have fun "filling in the gaps". The difference is that with a shared canon, you have a very particular kind of gap, which the reader can often fill via shared knowledge rather than by becoming a co-creator in the way he or she would have to with some of the Rhodes stories, but the participatory principle remains the same.

The other possibility Belatrix mentioned was "taking familiar things and putting new twists on them, making the reader see them in new ways". This, in the context, means especially reinterpretation of canon, which is a popular fiction trigger among fanfic writers, particularly if in the canon a certain piece of behaviour seemed out of character, or a scene intrinsically unlikely – or, in some cases, if it could bear a slash interpretation. And this reinterpretation motive too lends itself to short-short fiction, for, as she said, you don't actually have to set up the canon situation, merely suggest the new twist on it. An example of this is kerr_avon's *B7* drabble 'Zero-Sum Game':

> "You'll have to do better than that, Orac, if you expect me to kill them."
>
> Orac failed to make sense of Avon's statement until Gambit's circuit board was linked to him. A game between man and computer, ending in death, was a fascinating new concept. He was pleased that Avon had challenged him.
>
> He processed all the information he had on Avon from Federation sources, to analysis of Avon's actions aboard Liberator, to a psychostrategist's notes. Orac was ready to make his game-winning move.
>
> Orac said, "I have just received a message from Roj Blake on the planet Gauda Prime."[5]

In this brief compass, information from three episodes, 'Headhunter', 'Games' and 'Blake', is linked to suggest a motivation not implied in canon for the computer Orac's singularly unhelpful behaviour to its owners in the final episode. The remark at the start is Avon's, when Orac, panicking for its own safety, suggested sacrificing the lives of a couple of crew members. Gambit was another rather too sentient computer which played games with its owner. The idea that the catastrophic confrontation on Gauda Prime, rather than being more or less accidental, was set up as a sort of game by something incapable of emotion or loyalty allows the reader to look at the whole episode in a new way. And the final sentence, presaging the whole doom-filled last episode, is another example of Belatrix's "emotional-punch ending", this time merely implied in the writing itself and supplied by the reader from her own shared knowledge.

These methods and motives do strike me as specific to fanfic, or at least to any writing dependent on a shared canon. The business of "experimenting with how much I have to actually put on the paper, and how much I can leave to happen in the reader's head" certainly does happen in profic mini-stories, but in a different way. The Rhodes mini-stories of *Anthropology* leave you wondering about matters outside their compass, notably the nature of the "I" who narrates them. But if there is a back-story, it is one each reader invents for him- or herself, rather than one he/she already shares with the writer.

Of course not all fanfic mini-stories are geared to shared canon either. The motives that Rhodes cites can hold good for fanfic writers too. Mireille's *B7* drabble, 'The Other Side', is in the persona of an unidentified Federation army doctor: the only information needed is that he works for the regime, and against rebels, which is clear from the text:

> The medic didn't know what he hated more about this posting: the mud, the biting insects, the seemingly endless stream of wounded troopers....
>
> He hadn't been quite sure how he'd felt about the Federation's attempt to crush the rebellion until he'd got his first combat posting. Now, though – "Animals," he muttered, as he examined the bleeding wreckage that had been a young man. "They'll stop at nothing."
>
> "That's a rebel, sir," his assistant murmured. "We're to patch him up for interrogation."
>
> That was when he started only caring about treating the wounds, and not thinking about how they got there.[6]

This piece uses the spareness and concentration of the drabble form to point up one grim moment of realisation in a man's life, and it would not have to be fanfic, though it is typical of the genre's fascination with different points of view that it tries to give us an insight into the mind of the canonical enemy.

But Mistraltoes' *B7* near-drabble (it only uses 91 words) 'Gang Aft Agley' is in some ways more typical:

> He'd have to apologize. The others understood that he'd said those things to protect them, but to Cally it made no difference. His words were like knives to her, and she took them to heart, because she understood that at some level, he'd meant them.
>
> All right, then, he'd apologize. But first, he'd check out the abandoned ship with Dayna. See if he could find a way off the planet. It would be easier to talk to Cally after he'd repaired some of the damage he'd caused. After they were safe.[7]

This depends, firstly, on knowledge of the situation, which can be gleaned from the mention of the "abandoned ship". At the start of the episode 'Rescue', the crew is marooned on a bleak artificial planet as a result of an ill-fated attempt by Avon to find Blake (in the previous episode 'Terminal'). In the course of that attempt, Avon had discouraged his crewmates from following him and denied that he needed any of them.

Secondly one needs some knowledge of Avon's and Cally's characters. He is prickly and defensive but does have feelings, which he constantly denies, for his crewmates. She is telepathic and has in the past seemed to have more of a bond with him than most; certainly they have shown a mutual sympathy at times. For him to apologise would be difficult, though not unprecedented, and he would regret the loss of her friendship.

Most importantly however, we need to know, as we do and he does not, what happens next. Before he gets back from his errand to check out the abandoned ship, Cally will be dead in an explosion, so anything he might have meant to say will remain unsaid. "After they were safe" – as they are not and never will be again – is what Belatrix called the emotional-punch ending, and its impact depends entirely on *not* having to be spelt out or arrived at over a long period but dropped casually and brutally into the pool of knowledge its audience already possesses. Mireille's drabble could easily enough figure on the-phone-book's site or in any profic context; this one could only happen in a fanfic context.

There is one other way in which short-short fiction suits the specific needs of fan fiction. In this most inclusive of genres, it simply gives more people a chance to join in. It would be an error to suppose that short-short fiction is "easier" to write because of its brevity. Condensing one's utterance takes some skill, particularly when word limits are involved; it is far from easy to whittle 130 words down to 100 without losing anything vital. But it is undoubtedly less time-consuming than writing full-length stories, and may also be less intimidating for unpractised writers who are unsure of their ability to construct a plot or sustain a story at length. Hence it is sometimes a way into writing, and even more often a way for those who are normally readers rather than writers, like the "lurkers" on a fiction mailing list or in a blogging community, to participate actively, perhaps through fiction-writing "challenges". The three *B7* drabbles quoted above all came from a weekly mini-fic challenge, limited to 500 words and on set subjects, on the blogging community livejournal[8]. These challenges, referred to in earlier chapters, are common in all fandoms and if a form is specified it is often a mini-fic of some kind. It might be defined by a word limit, like a drabble, or it might be a time limit – see the "thirty-minute fic" challenge on the savegilmore website. And part of the reason for this is to encourage participation by those who may not have the time, leisure or online access to construct full-length fiction but still want to play an active part in the community.

At the other end of the spectrum from mini-fiction stands the novel-length story. These too are well represented in fanfic (as is the novella, a form unpopular with publishers because it takes up much the same shelf space as a novel while being less lucrative). It might be as well here to mention length criteria which are reasonably commonly accepted. For the purposes of the Screwz Awards, which relate to printzines, a "short-short" story is anything below 5 pages, a "story" is 5-20 pages, a "novella" 20 and upwards and a "novel" a work printed as a standalone zine. The Mithril Awards, associated with the Henneth Annun Tolkien website, define a novel as anything over 50,000 words.

From personal observation, plus the evidence of numbers nominated in the relevant categories of the FanQ and Screwz awards, I should guess that the short story is still far more popular than the novel in fanfic, which might seem the reverse of the case in profic. But then it is near impossible for a profic writer who is not already a recognised novelist to get a collection of short stories considered by an agent or publisher, so it is hard to tell whether profic readers really prefer the novel or just don't get much choice about it.

One aspect of the novel which has all but died out of profic is its initial publication as a serial. In the nineteenth century, distinguished authors were happy to be published this way in periodicals: now it happens only to the particular kind of fiction published in women's magazines. In fanfic, though, the serial is alive and well, thanks of course to the Internet. On many big fanfic sites, like fanfiction.net or savegilmore, you are liable to see stories in various states of completion, which are being posted chapter by chapter, sometimes as they are written. It does not happen in all fandoms, but often enough to be considered a normal way to publish in fanfic. The Horatio Hornblower fiction archive[9] contains many, and *The Bill* web archive savegilmore[10], set up to continue the story of the Gilmore character when it became clear he would leave the series, is home to several serial writers, four of whom, Clare, Bebe, Gill and Kethni, were kind enough to answer some questions about the way they worked.

Publishing along the way does strike me as a definite variation on normal profic practice. In some ways it is reminiscent of differing attitudes to posting work-in-progress on a mailing list. I mentioned earlier that this is commoner in fanfic. On litfic mailing lists many writers are shy of showing others work they do not regard as finished. I recall a comment from before the days of mailing lists, by a poet from whom a magazine editor had solicited some draft work for a feature. He declined on the ground that "the Muse is a lady and does not appear in her dressing-gown" (it was some decades ago).

Serials, of course, can perfectly well be finished before they are posted, and some are. Kethni, author of some of the many serials on the savegilmore website, believes in that method of working, saying (in private email) that there are enough half-finished serials online, to which she did not wish to add. (This is certainly true of some of those on fanfiction.net, which do not look like ever being finished.) But others on that site, like Bebe, do post more or less as they write, though they will generally have had it checked by their beta-readers first. Clare opted for a middle path:

> I never post until I've done at least 6 or 7 chapters, just in case it doesn't work out. All the time I was writing "New Horizons" I kept about 5 chapters or more in reserve.

Gill found her method progressing as she became more secure, having not originally set out to write at that length at all:

> The first fanfic I wrote was in serial form ('Aftermath'). I wrote three chapters and imagined that would be it. By then I had had some really positive feedback so I carried on and wrote three more chapters, to

> another possible ending. At that point I was enjoying myself so much I wrote a further three chapters. This was followed by a one-off epilogue 'Caught in the Act'.
>
> A similar thing happened with 'Soliloquies' which I intended as just a one-off reflective soliloquy from both men on their relationship – timed after Luke walked away from Craig at the hospital. Because readers wanted more I then wrote a prequel 'Chimera' expressing thoughts and feelings just prior to the stag night. Some time later, because there were readers still asking 'What happened in the end – did they get together?' I wrote the sequel, 'Restitution'.
>
> Whereas some planning went into 'Aftermath', and 'Soliloquies' just happened, by the time I wrote my next serial, 'What Men Need' I felt sufficiently confident in my ability to develop and finish a story that I wrote only one chapter ahead of sending it to go up on site. Similarly with my last serial 'Heaven Sent'.

One reason for fanfic writers publishing in serial form is simply that they can; if you publish on the internet it is easy and even convenient, given that each chapter is going to be a separate html page anyway. It means you can satisfy your rapacious readers more quickly and get feedback as you go along, rather than waiting till the end – and most fanfic writers crave positive reader feedback as much as profic writers do. If, rather than putting the fiction up on your own site, you are sending it to a site editor (like Sioux at savegilmore), it means the updates for her site will be both more frequent, which is more interesting for the site visitors, and of a manageable length, which is more convenient for her.

Some writers, as indicated, do fail to complete serials but for some they provide an incentive. "Readers wanting more", in Gill's case, led to an expansion of the original plan. Having not only got partway through the work but received feedback from those impatient to know more, the writer may be less likely to give up than if she were working in isolation from an audience. This is particularly important to less practised writers who need the confidence that feedback can give. On the savegilmore site, many writers, like Bebe and Clare, were first inspired to write by the Craig/Luke scenario (though Bebe has since gone on to creative writing classes and has had a profic story read on BBC Radio). Both have completed serials on the savegilmore site. Kethni, on the other hand, is one of those who has always written for her own enjoyment but had never considered publication, while Gill's real-life work involves writing (professional rather than creative).

Gill, unusually among fanfic writers, does not use a beta, but all the others do. Clare and Bebe use the same third party (Pete, himself a fanfic writer) as a beta/editor, while Clare in turn acts as beta to Kethni and other writers on the site. All are also friendly with Sioux, who, like many site editors, will sometimes make suggestions about work-in-progress. This all adds up to a close-knit and supportive group, which in itself must have been a help to newish writers. But all also testify to the importance of reader feedback along the way. Gill says "I haven't been influenced to change the direction of my stories by feedback – only to keep on writing them". But that "only" is fairly major; indeed it is clear from Gill's account of her first two serials that it was feedback which caused them to end up the length they did.

I wondered if feedback obtained while the work was still in process would actually alter it at all. Gill, as has been seen, did not let it change her direction. For Clare, it acted only as support and confirmation that what she liked was pleasing others too:

> I've been lucky, I had plenty of feedback as I went. You tend to get more from standalone stories, but towards the end of the serial it got really good.[...] Having said that though, despite feedback, I wrote what I wanted. It was for me although I had a pretty good idea what the others wanted to read. The feedback gave me enough clues after all.

Kethni, however, found another way to use it:

> Feedback can make huge difference. Sometimes readers pick up on things that I hadn't consciously noticed but that do make sense and really add to the story overall, so I steal them and pretend they were my idea all along!

This is a familiar enough scenario to a profic writer, though for them it usually happens after publication of completed work: a reader or critic sees some intention or undercurrent in the work that was not evident to the author while writing. Kethni's self-deprecating "pretend they were my idea all along" is typical of a fanfic writer's belief in art as a collaborative process, but no doubt what her readers saw was, in effect, already her own doing, though it may not have been consciously so. In this case the feedback, by recognising and spelling out what was implicit in the work, may have made the author more conscious of those elements and able to play them up as she wrote.

What none did was to go back and alter earlier chapters in the light either of feedback or of their own later writing, as a profic writer working alone on a novel would be liable to do. All had a pretty good idea at the outset of where the story was going (though Gill, Bebe and Clare had never intended their first serials to be so long) and for those who used betas, the beta-reading process had already edited the chapters to a state the authors were happy with before they posted them on the site. This would be the main difference between most fanfic writers and a profic writer with a work in progress. The latter, unless he or she had a sympathetic partner, would be unlikely to have it so closely edited before it got to a publisher. Partners, by the way, do sometimes edit for fanfic writers too. Clare gets feedback from her husband, as do other fanfic writers from theirs, though the husbands of slash writers tend to opt out of commenting on the m/m sex scenes. The few male slash writers, if willing to beta-read for others, are a precious resource for female writers anxious to get their facts right in this area and both Clare and Bebe make a point of stressing the value of Pete's assistance.

Most fanfic writers start out writing short stories and only progress to longer forms later, if at all (Gill was an exception, in that 'Aftermath' was her first fic, but then it did not set out to be that length). I was interested to see whether some of the techniques typical of a fanfic short story would survive the transition to writing at length, notably the use of the present tense, which many fanfic short story-writers prefer. So of course do some profic writers, but over a novel-length profic story that would be less common. In fact, of the four writers on whom I was concentrating, three tended to prefer past tense whatever they were writing. But Kethni, interestingly, liked to use present tense in short stories and had also done so in her longer serial fics, 'Sun Hill Fairy Story'[11] and 'Rapprochement'[12]. Indeed the latter, true to its title, is narrated for much of its length via, successively, emails, MSN Messenger and webcam, as the estranged Craig and Luke gradually grow closer until they finally end up physically together again. This interest in various – and often very modern – narrative methods has parallels within *The Bill* fandom (Kel, in her story 'Exhibit RHI'[13], uses a screenplay narration presumably derived from her TV source material, and Gill's serial story 'Heaven Sent'[14] interleaves poetry with the prose narrative). Most other fandoms, too, have their stylistic innovators. Executrix, in *B7*, enjoys breaking up a narrative into an unusual number of short scenes, again rather like a screenplay. But stylistic innovation is still uncommon: as in profic, most writers do not go beyond more traditional methods.

One thing that does seem to alter when an author undertakes longer stories is the extent to which original characters (OCs) are used. Kethni remarks that "serials give you the opportunity to have little diversions from the main plot and also to develop secondary characters". These secondary characters need not be OCs, but quite often they are. As has been noted in an earlier chapter, some readers are intolerant or at least ambivalent about OCs, especially if they threaten to overshadow the canon characters in the story. In a short format that result may be more likely, whereas the compass of a longer story can accommodate OCs without reducing the role of the canon characters.

It is interesting to look at the way fanfic authors create OCs and whether this differs from their way of presenting canon characters. A fanfic author whose audience already knows the canon characters does not, technically, have to go in for character drawing at all. If she merely mentions the name of Archie, Darcy or Gilmore, the image of the man in question will spring fully formed into her readers' heads, and all she need do from then on is ensure either that she makes him speak and act consistently with that image, or, if she wants to change her readers' perception of him, that she does so in a way they can credit.

You might think this would save a great deal of introduction, and sometimes indeed it is used to do so. But even within the compass of short-short fics like drabbles, many fanfic writers do not in fact avail themselves of this device. Like profic writers, fanfic writers sometimes see the introduction of character names into a narrative as a problem; it can look artificial if unsubtly done. Besides, if the reader can identify the character just from what he says and does, it is proof of the writer's success in capturing him, and certainly in some short-short fic it seems almost a point of pride to characterise in that way.

Even then, though, you would not find many fanfic writers going in for extended physical description of their canon characters. It would only happen in special circumstances, for instance if the character in question were being seen through the eyes of another character who did not know him. But no fanfic writer is going to use her own narrative voice to describe these people to readers who already have the picture in their heads. This is perhaps especially true of writers working with a source property from film or television, where the character's physical presence onscreen renders all description unnecessary.

Manna's "Administration" stories, archived at her website the

Mannazone[15] and also in printzines published by Knightwriter, are set in a dystopian futuristic universe that is inspired by, and in some ways resembles, the "Federation" of the *B7* fiction universe, but is not identical with it. You might say the Administration was an avatar of the Federation, in the same way that original fictional characters can be avatars of canon characters. One of the two main characters in these stories, Warrick, himself began life as an avatar of *B7's* Avon: the other, Toreth, is wholly original, an OC. In the opening chapters of the novel *Mind Fuck*, where both they and other characters are first introduced to the reader, it is interesting to see how this introduction is handled. Toreth, who works for "the Investigation and Interrogation Division" (i.e. he is a professional torturer who uses both psychological and physical methods) is first encountered doing his job:

> The prisoner looked up from his contemplation of the tabletop. He looked very much as he had at their brief meeting earlier, which was to say sullen, angry, and frightened. Toreth stood, impassive, letting his height and the breadth of his shoulders kick off the process of intimidation.

This is the only information about Toreth's appearance which will be vouchsafed for some time, and it is given only because it is relevant to his job and how he does it. Once Toreth's point of view is established we see others through his eyes, and he does not describe for the sake of it. Brief facts about his colleagues are dropped in only when they can be justified for some other narrative reason: he has to pay some attention to his assistant Sara's appearance because she has just challenged him to notice what's new:

> Sara spread her arms. "What do you think?"
>
> Trick question, because she was wearing the standard admin uniform of dark grey, with the I&I logo on the shoulder.
>
> He scanned her, letting his professional eye for detail pull out an answer. New hairstyle was a good first guess, but her black, glossy hair [...] was cut in a shoulder-length bob. No change from the last few weeks.
>
> That left one other usual thing to try, so he checked her hands. The new ring stood out at once.

The first time Toreth's viewpoint really gives us more information on someone's appearance than we might expect is when he first meets Warrick, and then the departure from normal practice is indicative of his interest in the man:

> "Excellent lecture, Doctor," Toreth said.
> The man turned his head. Impassive dark eyes looked at him out of a face dominated by high cheekbones, too much nose, and the most beautiful mouth Toreth had ever seen on a man. The mouth smiled just a little.

Ironically enough, in a *B7* universe rather than an avatar one, this description would immediately identify the character as Avon, which is why he probably would not be so fully described except in precisely these circumstances, i.e. through the eyes of someone who has never met him before.

Throughout these opening chapters, there is a concern not to "describe" for the sake of it, but only when it seems plausible that the point-of-view character would register such details and, preferably, when the description also serves some other narrative purpose as well. In many ways this simply parallels contemporary litfic trends: the nineteenth-century convention of telling the reader, on introduction, just what a character looks like has long fallen out of favour in literary fiction, though it survives in many kinds of genre fiction, notably the romantic and the thriller. Fan fiction has always resembled literary rather than "genre" fiction in this respect, preferring for purposes both of physical and character description to show rather than tell. The characters must be themselves; in fact for preference they must be definable and recognisable from their words and actions alone to earn the "that's so *them*" accolade craved by fanfic writers.

One fanfic form I have hardly mentioned so far is fan poetry. "Filks", which are essentially new lyrics set to an old tune, are something slightly apart from that. Serious filk lyrics do exist but most have a strong element of parody and fun: they are performance pieces intended for audiences at fan gatherings and conventions and nobody is writing filk lyrics with the TS Eliot Prize in mind. Actual fan poetry, as opposed to song lyrics, does exist, though as in the profic world it is a minority genre, and if I have kept off the subject it may be because the overall standard of fan poetry strikes me as depressingly low.

Until about ten years ago, I think this would have been true outside fandom as well. For the past thirty years or so I have now and then judged poetry competitions in the non-fan world, and for most of that time, most of the entrants, even when they belonged to local poetry societies, were recognisably in a different world from the Faber poetry list. They either did not read much contemporary poetry or did not let it influence them. They would use archaisms like 'tis or 'twas; they favoured rhyme but used it unskilfully so that their choice of words was driven and dominated by it and their free verse moved like prose in lines. But lately this has changed materially. Local groups these days discuss comtemporary poets in reading groups, they listen to them at readings and they go on creative writing courses at such places as Arvon centres. In the last couple of competitions I encountered, while the entrants might not be Simon Armitage or Carol Ann Duffy, their lexis and method was much the same; they knew what contemporary poetry sounded like and could make a very similar sound themselves.

Most fan poetry strikes me as not having made that leap. In fandom, as in the real world, poetry is very much a minority taste. It is easy for a fanfic writer to find a beta for a story, much harder to find anyone who feels capable of commenting on poems, even by way of feedback. In fact, in many reviews of printzines containing poetry, the reviewer will cover the stories fully but completely opt out of commenting on the poems. If a fanfic poet posts poems on her site or in an online journal, she will get feedback, particularly if the poems are better than the average, but it is liable to be uncritically adulatory feedback, a kind of stunned wonder that anyone can do that, rather than the more useful "I like this, but I think the line breaks in verse 2 are a bit dodgy".

Profic poets do tend to get the same kind of non-detailed feedback from non-poets. Even prose writers in advanced creative writing workshops often do not feel at ease commenting in any detail on poems. The poets are likely to have to get most of their feedback from other poets (whether this in itself perpetuates the divide, and the feeling that reading poetry requires specialised knowledge, I couldn't say). But here, for once, the profic writer has the edge on the fanfic writer, in that a profic poet would be able to find like-minded people to workshop with, either in the flesh or online. A fanfic poet is a minority within a minority and in a fairly lonely position. Of course she could join a real-world poetry group, but then her subject matter might isolate her from other, non-fandom, poets in it.

But there are fan poets who are better than the norm. Baxter's free verse poems, on the savegilmore website, are among them. In her 'Things I Love About Men', interpolated into Gill's story 'Heaven

Sent', mentioned above, all men fuse into the one loved man. The concept works in the context of the fanfic story and would also mean something shorn of that context:

> That my hand can span their
> back and never quite cover them; that
> their soft bristle scours mine, the heady
> soft of their lips amongst this roughness.
> The plank-straight hardness of their loins.
> The length of their feet, the steps they take,
> The sound of their swagger. Waking next
> to the heat their bodies make, the rise
> of their chests as they breathe, the length
> of their thighs, their square hands. Throats.
>
> All things of all men, in you they are one.
> All this and the rest, just you, all day long.

In the *Highlander* fandom, Devo has a long poem sequence, 'Book of Hours'[16], again in free verse and again concerning the development and intricacies of an m/m relationship. As with Baxter's, it is rooted in a particular situation and particular fandom characters, but again it is easy to see how the few fandom markers could be removed (filing off the serial numbers, as the fan phrase is) and how the poems would then be no different from love poems outside fandom:

> It was neither history, nor quickening,
> nor words, that in me knew,
> as if some wind of unimagining
> blew from your soul to mine,
> unmaking certainties,
> a vexation,
> and I would never be content,
> except at your side.
>
> And the blood came between us
> soon enough, and you stood in the street
> with my sword against your neck,
> and traveled, after, to find me,
> to wield my sword again at my own
> complacency and peace.

The favourite theme of fan poetry, like that of most profic poetry (especially outside the narrow confines of litfic), does seem to be love. It tends to associate mainly with 'shipper fic and especially with pairings which are seen as OTP (one true pairing): in the case of Baxter's poems on savegilmore, that of Craig and Luke, in Devo's sequence Methos and MacLeod, whose viewpoints alternate throughout. Indeed, although Devo and Baxter are recognisably distinct poets, they have similarities and those who enjoyed one would probably like the other. But unless they happened to be fans of both shows, it is unlikely that they would have encountered both writers, and the two writers themselves, who in profic might well have some contact, are just as unlikely to encounter each other, not so much because Devo lives in America and Baxter in Australia as because there is no "fan poetry writers" context that could override the barrier of different fandoms and bring them together.

Henneth Annun, the Tolkien fan fiction archive mentioned in earlier chapters, contains quite a lot of poetry. Much of it, especially the form poetry, couched like Tolkien's own in the style of an earlier age, amounts to little more than pastiche, but Wild Iris manages to achieve an individual voice in poems like 'The Dead City'[17]:

> A used battlefield grows quiet;
> among strange escutcheons
> the wind keeps silence;
>
> and if one should return,
> seeking the cold towers,
> the glutted drain,
>
> the windows that looked onto cliffs
> and cliffs beyond them,
> armed with steel and snow –
>
> then there are high seats for his rest,
> there are passes for the gates
> flung down like dice;
>
> there are robes of ivy
> and the seeping fireweed
> that he may claim, uncontested.

Other poets admired in their own fandoms include Danseuse Morte, who has written poems in the *Pirates of the Caribbean* universe which are archived on the LiveJournal site[18]. And of course the fic "Green Eggs and Hamlet", quoted in chapter 3, was in poem form and for all it was a metrical parody of Dr Seuss, its intent and tone were totally serious. It was also by its nature a form poem. These are not rare (especially on Henneth Annun) but good ones that do not slide into pastiche are. One polished form poet is Predatrix (*B7*), whose sonnet sequence 'Triptych' appears in the printzine *Fire & Ice 4* (ed. Kathleen Resch). These are form poems with a vengeance, not just sonnets but three linked pairs of sonnets, each pair involving two voices, one responding to the other, and using the same rhymes. This sonnet sequence would be unusual in any context, in that it uses strict form poems to express explicit material – see the second pair:

I kiss you silent, tongue you hot and hard
You have no time to think, let alone say,
That "No" inside you. That's right. Off your guard,
And off your feet – come on, the bed's this way.
You haven't bitten me. I must be right!
You must be eager (or at least not mind).
I get your clothes off. Even if by fight
I'll have you – glut my hands with what I find.
I ready you and take you where you sprawl.
I haven't even asked: I try to wait
(It nearly kills me). Then you take it all.
I plunge until you groan beneath my weight.
I feel you come as I do, clutch me deep,
And in the echo of my cry I sleep.

Your wanton tongue has me already hard.
I want to speak. The word I want to say
Is "yes." You hold me silent. Disregard
My words in favour of my mouth. This way!
Yes. Getting the idea, are we? That's right:
That opens here, and here. Don't rip it, mind.
I'll take my boots off – we don't need to fight.
Now we can be a little less refined.
Prepared with oiled and urgent hands, I sprawl.
You take possession, then you seem to wait.
I almost sob "Don't stop!" I want it all.
Stretch me and fall on me. I want your weight.
You plunder me, hot, glorious and deep.
I melt, you shout. Enough. Now go to sleep.

In this sonnet sequence the form is being used both to relate a narrative, the course of a relationship, and to point up, in each of the sonnet-pairs, the parallels and contrasts between the two personae. The concentration on relationships is typical of fanfic, and still more of fan poetry, but the specific use of *formal* techniques, like the echoed rhymes, to express it, is not.

In all the fandoms I know, really memorable poets are rare. That in itself does not differ from the situation in profic. What does differ, I think, is the standard of the rest, which in fandom is not as competent, and certainly not as au fait with contemporary practice, as in profic. I would put this down almost entirely to the poetry group and workshop culture which has sprung up in profic over the last 20 years or so. Not all poets are part of this; many of the most highly regarded are very much individuals who work alone, but the mass of what might be called amateur poets do seem to flourish and improve in that culture. And it is the one form for which such a culture does not exist in fan fiction.

No individual fandom I know of could support a group purely for poets, or possibly even for poets and poetry fans; it would need to cross fandoms, and though cross-fandom groups do exist, they are based around the kind of writing people do, rather than the form they use. Those whose interest in slash crosses fandoms have had groups like Britslash for some time; a more recent development is The Shipper's Manifesto[19], an online group for those whose main reading and writing interest lies in intense relationships. Its own manifesto dubs it

> a project designed to bring together 'shippers of every conceivable pairing and share with the world what it is that draws us to those pairings.
>
> This community's goal is to provide readers with a detailed listing of pairings, insight into the characters behind the pairings, and contextual understanding of what makes the pairing work.

Yet it would be wrong to suppose from this that fan writers' absorbing interest in their subject matter precludes a fascination with technique. There is great interest, among prose fan writers, in narrative techniques; if cross-fandom groups have not sprung up to discuss these it is probably because the writers concerned are getting enough contact with other writers and feedback from readers within their own fandom. Fan poets, by contrast, work alone and with feedback that cannot be helping them much; it is a wonder the best of them manage as well as they do.

For the demands, the feedback and to some extent the input of readers have a considerable effect on fanfic work. The serial writers quoted earlier stressed that though they valued the ego-boost of feedback they did not let it change the direction of their writing – "I write what I want". When in the mood, though, fanfic writers are often willing to write specifically what readers want. Gill's first stories expanded into serial fics more or less by popular demand. And in all fandoms, writers sometimes respond to "fic challenges" from list owners or individual readers asking for stories with particular elements.

An example of this is the "ficathon", in which a number of people on a mailing list or in a blogging community will sign up to both write and receive a fic. They will state perhaps three things they want or don't want to see in the fic someone writes for them (e.g. a request for a particular character, or a happy ending), and also what they themselves feel capable or otherwise of writing (perhaps no explicit sex). Then the ficathon organiser will try to match each reader on the list with a potential writer, from the same list, as well as she can, so that everyone both writes a story for some specific person and receives a story, not necessarily from the person they wrote for. One result of this is that, for all the attempts at matching requirements, many writers find themselves doing something they would not usually contemplate, perhaps writing about a character or a time zone of the series that they normally avoid. This, of course, is part of the reason they do it: for the challenge.

These challenges can, as I said in a previous chapter, also come via random generators which throw up a particular set of characters and circumstances, but writers also respond to requests from individual readers on a list or in a community and these, albeit in a less formalised way than the ficathon, will specify the kind of story they want – perhaps the characters, the sex level, the setting, a happy or unhappy ending. In this case the writer is more or less writing to order, and many, if in the mood and with enough time on their hands, are perfectly willing to do this.

Profic writers sometimes respond to challenges too, but these almost never emanate from individual readers. Rather they are set by competition judges, or by newpapers and magazines commissioning work on set themes or perhaps lining up a number of writers to produce instalments of a story. I don't think it is true to say that profic writers are less willing to compromise, to produce work to specifications other than their own fancy. Some will not, but most are willing enough to do so for a competition or commission – i.e. for money. Many, too, will not refuse to alter their vision to accommodate the demands of editors or publishers (even Charles Dickens altered his original hushed, downbeat ending for *Great Expectations* because his publisher doubted its commercial success). Patrons, whether the aristocrats of old or the present state-funded kind, have always been able to specify the kind of writing they wanted, as long as they are paying for it. Sometimes, too, a profic writer will write specifically for a relative or other loved individual and take account of their likes in his writing.

But I cannot think of many instances where a profic writer has written something tailored to feedback from ordinary readers. Even the children's writers I know do not do that. Only in one genre can readers habitually cajole writers into producing exactly what they want for love rather than for money. Or if not for love, perhaps for goodwill in the community, the near-certainty of pleasing the reader and getting positive feedback, or just for the challenge.

NOTES

1. *The Handmaid's Tale*, Margaret Atwood, McClelland & Stewart, 1985
2. http://www.the-phone-book.com/ 13.09.04
3. http://www.guardian.co.uk/online/story/0,3605,853645,00.html 13.09.04
4. *Anthropology*, Dan Rhodes, Fourth Estate 2000
5. http://www.livejournal.com/community/b7friday/35290.html?mode=reply 20.09.04
6. http://www.livejournal.com/community/b7friday/7899.html#cutid1 13.09.04
7. http://www.livejournal.com/community/b7friday/2004/07/01/ 13.09.04
8. http://www.livejournal.com 15.09.04
9. http://sarahb1.tripod.com/hharchive.html 17.09.04
10. http://www.savegilmore.com 15.09.04
11. http://www.savegilmore.co.uk/Sunhill%20Fairy%20Story/Sunhill%20Fairy%20Story.htm 16.09.04
12. http://www.savegilmore.co.uk/Rapproachement/Rapproachement.htm 16.09.04
13. http://www.goldweb.com.au/~bessie/sunhill/stories/exhibit.txt 16.09.04
14. http://www.savegilmore.co.uk/Heaven%20Sent/Heaven%20Sent%20Ch%201+.htm 17.09.04

15. http://www.mannazone.org/zone/index.html 20.09.04
16. http://enook.net/hl/devo/devo.htm 18.09.04
17. http://www.henneth-annun.net/stories/chapter_view.cfm?STID=2920&SPOrdinal=1 18.09.04
18. http://www.livejournal.com/tools/memories.bml?user=guede_mazaka&keyword=Poetry&filter=all 19.09.04
19. http://www.livejournal.com/userinfo.bml?user=ship_manifesto 22.09.04

9. Speak for Yourself

Fanfic Writers and Individual Voices

When readers and writers of profic ask me why I read fan fiction, one question that always crops up sooner or later is whether a fanfic writer, working with someone else's material, can ever develop her own individual voice and become more than a pastiche of someone else. I can sympathise with the question. After all I am myself a profic writer and anything but immune to the feeling, which has prevailed in literary fiction for at least the last two centuries, that originality and the personal, individual voice (not to mention the possibility of personal individual immortality) are, or should be, vitally important to writers.

Nonetheless, not all writers do think that way, and when this question is asked about fanfic writers the possibility of different motives must be taken into account. Some fanfic writers not only do not want to develop such a voice but would think it a serious disadvantage. Most of the denizens of the Republic of Pemberley and the Derbyshire Writers' Guild wish to hear not their own voices nor those of their colleagues but as near an approximation as they can get to Jane Austen's. Their mission statements make that clear. They want to "present Jane Austen's characters behaving as she wrote them in scenes we might wish she had an opportunity to write herself" (the Republic), because "we all wish that she had lived longer and written more" (the Guild).

In fact the authorial spirit is hard to keep in such bounds. The Republic's and the Guild's writers know well that the reason Austen did not write all-male scenes was not that she had no opportunity to do so. She chose not to, but that does not stop them making the opposite choice, fortunately, since this is one of the ways they can develop on what she did. I have stated already that for me, such restrictions limit both the scope of the writing and the enjoyment I can get out of it. But then I am a profic writer and, since I earn my bread elsewhere, am in the happy position of being able to write what I like without feeling I need some sort of agenda. Some profic writers do have an agenda – political, say, or ecological, or even commercial – and are used to subsuming some of their own individual personality to that end, though normally not as much as the Austen devotees of the Republic do.

"Individual voice" is not a priority for these writers and that is the main reason it is rare in the Republic. It is also rare in Discworld fanfic, again because it is not what the readers, mostly, want to hear. Both groups of fans basically want "more of" rather than "more from", and that presupposes a mimetic rather than an original voice. I don't think this necessarily means it could not be done. There are Austen fans, like those who post on Hyacinth's Garden (see chapter 3), who are happy to take the characters and relationships and set them in another time, which immediately precludes using the trademark Austen voice. It is true, though, that it takes an initial effort of will on the reader's part to forget that voice and accept that the story and the characters can exist outside it.

I have heard it suggested, and to some extent I concur, that "original voice", if you want it, is far harder to develop in book-based fanfic than in TV and film-based fanfic. It is true that with a book you are liable to have one author, with a strong individual voice and few constraints on it, which makes it harder to play variations on (at least variations that improve on or extend the theme). But it is not impossible, and one proof of it I generally cite to those who think they have never encountered fan fiction is the literary kind – Jean Rhys's *Wide Sargasso Sea*, George Macdonald Fraser's *Flashman* books. For the life of me, I cannot see these as being somehow a different *genre* from sequel and prequel stories in fanzines, simply because they were published for profit. Their authors were canny enough to choose writers out of copyright, and they were supremely good at what they did, but they were playing variations on another writer's characters and universe, and that is the genre I have been discussing throughout.

Both Rhys and Fraser chose a minor canon character's point of view and used it, to some degree, to subvert the original. Rhys's take on Rochester and Antoinette is emphatically not Bronte's, and the character voices in which *Wide Sargasso Sea* is told are not Jane's, though the passion in Antoinette's makes an interesting and poignant parallel with it. And the universe as presented through Flashman's eyes works on entirely different moral principles from those constantly preached at us by Hughes's *Tom Brown's Schooldays*.

This would seem to suggest that if you do want to develop your own voice, then you need to want "more from" your canon rather than "more of". There has to be something your canon author did not do with the canon, and which you want to, some viewpoint or insight that did not come through and that profitably might. For this purpose it is probably easier to start with a minor author, like Hughes, but Rhys's example shows that you do not have to. (I am tempted to suggest that this example also vindicates the Mary Sue, for Antoinette's vulnerable, addictive personality surely has elements of Rhys.) If you do choose a major author you may be able to get away from his voice by altering the *form* of fiction he uses: a truly mimetic Shakespeare fanfic would be in dramatic form and Elizabethan English (and some, disastrously, are). But the *Romeo and Juliet* fic 'Some Day', quoted in chapter 3, is in short story form and modern English. As the author, mintyfreshsocks, sardonically remarks in her note, "canst thou not see that 'tis not writ in the Elizabethan language?" and it therefore cannot help developing something of a voice of its own.

If Austen and Pratchett fanfic authors wanted to subvert and extend their canon, they could. Austen's world can be subverted by being seen through the eyes she does not choose – male eyes, or those of the servants, traders and workers who are present but silent in her books. What does Emma's Highbury look like to the Coles, who, having made their money by trade, take ten years to be in a social position to invite the landed neighbours round in the evening? Pratchett's world is more inclusive than Austen's, and becomes more so with each book, but it too could be subverted. Pratchett, so far, has fought shy of the irreversible death of main characters, and that is a gap someone could profitably exploit, in a fanfic universe where character death is less of a taboo than in many.

There are, as I have mentioned earlier, some Austen fics that focus on men, though most of her fans seem no more interested in the working class than she was. There are a few Discworld fanfic writers trying to write not just scenes Pratchett might have written but ones he would not have done. It seems doubtful, on the face of it, that he would, like JD in 'The End'[1], write a scene where Vetinari not only dies but admits to being in love with Vimes. But mostly, writers in these two fanfic universes are more mimetic than original, because they want to be, and they don't very often try to subvert their canon writers because they like them too much. This situation may be more common in the world of book-based fanfic, but as I hope I can show later in this chapter, it doesn't always happen. The effect it has on the quality of fanfic writing depends a lot on the quality of what is being imitated. There is a website, Henneth Annun[2], for *Lord of the Rings* fan fiction based on the book canon rather than the films. The fiction on it is in the main highly literate and thoughtful but it suffers, in my view, from being too faithful to Tolkien's written style, especially when it comes to dialogue. As a writer he has his points, but dialogue is not one of them. As often as not, it is overblown, faux-archaic and faintly embarrassing. Some of the fan writers on this site also work in other fandoms, and their handling of dialogue is a lot better when they do not feel obliged to sound like Tolkien.

In the world of film and TV-based fanfic, things are different. There are still plenty of fans in these fanfic universes who want "more of" – more cases for Holmes to solve, more arrests for *Starsky & Hutch* or *The Bill* to make, more French ships for Hornblower to fight or more vampires for Buffy to slay. And for these writers originality is no particular virtue. But there tend to be a lot more writers in these fandoms who want "more from", who see possibilities not explored in their canon and want to rectify that. And this is where individual voices do tend to develop. I know five fandoms well and have read in a number of others for this book, and I still know only a fraction of the fan fiction on the web or in fanzines. Some of the biggest fandoms (eg *Star Wars* and Harry Potter) I hardly know at all. So if I can fairly easily find developed individual voices in the fandoms I know, it would seem logical to suppose that there are many more in the ones I do not.

By way of example, I would like to discuss here some individual writers who do seem to me to have very individual, identifiable voices. I should stress that I am not aiming here to provide a complete potted critique on each; I want to focus on those aspects that make them particularly the writers they are, the signatures that tell a reader immediately that such-and-such a fic is by this writer and no other.

Kel, who writes in *The Bill's* fanfic universe, is Australian and works in a library (not the fiction kind). There are, by the way, other Kels among fan fiction writers but this is the only one in *The Bill's* fandom. Her stories can be found archived at the Arjuna site.[3] Their most obvious characteristic is a sense of place intimately linked to an intense lyricism and the mood of whichever character's viewpoint we are in. In an earlier chapter I quoted the opening of 'Sins of Omission', where the introspective Alistair's detached mood is mirrored in the view from Sun Hill's fire escape at dusk. At the start of the story 'Golden Boy', PC McCann is pursuing a suspect, not long after failing his sergeant's exams (this failure was canonical):

> It was dark in the corridors, dark and damp and grey. McCann felt his way slowly through the ruined factory, baton raised, listening for the hurried steps, the ragged breathing of the youth. Dammit, where was he? Over the trellis, into the forecourt of the abandoned estate, then bang up to the fourth floor, sliding on rotted timbers as he scrambled up the old cast-iron fire escape. No working lifts, and local kids had put their Doc Martens through the other stairs years ago... he *had* to have come this way. There was nowhere else to go. [...]
>
> It wouldn't have been so bad if there'd been someone he could talk to. None of the other guys understood, really; they thought he could just get on with the job, just get back on the horse. They didn't understand how hard it was to be knocked back. He'd never failed anything before, never. His parents had been great, said of course they understood, better luck next time, probably a good thing in the long run, all that stuff... but there was always the faint tang of disappointment, that indefinable sense that he had let them down. He hadn't, he knew he hadn't. But still... *You're not the golden boy anymore, sweetheart.* [...]
>
> Cursing silently, he edged along the hallway, out into an open area branching out into small offices. Once a shining example of the Eighties' communal workspace – partitions, desks, photos of children and girlfriends, the obligatory potplants – now, it was just so much scrap. Anything the local kids hadn't smashed or burnt had long since begun rotting from the riverside mists, which even now curled in through the broken windows, weaving patterns through the rain which dripped and poured steadily through cracks in the ceiling. A thousand managerial dreams washed away into piles of splintered, mouldering chipboard. A thousand places to hide.

There is an extra edge to McCann's failure which does not need to be spelled out to any *Bill* fan: he is one of the Met's relatively few black officers and consequently feels more pressure to succeed. The lingering, lyricising delight in decaying urban landscapes here is characteristic of Kel's writing. It appears again in 'Sins of Omission' and in 'Somewhere Within', quoted in earlier chapters. And it is, necessarily, an extension of its canon, because it takes a different fictional form. In the TV canon, the camera may linger on London's landscapes but characters who pass their lives there are not liable to talk or think about them much, so they are never realised in words as they can be in a fic.

Another Kel characteristic is a laconic, disjointed syntax reminiscent of a man taking notes. This may well have been suggested by the police context but tends to appear particularly at moments of stress when the speaker, like the syntax, is breaking up. At this point in 'Team Player' Jim Carver, fraught after the break-up of a relationship, is struggling to keep up at work and taking risks outside it:

> === Sunday ===
>
> Passes silently. Dustily. Paper, people. A heated altercation with a young and poisonous football hooligan settles his mood, keeps him focused. He stays late, very late. Boulton remains unmollified, at least outwardly, although Jim puts that down to other things... the ram-raid renaissance, David Wilson up for sentencing, all sorts. He knows he's behaved himself today. Mostly.
>
> On the phone to an informant, he watches the DS leave, crumpled, subdued, tired. Resolves to be a little more polite tomorrow, then swears as he remembers something. Rings and leaves a message about overtime documentation.
>
> Jim goes back to the park. Third time lucky.

Sometimes, too, she uses the narrative techniques of her source material; her fic 'Exhibit RHI' mimics the layout of a screenplay:

> 0000 static
>
> 0013 Garden path, cobblestones, out of focus. Muffled voices in background.
>
> 0020 Shot out of a window, overlit. Birds in background.
>
> 0022 static
>
> 0039 Long shot, small bedroom. Fuzzy yellow light, overexposed, in one corner of the room. Makeshift brick and plank bookshelf on the right, with one sad-looking indoor plant drooping over the edge. Old, tatty Professionals poster on the wall, black and white. Torn corner of football poster just visible in upper left frame (can't see which team). Hastily made double bed disappearing off left of frame. It's all a bit fuzzy, really.

Kel is a slash writer, and so, sometimes, are other writers I have chosen as examples in this chapter. This is liable to annoy some in the fanfic reading and writing community, both because some object to slash and because it is a small part of fanfic as a whole (though not as small as it used to be). But I was looking here not only for good writers but for writers who had developed a strong individual voice. And in my own reading, which, as I have said, I don't claim to be comprehensive, I have come across more slash than gen or het writers who fit this bill. Not that they are always writing slash when they fit it – many write gen as well. But I would tentatively suggest that the *willingness* to subvert, to read subtexts and stretch the characters to that extent is indicative of the kind of writer who wants "more from" her canon and feels she has something new to add to it. Executrix says something similar in an unpublished essay:

> I would posit two main impulses in fanfic writing: concordant and discordant with canon. Concordant fics (which are often, but not necessarily, gen) express the writer's pleasure in the canon universe, and a desire to inhabit it a little longer, whereas discordant fics (often, but not necessarily, slash or het) are "fix-it fics" that seek to change some important aspect of the show.

The same lyrical quality with which Kel treats urban landscapes surfaces in her treatment of bodies. When slash writing becomes risible, which it easily can, it is generally because it is either too mechanical ("fit tab A into slot B") or too sentimental and over-romantic. Kel's technique for avoiding these pitfalls seems to be to treat lovemaking like any other activity through which a writer might want to let her character express his nature: what actually goes on in bed is firmly anchored in the context of the characters' personalities and relationship. In 'Something Within' Jim, who tells the story, is an incurable romantic, given the chance:

> Tungsten light falls through the tiny windows, golden, playing on his eyelashes, complementing stubble on his face, his softened angularity, the man made boy, lost boy, lips parted as I thrust back, harder, further, deeper. It's a light made for him, made for nights like this, so calm, so warm, so at odds with the man beneath me and everything we do. It catches him, catches fire from him, stops my heart, unwelcome.

But he has to curb this romantic tendency fairly brutally because his partner Loxton won't have it and the relationship is being conducted on his terms, to satisfy his taste for mental and emotional (though not physical) domination:

> In my arms, he revels in dissatisfaction; his, mine, it's all one in the end. No kindness, no fluidity, just explosion and collapse, torn for breath, unheld and buried in him, devoted, rejected, alone. His discipline

> astounds me; impatient, restless, yet still, saturated in my sweat, my semen, my soul. I am unforgiven. I never meant to care.
>
> When I fail him, when I come too close, he leaves. No argument, no anger, just an unspoken disappointment that chills me, stops me, shuts me down. On these nights, these bleak and lonely nights, I back off, withdraw, free him with bowed head and trembling, clumsy hands, stand numb as he dresses and walks wordlessly into the dark. Like to like. He leaves me older, empty, weighed and greyed by silence.
>
> There are rules. He is never untied, never in me, never kissed, never held. I am never tied, never filled, never kissed, never held.
>
> I stroked his cheek, once, full of emotion and daring and unbelief – this was early on, before I knew better. I confused our fucking with lovemaking, and he left. Called him by name, and he left. Kissed him lightly, sure he'd never feel it, never know, and he left.

Kel's writing is a world of urban landscapes and inner landscapes, both fairly desolate. Sun Hill's dingy fire escape, a derelict warehouse, the pockmarked tiles on Des Taviner's bedroom ceiling reflect stalled careers, missed opportunities, relationships which do not satisfy. Characters making love (or having sex, which as Jim notes above is not the same thing), are frequently not getting much pleasure out of it -– or what pleasure there is will be feverish, clandestine, transient or otherwise flawed. By and large, a sex scene in a Kel story is liable to epitomise the tensions and problems in a character or relationship. Alistair will be too hesitant to take the chance of happiness while he can; Jim is stuck in an addictive, painful subservience. Even Des, who has Reg's devotion, is tormented by the knowledge that he doesn't actually deserve it. Quite often, action in Kel's stories takes place in darkness or subdued light, which is authentic enough in the context of police work but also seems emotionally appropriate.

Though her dialogue is as authentic as need be, she works less through it than many fanfic writers do, and makes more use of interior monologue. She nearly always narrates either in first person, as in 'Somewhere Within', or third person intimate, as in 'Golden Boy', where the point of view is McCann's, and 'Suburban Wing', where we are throughout in the guilt-tortured mind of Des Taviner. This closeness to the protagonist and his immediate concerns is probably also one reason she often writes in the present tense. Like all fanfic writers who specialise in angst, she is interested in the inside of people's heads, their struggles with guilt, inadequacy and unrequited feelings. Her special talent is to be able to convey these, via her use of external conditions to create mood and also through her handling of imagery and the rhythms of language, without the writing becoming static. This despite the fact that plot, as such, interests her very little. A lot of her stories are PWPs, though not always in the sense of "sex and nothing but" which that phrase sometimes conveys. The point of a Kel story, generally, is not for anything to happen but for something to become clear to a character, or to the reader, which wasn't clear before. In 'Golden Boy', McCann becomes alive to the possibility of leaning, literally and figuratively, on someone else; in 'Somewhere Within' Jim ends up painfully clear not only about his own situation but about the fact that unhappy as it is, he prefers it to the alternative.

The second writer I want to discuss is Executrix, who works mainly in the *B7* fanfic universe, in which she has been writing since 2000, though she has also written crossovers into the *Buffy* and *Firefly* universes. She is American and, as mentioned in chapter 7, works in the legal profession. She is also a great Anglophile and can write the very BBC British voices of Blake and his crew as unerringly as the antipodean Kel does London accents. Some of her literary influences are British – Austen, Shakespeare, Dorothy L Sayers – but she also has an encyclopaedic knowledge of films, songs and musicals from which inspiration is just as likely to come.

Her wide reading and consumption of fiction in other forms are basic to her writing. I have previously quoted her as saying that she likes to do pastiches for the light that one character or situation can shine on another, and that she uses allusions "because of the ability to incorporate by reference". Even in a genre where this happens a lot, her writing is more allusive and intertextual than anyone's I know. She also, like many fanfic writers, gains inspiration from other fanfic stories and writes variations on them:

> I think of this as either an "over the shoulder" (i.e. the other angle in a two-shot) or a "carport" (i.e. it leans on an existing structure). The interesting thing about these stories is that they have virtually nothing in common with their "substrates" and sometimes it wouldn't be obvious when read side-by-side that they're "the same".
>
> – From an essay, 'Reading between the Loins' (RbtL) reproduced at Appendix 4

That may perhaps be a clue to the odd fact that, as referential as she is, she has a very distinctive writing style: her material and inspiration may come from all over the place but her voice is unmistakably her own. Part of its stamp is a sardonic and irrepressible sense of humour. Executrix claims not to like angst, though she has written a fair amount – in this darkest of fanfic universes it is hard not to. But even when writing about serious themes, she is unlikely to do so in a completely sombre vein. The fic 'Her Father'[4], a PGP in which the rebels survive and the revolution goes on, is angstier than most Executrix stories. In it Avon, though still involved with the revolution, has become a priest. This is in keeping with a long-running Executrix thread about him having been brought up a Catholic. There is no canonical basis for that; in fact the position of religion in the Federation is uncertain, but it fits quite well with his penchant for guilt and remorse. This fic is very much about guilt, about relationships that don't work but can't be laid aside, and the irrevocable nature of the past, the problem being that you can neither go back and change it nor ignore what it has done to you. Yet, autumnal and brooding as it often is, this is its opening:

> All of the delegates to the Contrafederation Information Technology Conference were required to check their weapons at the door. Quite apart from the predictable presence of Central Security plants and double, triple, and higher-power agents, the mere fact of opposition to the Federation didn't lead to harmony. That was evident from the glares being exchanged between the Jihad of Blood Women's Auxiliary (huddled behind a hedge of lesbian separatists) and the Intergalactic Zionist Verein and their picket fence of Young Spartacists. But it seemed that every day a new rebellion sprang up, and together – if they could stop trying to kill each other for a minute – they were more and more likely to achieve final victory (and then fall to squabbling over the results).

Later, with Avon now living according to rules of chastity, the fic flashes back to earlier times in his life:

> Over a fairly good run, approximately two decades, Avon usually found sex to be a delightful demonstration of the Magic of the Free Market. An Invisible Hand Job, as it were. It was like going on holiday in some picture-postcard country, where you'd turn over a handful of coppers and receive fragrant, crusty fresh bread or exotic orchids or hand-painted pottery. Both participants wouldn't just accept it, they'd be delighted by the exchange.
>
> However, the marketplace was located on a road bracketed by a

> casino at each end. By the time he met Blake, Avon already knew what happened when you crossed the threshold. There would be a few minor coups, just to keep you interested, and then, gradually or suddenly, you'd lose everything. But then, like any real gambler, Avon knew that whatever money you might win was only the cellophane wrapping. The sweet inside was the catastrophic loss.

Perhaps when she says she dislikes angst, she means she dislikes the wallowing in emotion which angst at its worst can be. She is more likely to undercut emotion with humour or colour it with figurative language, as here. Nor will she let her characters brood for long; the characters in this fic, as in most of hers, are not entirely happy with their lives but they get on and live them anyway, as most of us have to in real life. It's arguable, in fact, that for a writer in an SF fanfic universe she is more rooted in real life than most. Her stories are more conscious of the senses, and of sensual pleasures, than many SF-based fanfic stories. The food references in the extract above are typical: such sensual references to foods or materials are a signature in her fics. She is alive to atmosphere in the same way that Kel is, though her preferred settings are different, and she identifies a lack of this awareness in some SF-based writing:

> One thing that leads me to label a story as disappointing is that its setting doesn't seem to be very clearly visualised. One of the nice things about fanfic is that you can instantly build a rose-red city half as old as time, and it doesn't cost any more than sending them down another naffing quarry.
>
> – RbtL

In fact, though the setting in her fics is likely to be urban, the city in question isn't often anything like Petra. Most of her locations have a twentieth-century feel: some SF writers of both profic and fanfic give the impression of wanting to get as far away as possible from their own time and place but she is not one such. In 'Purple Haze'[5], the protest is about a planned war with another star system, but it takes place on what is effectively an American university campus of the Sixties:

> "No Andromedan ever called me nigger," Hal Mellanby told the small group assembled around him.
>
> A little girl in a pink dress, a redolent diaper protruding beneath, toddled around barefoot, one chubby fist in the air. Eventually, one of

> the woman students picked the girl up and sat her down on her lap, nuzzling into her sunflower nimbus of soft hair.
>
> "Dig, the Federation is a wartime state. They have to have a war, someplace. Either they need conquests so they can exploit the resources of new planets, and send out colonists to planets that haven't been poisoned by the Atomic Wars, or they need to stir us up into a frenzy of hate so we won't notice that all the resources go to the Alphas. Otherwise, we might think that all the Grades had some common cause to make. This way, we just stay put and we put up with the shortages they create because it makes us feel patriotic. And we put up with our boys and girls dying in those wars, because otherwise there'd have to be jobs for them, and housing for them, and education for them, here at home.
>
> So just shut down the war machine. Resist the draft. Stop the war."

It isn't just a place that is being evoked here but a place at a certain time, and the spirit of that time. In 'Wanderjahr', mentioned in the previous chapter, it was the decadence of Isherwood's pre-war Germany, in 'Baccalaureate'[6] it is a Dorothy L Sayers England, complete with punts and picnic baskets. To a certain extent, this is the curiosity and endless seeking for alternatives of a fanfic writer: what if these characters had lived in this era rather than that? But in this case it is also a constant reminder that people are much the same whatever genre and time you put them in:

> Strictly speaking I can't be classed as a science fiction writer and not even really as a *B7* writer – most of my output was either instalments of an unauthorized Avon biography or a bunch of little sub-*New-Yorker*-y stories about a couple of guys having an unhappy love affair in a big spaceship in stationary orbit over the suburbs. There's probably a good reason why nobody ever tried to become the John Cheever of *B7* before.
>
> – RbtL

One odd result of this setting of the canon characters and situations in other places and times is to make them seem more timeless. In 'Purple Haze' the references are very specifically to the Vietnam war. At the time of writing (early 2003) the relevance to America's proposed war with Iraq is positively disconcerting. Since the *B7* canon involves a Robin Hood situation – guerilla fighters against a totalitarian government – you might suppose its writers would all be politically left-wing and anti-elitist. In fact they aren't all, but a fair number are, and she is among them. In 'RbtL' she states her preference for addressing serious themes through the medium of comedy rather than tragedy, and some of her reasons seem to tie up with her previous observation (see chapter 7) about the democracy of fanfic versus litfic:

> Traditionally, tragedies are about gods and heroes and kings – someone far above the audience. And one theory is that comedy is either about people at audience level or below it [...] this involves a certain degree of normalization, deglamorization or, it might be argued, dragging things down to my own level.

True to this aim, she admits to being "much more interested in things like the Liberator washing-up roster than in techno-neep" (RbtL). If she decides to use action as a means of illustrating character it is liable to be something as down-to-earth as the way someone packs a picnic basket. In fact that paragraph of description, from 'Baccalaureate', combines several features of her writing: its awareness of sensual pleasure, its humour, and its referential habits – the syntax echoes *Wind in the Willows* but the contents are clearly packed by a hand other than Ratty's:

> There were blue-and-white china plates and teacups and cranberry glass tumblers. There were napkins. There was ivory-handled cutlery of all descriptions, including a formidable bread knife. There were salt and pepper shakers. There were five kinds of sandwiches, a lavender-blue stoneware crock of potted shrimps, an immense vacuum flask of tea, a piece of white Wensleydale, black grapes, ginger biscuits, and a slab of bitter chocolate.

Executrix writes both het and slash, which isn't all that usual – for many fanfic writers of adult material it is either/or – and though most of her work has some adult content it is often not very explicit. Sex tends to be another sensual pleasure like food, and much of the enjoyment of both comes from looking as much as tasting, from prospect and retrospect as much as from the moment. The picnic in 'Baccalaureate' slides into sex, but very obliquely:

> They were both hard, it would take more than flannel and linen to disguise that fact, but it didn't seem necessary to do anything about it. Indeed, Blake felt that it seemed to concentrate all of the other senses – hard wood underneath him, the warmth of the day and

> Avon's body, sunlight reddening his closed eyelids (when they weren't overshadowed), Avon's hands, one of them holding Blake's hand (the one that wasn't sweeping up and down Avon's back), the other caressing Blake's face with desperate gentleness.

The site this is archived on describes it as "very mild slash"; myself I would say that it leaves a lot to the reader's imagination and recognises that "explicit" and "erotic" are close to being antonyms. She can write very erotically, as can Kel, but the two could not be more different. In an Executrix story the participants are quite likely to be having fairly unalloyed fun, as they might if enjoying some other sensual pleasure like food. Generalisation, as ever, is flawed: Kel sometimes lets her characters play and an Executrix story can be brooding and haunted – but rarely so much so that the narrative voice or one of the character voices cannot come up with a bon mot about the situation.

All the examples here are narrated in the third person and that is typical for her work. As an avowed non-angst-fan, she cultivates a more detached and less emotional style of narration. But I also suspect that, like Terry Pratchett, she would find a character voice inhibited her own very individual authorial style, particularly its humour (she has, in email, observed that "Robertson Davies talks about 'Merlin's Laugh' – the outsider's ability to discern the ironies in a situation"). From her omniscient-narrator standpoint she likes to explore different characters' viewpoints and often uses ensemble casts. She makes an interesting comparison here (again via email) with her professional writing:

> Actually one thing I like about writing lawbooks in real life instead of practicing law is that I can observe all sides of a question instead of being reduced to making the arguments for only one side.

Executrix believes strongly in the categorisation that separates fanfic writers into those who want "more of" their canon and those who want "more from" it. (She also observed, in private email, "*Source property is a complete load of bollocks that desperately needs our help* is a possible attitude towards canon, y'know".) She is definitely one of the "more from" camp: she likes to push her characters and their universe in all manner of directions that would never have occurred to the BBC.

My third writer is also from the *B7* universe. This might be the moment to mention that the *B7* fanfic community has a conviction that it produces better fanfic writers than any other domain. This is the sort of assertion one investigates in the gleeful expectation of disproving it. In fact, after a lot of reading in a lot of fandoms, I would have to admit that in some ways they have a point. The most consistently *competent* fanfic, once one excludes the orthographically challenged teenagers, comes, I think, from the Discworld, though I don't think the standard often rises far *above* competent. My favourite individual fanfic writer, most of the time, is Kel of *The Bill* (but then I am an angst fan). But if I were looking for a domain that produced a number of interesting, sophisticated writers many of whom had clearly defined original voices, *B7* would be a better place to start than most.

Why this should be is debatable. I have heard many suggestions, including the fact that the authors are mainly somewhat older and more experienced than, say, in the Buffyverse; also that "dark" fandoms produce better fic than happier ones! It may well have to do with the source property, inasmuch as, like all the best canons for fanfic, *B7* was more promise than performance. It created interesting characters and situations but then failed to exploit them fully, thus leaving gaps for fanfic writers to do so.

Some also point out that this fandom has been producing fanfic for a long time, so that technique has had a chance to develop. As someone put it on a mailing list, the really inept stuff got written years ago. This is an interesting theory, because it doesn't just mean that individual writers get better with time – which would scarcely be unexpected. As in most fandoms, many writers cease writing or move on to new fandoms after a while: some do stay for years, but of the writers appearing in current fanzines like *ttba*, few will have been around 10 years ago. Executrix, as mentioned above, has been writing only since 2000. So if true, this theory would mean that new writers in the fandom were learning from what is there already, building up a literary tradition.

In order to do that, they need to have read a lot of fanfic, which is certainly true of my third writer, Nova. But she too came to it fairly recently; like Executrix she has been publishing fan fiction since 2000. She is Australian and has been writing fiction professionally for many years, in genres mostly unconnected with the SF of her fanfic domain. She writes slash, both m/m and f/f, but unlike Executrix she is a non-het zone.

Of the writers I am discussing here, I should say she was the most interested in narrative technique. Because of this, she is not at first sight such a recognisable writer as either Kel or Executrix; she is more protean than either. It is rare for Kel not to be in the closeness of first person or third person intimate and equally rare for Executrix not to be playing detached and omniscient narrator. But Nova will use either, and whatever else the story seems to need, or that might be fun to try. Alternating narrative viewpoints between characters, as she does in 'Body and Soul'[7] is relatively straightforward. Some of her narrative strategies are far more complex. Her zine 'Bend Me, Shape Me'[8] consisted of seven stories each giving a different viewpoint on the same relationship.

In 'Evidence'[9], she uses as narrator a canonical character called Carnell, a professional mind-manipulator officially known as a psychostrategist and colloquially as a "puppeteer". Carnell, as keen an observer of his own reactions as of other people's, is dictating his feelings of unrequited love into a voice recorder and, as if that were not enough, getting progressively drunker as he does so:

> I shall enjoy solving this puzzle.
>
> [The tape records a dozen clinks of glass on glass, switching off between each clink.]
>
> No, I won't. Can't enjoy anything, without Vila. Getting shozz – I mean, sozzled on soma and adrenalin now, because he said he liked it, but still feel as cold as his mouth, when I kissed him. Should've guessed he'd had bad experiences with men – statatisticly likely, after reform school, then several prison terms. Should've set up a scenario that was different from prison powerplays. Not sure what but should've. But wanted to touch his hair. Couldn't wait. Stupid Nik. Stupid. Bad puppeteer. Oh, hell ...
>
> [The tape records a distant sound of gagging and a rush of water.]

Later, Carnell lists ways he might be able to gain the object of his affections:

> – I could slip him an aphrodisiac.
>
> – I could arrange to be stranded with him in an icy cave and make love to him as a way of keeping us warm.
>
> – I could suggest that he might overcome his fear of sex with men by tying me to a bed and taking me, relentlessly and repeatedly.
>
> – I could infect myself with a horrific ancient disease and – no, hold on, I used that one on Blake.

What he, and Nova, are doing here is listing time-worn slashfic devices for getting two characters together. The "cave" in particular is a notorious cliché. Nova has made a study of earlier *B7* fanfic, both gen and slash, and is obviously fascinated by its narrative devices. In 'To Tell the Truth'[10] she plays with another, one of the many ways devised to counter Avon's reluctance to discuss his feelings about anything that matters. In a futuristic setting, truth drugs are one obvious way around this, and have often been used in fanfic. But mostly they are used as a quick fix to make the man say something he wouldn't normally. Few writers have been so interested in *exactly* what they would do to the utterance of a reticent person compelled to say what he thought, or in what the appropriate response of a decent person would be:

> 'Avon,' Blake whispered, on the edge of a terrible realisation. 'Avon, why are you telling me this?'
>
> 'Because I have no choice,' Avon said. 'Believe me, I would not willingly expose myself in this fashion. However, Servalan's tame medico injected me with fast-penta, a few seconds before you burst through the door. Consequently, I am obliged to answer any question you put to me. Go on, Blake. What else do you wish to learn about me, while you have the chance?'
>
> Blake winced, wounded by the acid mockery. 'Nothing, Avon,' he growled. 'I'm not going to take advantage of this. For God's sake, what do you think I am?'
>
> 'I think you are an honest man, a quality which attracts me almost as much as it terrifies me,' Avon informed him. 'I know you are a natural leader, because you activate a desire to follow that I previously managed to conceal from everyone, including myself. I also know you have a charisma that is all the more powerful for being unselfconscious. I resisted it for as long as I could. Then I left.
>
> The words spooled out, smooth and unstoppable, but his eyes glinted resentfully. Blake lifted a hand to his mouth and bit down hard on the thumb joint, using the pain to focus his thoughts. He wanted to hear more – wanted it so badly that part of his brain was preparing half a dozen simultaneous rationalisations – but at the same time he knew that every sentence was building an irrevocable barrier between him and Avon. So, really, there was no other choice
>
> 'Avon,' he said, interrupting the flow of words, 'will you tell me how the Liberator's deflector shield works?'
>
> Sudden as a puppet whose strings had been cut, Avon relaxed back in his chair and began to reel off data and statistics.

"The words spooled out" – one of fanfic's favourite metaphors, the tape playing. The author is very aware that she herself is her character's real interlocutor, and truth drug, just as in a sense she was Carnell's voice recorder (and Vila, who eventually steals it from him, complete with the "evidence" of the title). This metafictional awareness of fanfic as a genre, and of many fanfics as being on some level about the writing process, is not unique to Nova but it is characteristic of her writing. It is also characteristic that she tends to refer to fanfic clichés not to satirise them but to try to breathe new life into them. In 'Five Easy Pieces And A More Difficult One'[11] she takes five often-written slash scenarios for getting Blake and Avon together, all of which are in some way excuses (e.g. the Planet With Odd And Faintly Grecian Social Customs which figures in many futuristic slash domains). The sixth, which is the "more difficult", is getting them to simply admit that they *want* to be together. The "excuse" scenario, though it was often used in the early days when slash tended to involve men who thought they were straight, seriously annoys many modern readers and writers, particularly gay ones, because it could be taken to imply that such a thing couldn't just happen on its own. (Besides, most of the excuses have been used to death). And Nova's title itself implies that this kind of scenario can be seen as a cop-out. But when writing each of the sections, she treats them with equal seriousness and brings all her craft to making them convince.

Another Nova signature is a liking for positive endings. She does not claim to hate angst as Executrix does, but she probably writes even less of it. In fact she coined a term, HEX (Happy Ending eXpediters), for *B7* writers who, as she put it in the introduction to 'Bend Me, Shape Me', "admired the harshness of the series' ending" (the episode 'Blake') " but couldn't bear it". (The opposition promptly invented the SADists, who get their buzz out of ratcheting up the angst factor.) In her rationale for HEXing (in correspondence on an unarchived mailing list) she suggests that her motive for HEXing is essentially the same as for slashing:

> Me personally, I slash because I see a m/m subtext and I write stories with happy endings because I see a lot of ways in which Gauda Prime could have been averted. [...] I know angst but I need all the practice I can get in working out how shit might, just possibly, if one were creative enough, not happen. [...]
>
> The truth is, I still don't fully understand why people write SAD *B7*, when they can slip a "Blake" cassette into the VCR.

In other words, she sees HEXing as a way of subverting the canon, for getting "more from" it, whereas, in this fandom at least, angst amounts to "more of". It's an interesting theory and would seem to some extent to be borne out by the fact that in this darkest and angstiest of fanfic universes, the two writers I chose to illustrate original, characteristic voices are atypical in that regard. She also sees a "creative" challenge in working out how things might *not* go wrong, how people with a proven penchant for misunderstanding themselves and each other and generally fouling up might overcome those factors.

That is not to deny those factors, or the reality of the sadness they produce. There can be a lot of grief on the way to a Nova ending, and though it wouldn't fit the acronym I would say myself that most of them were "positive" rather than "happy" endings. In other words, people don't generally get exactly what they want, but they do find a way of living fairly contentedly with what they get – as most of us have to in real life.

An example would be the end of 'Before and After'[12]. This is in the voice of Vila, who works well as a Nova narrator because he is a natural survivor. The story is a PGP in which Vila and Avon survive the massacre on Gauda Prime, but Avon, having shot Blake, is judicially executed by his followers. The leader of these is Deva, who is, like Avon, a computer expert and who in Nova's story had loved Blake (there is the odd vibe in the relevant canon episode). Vila, meanwhile, had cherished feelings for Avon which fear in a homophobic society made him repress. (There is no canonical evidence as to the futuristic Federation's attitude to sex, so writers are free to speculate.) Vila is feeling regretful and miserable, at one point almost suicidal. But he is used to making the best of a bad job. So when Deva suggests the two of them might be able to act as substitutes for each other's lost loves, Vila, despite his initial reaction, is not immune to the sense in it:

> "You stupid bastard," I choked out. "No one can take their place. They were giants. We're just little people, you and me."
>
> "You may be right," Deva said, looking even sadder. "But they're gone and we're still here."

It does not take long for Vila to stop resenting the truth of this and to recall his aunt's dictum of long ago: "better a live dog than a dead lion". The end, though downbeat, is positive:

> As for me – well, I suppose you could say I'm happy. Funny thing, I fell for Blake's computer tech and I ended up with Blake's computer tech, just not the same one. Mind you, that little joke shows you how, even though I'm still with Deva, I still think about Avon. It'd be kind of embarrassing, if I didn't sometimes catch this faraway look in Deva's eyes that tells me he's still thinking about Blake.
>
> When that happens, we tiptoe round the place for a while, giving each other a bit of space, making sure we don't accidentally drop a mention about the past. We concentrate on our jobs at Deva's training school for budding revolutionaries – revolutionaries being Gauda Prime's main export, now we've kicked the Feds off the planet. (Deva runs the school and teaches theory and computer hacking. I teach lock-picking, pick-pocketing and survival tactics.)
>
> Then we come home and cook ourselves a nice meal, open a nice bottle of wine and sit by the fire, being kind to each other. "Every dog has its day", my auntie used to tell us kids and she was right about that. Deva and I are the living proof of it.
>
> But we miss our dead lions.

I once remarked to Nova in email that in her version of Cinderella, the girl would dance all night with the prince, then come home next morning and marry the postman (or postwoman). She'd probably be happier, too. There is, I think, a moral dimension to Nova's writing, and particularly to her preference for endings where people find a way of living with what they have. It reminds me a little of the nineteenth-century German Biedermeier writers in revolt against the excesses of Romanticism, letting their heroes find happiness and fulfilment in small actions and familiar places.

The last piece of writing I want to discuss is, I hope, one which shows that achieving an original voice in book-based fan fiction, though difficult, is not impossible. It is 'Make With Your Hands', on Team Bonet's site, Oki Doki.[13] Team Bonet consisted of seven U.S. writers, (some of them sisters and cousins from the same family, hence the name) who, as stated in chapter 7, set up a website together and signed their fiction collectively. But the stories were written by individuals. Many were based on anime and manga originals, but this story, by Maria Bonet, was, to quote the note on the fanfiction.net site, "based both on Alexandre Dumas' original novels and the 1998 Randall Wallace film *The Man in the Iron Mask*". It is thus, like many fics, multi-media-based, and its book base is several novels covering a long period. Essentially it is a Musketeers fic, based on the fanfic author's perception of the characters at a certain time in their lives, but in terms of any canon it is in some respects an AU. It treats the canon as Dumas himself treated history, as a good place to start. It is also gen: Dumas is very slashable territory but for all its emotional intensity this is not a slashfic.

Its book base was also that of an author being read in translation, and I think this may be relevant to why it worked better than most book-based fanfic for me. Among Austen fics, the one which struck me as being most successful at developing a voice which, though it suited Austen's world, was not obsessed with trying to reproduce her voice exactly, was Martine's 'Le long retour vers Donwell', originally written in French. It may be that the distance interposed by a different language makes an authorial voice seem less daunting and inevitable.

Yet even in translation, Dumas does have a quite distinct voice. He is an author who reminds you of his presence, periodically turning up in the narrative and giving a quick history lesson, often prefacing his remarks with some such phrase as "we have already noted" (which might be a guilty nod to his collaborators or an association of himself with his reader). In either event, 'Make With Your Hands' does not, ever, try to reproduce this voice. There is no authorial "we", no intervention; the unseen and unobtrusive narrator hides in the character voices.

The fic is set in 1662 and narrated alternately by Athos and Aramis. The three Musketeers plus the escaped Philippe (the former Iron Mask) are hiding out with the Jesuits and hoping for a revolution which looks unlikely to happen. Athos' son Raoul is dead and D'Artagnan estranged from them. The time is spring and early summer, but in all other respects this fic is very autumnal. Athos himself is not only ill but has had a recurrence of the canonical guilt feelings about the murder of his wife which struck him in *Twenty Years After* but which Dumas more or less forgets about in *Le Vicomte de Bragelonne*. He is obsessed with what his hands have done (the attempted hanging of his wife) and what they have failed to do (prevent the death of his son) and he needs something to do with them; hence he has taken to preparing and cooking their meals. Aramis meanwhile uses his rosary much as Athos does the kitchen knife: to keep his hands busy and his mind off more important things:

> He pauses in his work, lifting his head to gaze at me. I can feel his eyes on me as I roll the rosary beads along my fingers, counting out each *Ave Maria*, ignoring him as I ignore Porthos. It's easier to ignore

> Porthos. Athos has an unsettling way of looking at you, as if he's debating whether or not you exist, or if he's imagining you, as if you were at fault with him somehow. I don't think he realizes this.
>
> "What do you pray for, Aramis?"
>
> I pause in my prayer. The question comes softly, coloured by a genuine, almost childlike curiosity. An uncomfortable feeling crawls down my spine, lodges momentarily in my throat. My lips move, forming no words. Thoughts, answers, stir up in my mind. *For our safety, for a good life, for happiness*. None of it makes any sense. He's looking at me, his expression frank, but expectant. I sigh, lowering my hands.
>
> "Athos, you know me. I pray because... Because I *pray*. There is nothing I pray for. It's just... words. Words to repeat because it gives me comfort to repeat them." I turn to hold his gaze. "Is that enough for you, is that a good enough reason to pray?"
>
> He cocks his head to the side, apparently lost in thought, his eyes still holding mine. At length, he turns his attention back to the potato in his hand, half peeled. He doesn't say anything. Just sits there, peeling away, the sound of knife against the potato's skin hanging, magnified, between us. The skin scatters down over his lap and onto the floor. Words hang in my lips, unformed, not daring to form. I don't understand him, I find that I don't want to. I finger my beads, turn my gaze towards the crucifix at the far wall again, picking up where I left off, almost mechanically.

(The potatoes, by the way, are anachronistic; they were not commonly grown in France until the 18th century. But the anachronism is Dumas's own: he has them growing in *Le Vicomte de Bragelonne*. Dumas regarded historical fact as the raw material of fiction; he seldom felt bound by it and did not feel inclined to stop and do the research when his tale was carrying him along.)

The alternating narrative voice constantly shifts the perspective: sometimes the narrator gives us a new angle on himself, sometimes on the other man. (Though Porthos and Philippe have roles in the story, it is essentially about the two narrators.) In Athos's voice the sense of ageing, of illness and despair predominates:

> It took me a long time, you know, till I finally convinced Aramis to let me come down to the kitchen. I missed my work, I told him, not doing anything would kill me. He wasn't pleased with the decision he took, but he did allow me to come down from my room. I pulled up a stool under the window and peeled my potatoes and chopped my tomatoes on the first day. I have done little else since. But it's fine that

way. If I stop working with my hands, I start thinking and the sweat starts to break out again till I can't breathe. So I shuffle across the kitchen, cooking and coughing, trying to keep busy.

Today I want to do something different. There are no more potatoes to peel. I would tend to the Jesuit's garden, but the work tires me out too much. My fever comes and goes. Aramis can't explain it. Some days I can walk around the garden or even down the house's gravel path, but most days I find that I don't even want to get out of bed. I'll lie there all day, the sweat trickling down my neck, eyes staring out into nothing. It hurt, once, that Aramis seemed to be annoyed at me and my weakness, but I don't think I mind all that much anymore. I want to be alone. I want to take a walk.

I push myself up from the seat with difficulty. The world spins around me for a while, taking my breath. I cover my eyes, feel my body sway, searching for a place to rest. I ignore it, take a few steps forward, pulling my blanket closer about me. I know I can make it to the door. It hurts, God, it hurts to just take a step today, but I know I can make it. I don't want to spend another minute inside this house. And the door is just in front of me... right there... just a couple of steps away. Almost within reach. Almost... one more step. There.

The sun is too bright. A heady scent hangs in the air. Smoke from brush fires. The Jesuits who pass by our house occasionally come talking about the wild fires spreading throughout the countryside. The heat is too great. The worst summer in years. I only feel cold. A shiver runs through me and I have to crouch down, teeth shattering. For a moment, I consider going back to the house. I almost turn, reach out for the door handle... But no. I don't want to be Aramis' invalid old man anymore. Wrapping the blanket tighter around me, I make my way slowly down the gravel path. It leads down into a grove of sycamores. I think they're sycamores. I can't be sure in this light. It blurs everything.

Aramis is deeply worried about his old friend's condition, though he is not the kind of man who could say so either to Athos or himself. So it has to come through his actions:

"Up you come. That's it. Just like that. Here, lean on my arm. Can you manage that?"

Athos waves away my words with his free hand, a tired smile playing across his lips. His body rests heavily against my own, but I can see he's lost a lot of weight. He doesn't say a word as I lead him down stairs, his hand feeling his way along the walls. For a moment I worry that perhaps the fever has done something to his eyesight, but at the stairs' landing he points outside the hall window. He wants me to look

> at a blue heron perched on a fence. I turn my face away after I look in obedience to his request, thankful that he can't see the expression on my face. The relief.
>
> I have little else to feel relieved about. Athos' condition has improved only somewhat. Some days he will limp down from his bedroom to have supper with Porthos and me, other days, and these more often than not, he will remain in his room, gazing out the window in silence. Oblivious to everyone and everything around him. Lying in his bed, grey hair spread over his pillow, eyes sunk into their sockets, the sweat still glistening on his skin, he looks close to death. I can't bear to look at him, so I leave him alone. It's what he wishes. I can't do anything more for him
>
> Now I lead him down into the kitchen, one hand closed tightly over his elbow, supporting him without letting him know that I do so. I lead him to his chair. He grunts as he sits down, pulling his blankets closer about him. He looks lost. He darts a few looks around the kitchen, taking in the disarray his absence has brought to it. I turn away from him to prepare his medicine. I don't need the other priests to prepare it for me anymore. It's become second nature to me. I pound the ingredients into a clay bowl, mixing them with water till I've recreated the white, thick medicine I know Athos hates and does not drink unless I watch him.

I have quoted extensively, because the sense of ageing, of disappointment and grief but also mutual regard and need in this fic is cumulative and powerful. Not only are the character voices not rigidly mimetic, occasionally they slide into US English (as in "out the window" above). When one is absorbed in the story, it is as hard to notice as the dodgy chronology of the Dumas books. In fact, after a while it seems unimportant, because these men and their situation have universal elements which transcend national speech. In the end, Athos's grief is partly healed by his (very canonical) paternal impulses, in this case toward the lost and vulnerable Philippe who becomes a substitute for his dead son.

This fic gets "more from" its canon, in that the Musketeers in old age and at rest are shown in a depth which the books, in particular, only attain for brief moments. The characters are very recognisably those we know from Dumas, but the authorial voice is not his. It is more reflective and, because it uses two first person voices, more introspective and analytical. I find it convincing: if Athos and Aramis, in old age, could come alive and talk to us, I think they might well sound like this. But it isn't necessarily how Dumas would have done it – it is true to the characters rather than to the author they have moved beyond. It is a new angle on the material, fanfic with an individual voice.

NOTES

1. http://discfanfic.tripod.com/jd/end.htm 9.12.02
2. http://www.henneth-annun.net/index.cfm 25.04.03
3. http://www.goldweb.com.au/~bessie/ 5.7.04
4. http://www.liberated.org.uk/1130HerFather.htm
5. *ttba*, ed. Tavia, 2001
6. http://www.blakes-7.tv 20.01.03
7. http://www.liberated.org.uk/1025body.htm 21.01.03
8. ed Pat Fenech, 2000
9. *Tales from Space City 4*, ed Helen Patrick, 2002
10. http://www.liberated.org.uk/1061truth.htm 21.01.03
11. http://www.liberated.org.uk/1014five.htm 21.01.03
12. in the fanzine *No Holds Barred*, ed. Kathleen Resch, 2002
13. http://www.geocities.com/ayafujimiya/mask/athos.html 20.12.02

10. A Good Reader Also Creates

"Then the Characters are independent?"
"Slightly! Have you never known one of your Characters – even yours – get beyond control as soon as they are made?"
– Kipling: "The Last of the Stories"

In the introduction to the "Apocrypha" section of her *Archieology 101* web site[1], Catherine the Terrible writes:

> The phenomenon of fan fiction arises from an audience's need for more than whatever the film, TV show, book, etc. is providing. We want to know what happened before, what happened after, what happened in between. Fan fiction satisfies the craving for further adventures, explores new territory, develops characters and relationships, fills in gaps, corrects perceived errors, and even (in extreme cases) "un-kills" beloved dead characters [...]. Above all, fan fiction is written out of love, not for profit.

This is a pretty comprehensive explanation of what its audience wants from fan fiction. What is interesting is that Catherine, who is herself a writer, does not specify whether by "we" and "audience" she means those who read fan fiction, those who write it, or both. Perhaps this is because in fan fiction the two groups and their motives overlap far more than they do in most genres. Those who *read* Mills & Boon presumably want a romantic fix; those who *write* it want a cheque. A litfic author may choose to write a particular book or type of book for all sorts of reasons, many of them personal; his readers may choose it as reading material for completely different reasons, some of which might strike him as irrelevant. With some genre fiction we are perhaps a little closer to concordance; it is a fair bet that an historical novelist will be fascinated by the period she writes about in much the same way that her readers are. But in fan fiction the would-be readers themselves became the producers of what they wanted, at first because that was the only way to get it and later because they found the act of producing it pleased them for its own sake.

Most people begin reading fan fiction in a particular fandom, because they are fascinated by the characters or the universe portrayed in it. As we have seen in previous chapters, some then find themselves fascinated by the writing itself and will follow favourite authors into other fandoms, even other genres. And similarly there are writers who, whatever the reason they first took to fanfic, stuck with it because it felt to them like the genre in which they could best address their concerns and write the kind of fiction they wanted.

The kind of literature that fan fiction is did not spring fully formed into being in the 1960s and 70s, though some journalists still seem to think so. Throughout this book I have been stressing the link, in literary terms, between fan fiction and any other fiction based on a shared canon – such as history, contemporary events or Larkin's "myth-kitty". It is clear from the comments of fan fiction writers like Ika and Belatrix Carter that one major attraction of this genre for writers is the sense of having a complicit audience who already share much information with the writer and can be relied on to pick up ironies or allusions without having them spelled out. Writing based on the canons of myth and folklore can do this too, though as Belatrix Carter pointed out in chapter 7, these canons have been so extensively used for so long that it is becoming harder to do anything with them that feels original.

But there is another point, implied in Ika's remark in chapter 2 – "What I like about fan fiction is that you still get that very highly trained audience that can understand very, very complex and allusive things". The use of "still" alludes to the undoubted fact that for the traditional canons of myth, Bible, history and folklore, this "very highly trained" audience is not as reliable as it once was, because the canon information is not as widely shared as it used to be. There are generation gaps: particularly with a younger audience, a writer can no longer allude to Lazarus, Circe or Alexander and be reasonably sure that most of his readers have in their heads the thoughts, stories or images for which he was aiming. The human need for heroes and archetypes does not go away, but their faces change with time, and one avatar takes the place of another. Ika's point is a shrewd one: in an age of fragmented rather than shared cultures the fan fiction audience is unusual in having as thorough a knowledge of its particular shared canon as a Bible-reading or classically educated audience once did.

And this matters, because fanfic writers do not see their readers as passive consumers. According to Belatrix Carter, there is a Swiss proverb – "a good reader also creates". Fanfic writers all started as readers who were not content simply to consume the fiction put before them on the page or screen; rather they wanted to add to it, to fix what they felt to be wrong with it or missing from it and to extend its range. They expect *their* readers to take that attitude too – as Belatrix herself remarked in chapter 7, there is that which you put down on paper and that which you leave to happen in the reader's head. Or to return to what SA said in the mailing list debate recorded in chapter 6, you write what you want to and the reader reads what *they* want to. In the context of the debate, this meant that writers should not waste too much time trying to tailor their fiction to audience preferences. Even a skilful writer cannot always hope to persuade her audience to read the kind of fiction she herself prefers to write, since they may have other preferences – angst rather than complex plot, gen rather than slash, character A rather than character B. That being so, writers can only write what pleases them and trust that enough readers *will* share their preference.

But it is possible to interpret the remark differently. Not "people will not all want to read a particular story", but "people who do read this story will not necessarily get out of it exactly what the writer thinks she put in". You write what you want to, but then comes the reader's interpretation, and what is read will not always be what the writer expected. Some writers, even post-Barthes, cannot live easily with this, which is one reason they dislike fan fiction based on "their characters". In Michela Ecks' Internet article 'Fan Fiction, Novels, Copyright and Ethics'[2], an American author for children and young adults, the devoutly religious Kristen Randle, is quoted. Randle tolerates fan fiction, but within limits:

> I do not wish anything that comes from me to be used in a way that I would judge to be outside my moral view. I would be extremely upset to find my characters sleeping together, for instance.

This attitude takes it as a given that the author *knows* the characters she has created wouldn't ever take her by surprise by sleeping together. Many authors do feel they know their characters that well; others have always taken an opposite view. In 'The Last of the Stories', published in America in the collection *Abaft the Funnel*[3], Kipling imagines a writer's version of hell in which he meets the most famous characters from his short stories, including Mulvaney and Mrs Hauksbee. They do not look quite as their creator expects them to, and the more he talks to them, the more he realises that he never fully understood them. At one point he unwisely remarks to Mrs Hauksbee "I made you, and I've a right-", provoking her reply:

> "You have a right? [...] You made me! I suppose you will have the audacity to pretend that you understand me – that you ever understood me.[4]

It is, obviously, this latter attitude which is more typical of fan fiction writers. Very often, on a mailing list, a fanfic writer will speak of the characters, both canon and OC, "talking" to her, insisting that she write a particular story from a particular viewpoint or refusing to co-operate with the author's plans for them at all. Belatrix Carter, in chapter 7, spoke of story ideas "jumping up and down waving their arms at me until I had to write them down just to get them to shut up and leave me alone". (The tendency for fanfic writers to be devotees of the Maxis computer game *The Sims* is unsurprising. Sim characters are generated and controlled by the player, but they are also programmed to have a degree of autonomy. Now and again a Sim will simply refuse to do what the player asks it to, and the level of autonomy can be increased if the player wants "her characters" to pose more of a challenge.)

Now all writers, profic as well, have had something of this experience, when a story or a character within it seems to have a will of its own and to subvert the author's original wishes. In the case of a fan fiction writer that experience is likely to be reinforced by the degree of reality the canon characters already possessed in her mind before she ever got to work on them. With TV characters, this reality will have been created by a combination of writers, script editors, actors, producers, make-up artists and wardrobe mistresses, not forgetting the audience itself and previous writers in the fanfic domain in question. When a series of books is filmed, as with Harry Potter, it is possible for the adaptation to influence the original – several reviewers of *Harry Potter and the Order of the Phoenix* suggested that the once-villainous character of Snape had been subtly modified to accommodate the fact that readers who have seen the films now "see" him as the charismatic Alan Rickman. And though, with a book, there may be a single named author, even if said book has never been adapted for performance there are still the readers and previous fanfic writers adding their take on the characters.

The whole process might be compared to different streams flowing into an ocean, making it more than it was before. A character cannot accommodate all views of him; some will be so off-target that they will be rejected and cast up on the beach, as it were. But if he was convincingly and vividly enough realised in the first place, he can go beyond his story and, arguably, his original creator to exist in other stories, and he will still be recognisably the same person; indeed some depth may have been added to him. For me, this is what happened to Athos and Aramis in the fic 'Make With Your Hands' quoted in the last chapter. (And it reminded me that, just as V S Pritchett was certain Thackeray was misrepresenting Becky a couple of times, so I had always felt Dumas was sometimes wrong about Aramis.) The mimetic tendency in fanfic is understandable; the genre originally came about because readers and viewers wanted more of, as well as more from, what they heard and saw. But sometimes a fanfic writer is so sure of her own take on the characters that she can make them be themselves in times, places and situations their creator never put them in and, above all, without feeling a need to imitate that creator's particular narrative voice. And for me, fanfic posts its most surprising and thought-provoking achievements when that happens.

Two of the basic premises of fan fiction are the beliefs that (a) fictional characters and universes can transcend both their original context and their creator and (b) the said creator cannot claim to know everything about them. Believing this as they necessarily do, fan fiction writers cannot really play the Omniscient Author, nor claim to have a greater insight into the characters and universe with which they play than their readers, who know the canon as well as they do. Opinions differ: one person's take on a character or an aspect of the fanfic universe will not be another's and few people in today's fanfic climate would claim that a reader's take had less validity than a writer's. (Original writers in a book-based canon are admittedly a special case. The fiction guidelines on sites like the Republic of Pemberley and Henneth Annun are still restrictive. But there are writers even in those canons trying to push boundaries.) There are generally views of characters and events that are widely held by the fans in a particular domain, but there is always room for alternatives. A fairly common intro to a fic, where the writer is conscious that her take on character X may prove controversial, is "Your X may vary".

So fan fiction is a genre in which the boundary between readers and writers is shifting and easily crossed. The reader is unusually empowered and may indeed, by dint of playing in the fanfic writer's sandpit, herself become a co-creator. It is in this sense that Executrix calls fan fiction "democratic". Though its roots go much farther back than the 1960s and 70s, it was then that it really took off in the form that we now know. This coincided with the rise of mass entertainment, particularly television, which created new, widely known canons and heroes (or new avatars of old ones). It also coincided with a post-war improvement both in educational standards and people's expectations for themselves. People reading books and watching TV shows in the 70s were beginning to think "I could do that", rather than largely accepting, as an earlier generation might have done, that the clever men at Oxford, or their equivalents, produced "fiction" while the populace at large consumed it.

These viewers and readers were also beginning to *do* it, writing their alternatives to the canon down on paper and communicating them to others rather than just thinking them in their heads as readers have always done. The author profile of Bubbles, on the gen fanfic site for *The Bill*[5], summarises the experience of many who felt empowered by finding a community they had not known existed:

> I can't remember a time when I wasn't 'writing' stories. Okay, so I wouldn't actually write them down but I would write them in my head. Maybe at night when I couldn't sleep I would pick a show from tv that day or a book and then re-write the story and characters to my own tastes, it could be very satisfying at times!
>
> Anyway I began to watch *The Bill* and soon I had a story bursting to be written, [...] so I went for the computer and lo and behold I wrote the thing in two weeks, all 80-something pages of it! Of course it was drivel and won't be seen.
>
> After I wrote that I just wanted to keep on writing. I found this site and saw I wasn't the only one (previously I had considered myself quite mad for trying to re-write a well established drama) and so I wrote more.

I suggested in chapter 7 that some fanfic writers are nervous of trying the profic waters, and from the evidence of personal correspondence I would stand by that suggestion. But it should not be forgotten what a daring and positive step it was for them in the first place not only to become writers but to share their writing with others.

And this self-empowerment means fan fiction is also a genre where hardly anything ever ends – the metaphorical ocean referred to above need never stop expanding. If readers are not yet ready to see a fictional universe closed by the end of a novel or TV show or the death of its creator, they can, simply by becoming writers, re-open it. If they cannot live with a character's death, either in the source material or the fan fiction spinning off it, they can make it not be so. If they see a possible direction for the source material that was never explored by the original writers, they can take it there. If one book a year in the Discworld or two made-for-TV *Hornblower* films every few years are not enough, they can create more. This is just as well, since the contemporary demand for sequels discussed in chapter 7, the refusal to let something end, goes beyond the ability of individual authors to supply; it would have taxed even the Dumas novel factory. In these respects – their unwillingness to let things go, their refusal to sit back as passive consumers and wait for fiction to give them what they want – fanfic writers recognisably belong to a time when consumers in general were becoming more demanding and less passive. Fan fiction, which makes no money for anyone, is in a way the triumph of market forces, readers and viewers finding that the product on offer did not entirely meet their desires and manufacturing one that did. Sometimes they even managed thereby to influence the creators of the source material and get it tailored more to their mind.

The feeling that there is no one right version, plus the reluctance to leave a universe they enjoy, both contribute to the fanfic writers' habit of endlessly trying out alternative scenarios and relaying scenes from different viewpoints. So much fan fiction is based not on what *did* happen in the canon but on what might have done, or what must have done but wasn't shown. The AU is an obvious example, a whole sub-genre of "what if", but fan fiction's obsession with point of view is equally relevant. One reason the ocean continues to expand is that fanfic readers and writers are never satisfied with one side of a story. If Austen gives them the story from Elizabeth's viewpoint, they will want it also from Darcy's, Charlotte's, Wickham's and anyone else they can get, and it will be a slightly different story each time. Some of the fiction on the Sarah B *Hornblower* site[6] derives specifically from mailing-list exercises in point of view.

Fanfic writers are also fond of extending the ocean by going over and over an incident working out different possible resolutions for it. Again this may be a collaborative exercise in which one writer will take another's story and resolve it differently (e.g. the HEX response in *B7* fan fiction), or simply tell it in another way, throwing a new light on it. In 'Much Ado'[7], Nova and Executrix each present a version of essentially the same *B7* story with a plot based on *Much Ado About Nothing*. Nova's story, 'A Lot of Fuss about Nothing' had been written first, as a Christmas present to Executrix, and accordingly paid homage to her writing style, using the short scenes, quotations and shifting viewpoints more characteristic of Executrix than of Nova. It happened that at the time the two had been engaged in a discussion "on whether the way a writer structures a story is as individual and distinctive as the language the writer uses". "Then 'More Fuss about Less' was obligingly produced by Executrix [...] demonstrating this point to perfection by producing a genuine Executrix version of my would-be Executrix story"[8].

Something of the same can be seen in the explosions of fanfic in the *Hornblower* universe when Archie died, and in *The Bill* when the Craig Gilmore/Luke Ashton storyline took off (and still more, when it went in what the fanfic writers thought the wrong direction). There are innumerable different rewrites of Archie's death-episode 'Retribution', and still more of what might have happened, but didn't, to Craig and Luke after "The Kiss" and, later, "the stag night". (In canon, on Luke's stag night he slept with Sgt Gilmore, but in the morning he once again backed off from the thought and went ahead with his wedding.) The fic writers seem to agree on one thing: they didn't like the solutions put forward by the series writers. Beyond that, the possibilities are endless – there may be wrong answers, but no indubitably right ones.

The Nova-Executrix exchange of stories mentioned above derived partly from a discussion of writing style. Fan fiction as a genre may, by stressing the participatory and creative role of the reader, seem to diminish the power of the writer over "her" creation. Yet it is also a genre very aware of itself as fiction and of the role of the writer in making things happen. "The Writer" stories, in which we see the author openly participating in the story and manipulating the characters (literally, in some cases), are common in all fandoms. Mary Sues, it would seem, are excusable when clearly self-aware and ironic. Fashions in writing reflect in fan fiction as in any other genre, perhaps more so given the prodigious and multi-genre reading of many fanfic writers. If the litfic Book of the Moment is into fairy-tale, irony, second-person narration or telling a story backwards, fanfic writers will translate those trends into their own work. It is not surprising, then, that fan fiction tends to be a very self-aware kind of writing; it is of its time.

Using the writer as a character is also a way of blurring the boundary between fact and fiction – as is using real people as characters or making fictional ones cross over into a real universe. This blurring of boundaries is intrinsic to the genre. Dumas, like many another writer, used history as his canon base and then played variations on it. Writers like Emma Tennant, Kate Moses and Colum McCann, discussed in chapter 7, used biography in the same way. Both they and Dumas were taking a base of fact and then fictionalising it. Fanfic writers do the same, except that their canon base was fictional to start with. Yet, because it is the canon, it acquires some of the status of fact. That does not mean it can't be altered; on the contrary, as I have indicated above, altering it creatively is one of the main points of the exercise. But it does mean that fanfic writers discussing their canon find themselves agonising over the interpretation of some action, or speech, or character, as if these things and people had been "real", or rather factual, historical.

The definition of "real" is crucial to fandom as a whole, especially when fans are defending their activities to mundanes. Are persons or universes "real" only if they have an independent physical existence? Or does having a measurable effect on the lives of those who follow their fictional careers confer some degree of reality? A verb sometimes used in the fan community to describe what someone does when she leaves fandom is "gafiate". It is formed from the initials of the phrase "getting away from it all". From a mundane's point of view, it might seem perverse to describe turning from fandom back to real life in terms which normally suggest escapism – surely such a person is getting away *to* it all? But then it depends where the most important realities of your life lie. As "Kristina" remarks on the "Requiem" section of the *Archieology 101* website, about the "death" of Archie Kennedy:

> A fictional character yes, but sometimes a fictional character crosses that fine line we as humans constructed, that line between what is real and what is not.[9]

At a convention of science fiction fans, I attended a panel on recognising "life forms" and was surprised, being no scientist, to find that definitions of what constituted a life form had gone far beyond the indisputable "seven characteristics of living things" I dimly recalled from school biology. Indeed there seemed to be room for considerable dispute; at one point biologists and computer experts were debating whether Sims, the computer-generated characters from the Maxis game (see chapter 6 and above) could be defined as alive, and by some of the criteria they were using, it didn't seem impossible. Sims have always been able to have sex, procreate and die by illness or accident, but in the version released for 2004, Sims2, they can also age, die a natural death and pass on their unique "DNA" (Maxis' phrase) to their children, who will physically and in character be a blend of their parents.

Science fiction fans may be particularly open-minded on what constitutes "real life", but all fanfic writers, who have an inexhaustible appetite for fiction and are accustomed to using it as the background of reality against which they write, are conscious that the boundary between real and fictional is a fluid one. In Brenda's real person slashfic 'Relax', quoted in chapter 7, the words of Tolkien's *Lord of the Rings* are filtered first through a film version of the book and then through another fiction, a story not about the characters but about the actors playing them. Words that were really spoken by the actors, but in character, are borrowed to apply as if they had spoken them in their own persons; the "real" event on which the fic is based is the film adaptation of another fiction and the "real persons" in this RPS are actors doing their real-life job of pretending to be someone else. In a fairly early *B7* printzine, *The Totally Imaginary Cheeseboard* by Jean Airey and Laurie Haldeman, an actor and the character he played are transported into each other's universes. The character ends up at a fan convention, and one of the first things that tells his companions he is not who he seems to be is that he is taller than the actor. Logically this may be nonsense, but it reflects a widespread perception at the time; the character had his own perceived physical reality and it was not identical with the actor's. On the *Archieology* "Requiem" page, many fans left two tributes, one to Archie and one to Jamie Bamber, the actor who played him. They knew, in other words, that he was a fictional construct, but that did not stop him, in his way, being as real to them as the actor – witness the message from Natalie, "I love you, Archie and Jamie".

The same blurring of boundaries may be seen across the fanfic/profic borderline, in the current litfic fashion for fictionalised biographies. But as we saw in chapter 7, some litfic critics are worried by novels which seem to be confused about their textuality and which don't fit neatly into existing pigeonholes. Oddly enough, this attitude is not wholly unknown in fanfic. It is that of those readers and writers who will have nothing to do with AU and crossover, for whom the canon is effectively fact and cannot be departed from. But it is a rare attitude, and, I think, getting rarer. Most fanfic writers like pushing and dissolving boundaries, and the one between "real" and "fictional" most of all. Their links to computer culture may also be relevant here. After the initial explosion in fanfic in the late Sixties and Seventies, coinciding with widely syndicated TV shows which created a new shared canon of information, the next exponential increase came with the rise of Internet and email communities. Many fan communities exist online, among people who "know" each other by email and may never have met in the flesh. Yet their relationships are as real as if they had, and the boundaries of geography that in the "real" world would keep them apart do not exist in the virtual world. It is hardly surprising if the characters they have seen and heard on screen are as real, in their way, as the e-friends known only by a name, which in many cases is not the person's "real" one either.

Another boundary capable of being blurred is that between authors. In a genre which grants the original author no particular primacy, and which has traditionally been practised in supportive groups, it is perhaps unsurprising that collaboration is so widespread. Nova, who practises both fanfic and profic, has remarked on what an unusual genre fanfic is in this regard. In profic it is not easy to "sell" a co-authored work of fiction to publishers, mainly because the publishers themselves are convinced that works with a single author's name sell better to the readers. This was apparently one reason Dumas's collaborator Maquet did not press for his name to be credited on the books; Dumas's name alone sold more copies, which was more to Maquet's advantage (or would have been had Dumas not got behind with the payments).

It may be that this commercial consideration, rather than any issues of ego or unclubbability among the writers, accounts for the relative rarity of literary collaboration in profic. On mailing lists for poets and fiction writers, works finished or in progress are sometimes posted, and other list members will offer comments. But I have never seen one ask if he or she could continue the story, or tell it from another viewpoint, as would happen on a list where fan fiction was mailed. Nor can I see such a request getting the agreement of a profic writer, who would inevitably be thinking, "where can I get this published, when it's finished?" The fact that fan fiction isn't written for money causes it to be held in low esteem by many who have never read any, but are convinced that writers who were any good would be getting paid. But this same fact also gives fan fiction writers a degree of freedom denied to those who have publishers to please.

Both sets of writers, however, have readers to please, and fanfic writers, who get far more feedback on their work, are very conscious of the fact. Most of the ones from whom I have read comments on this matter say that being aware of their readers' preferences doesn't directly affect their writing; they write what *they* want to write. It may be, though, that being part of the same fan community as their readers, they share many of those preferences. I have often heard writers and critics of literary fiction complain about a kind of audience response based on criteria which strike them as irrelevant and non-literary. Readers, often enough, dismiss a book because they do not like the subject matter or the setting, or find they cannot sympathise with, or care enough about, the characters. This last objection seems particularly to irritate professional writers and academic critics, who will often rejoin that it isn't necessary to do so, and that this is not how the writer's success at his craft should be judged.

Yet the need for characters who are not only credible but can engage our emotions is a fairly basic one to most readers. It is also natural enough that someone who is about to spend some hours in a fictional world will choose one he or she expects to find congenial for one reason or another. Readers looking for escapism may avoid novels with a setting familiar from their own lives; others, who like fiction to mirror their own experience, may conversely steer clear of anything exotic. More adventurous readers will give a writer the chance to convince them via craft, especially if the writer's work is already known to them, but very few general readers choose or enjoy a book *purely* for the writer's technique. Other criteria do come into it, and if these are not "relevant" to writers and critics, they are to the reader, who is the one looking for enjoyment.

In this search fanfic readers have a head start, owing to the categorisation habit mentioned in chapter 6. In some online fanfic libraries readers can not only call up stories by named authors but set criteria for which characters are featured, the point on the canon timeline, the exact amount of sex involved and whether this is m/f, m/m or f/f. They can select for humour or angst, allow or disallow crossovers, AUs or character death and even stipulate happy endings.

As I said in chapter 6, I do not think this is an unalloyed blessing either to writer or reader. For writers, it can make less classifiable fics harder to home, though a good fic will always find a place somewhere. And for readers, such choices can become limits, if they never read in a more adventurous way and allow the writer to surprise them. But there is no denying the degree of empowerment and participation it confers on the reader, who can to a considerable extent control and personalise her reading experience. Of course all readers in all genres can do this to varying degrees. They can choose a book according to whether it is on the science fiction or historical novel shelf, or by what is said in a review or on the back cover, and if the book disappoints their expectations they can put it down. In between, though, they are pretty much at the author's mercy. But fanfic readers are less so than most – in the genre written for love, with no commercial considerations or restraints on what writers do, the consumer, paradoxically, is king.

Indeed this emancipation of the reader may have unexpected and even unwelcome results for the writer. In most film and TV-based domains, if a writer's view of the canon does not please her readers, they will simply try something else. But if she happens to want to write in certain domains, notably book-based ones, she may actually find her audience declining not only to read it but to let her post it in the community. This does happen, witness the hostility of some major Austen fiction sites to AUs, and the selection process on Henneth Annun. Of course this does not prevent her posting it on another more liberal site, or creating her own, in the same way that a profic writer who cannot persuade a publisher to back her can self-publish. But profic writers, who might otherwise envy the fanfic writer's freedom from having to please marketing men, may note that even when one speaks direct to an audience, one may find them just as unready to branch out and try something unaccustomed. Audience taste can be just as tyrannical even when no money is involved.

The fact that fan fiction is not written for money has some relevance to the moral arguments still sometimes advanced against it. Profic writers use as source material their own imagination, history, myth and folklore, their own lives and the lives and characters of other real people, though if these latter are still alive they generally refrain from identifying them. They also, sometimes, use the fictional constructs of other writers, provided these are out of copyright. All fanfic writers do differently is, firstly, that they extend the pool of source material to fictional constructs not out of copyright and, in the case of "real person" fan fiction, to named and still living people, and secondly, they don't do it for money.

This extension of source material may raise a question of manners, but it surely cannot raise one of morals, unless that applies to profic writers as well. If there is no *moral* objection to creating a character called Cardinal Richelieu, based on the real Cardinal, and having him do things that Richelieu never did, then there can be none to characters based on the recently dead, like Sylvia Plath, or even the still alive, provided it is made clear that the writing is fictional and the character not identical with the person whose name has been used. If there were, then what would be the cut-off point – how long need someone have been dead before what is objectionable becomes acceptable?

Even using named living people as fictional characters is not of course unknown in profic, provided one has their consent – Kinky Friedman's *Roadkill*[10], for instance, uses the singer Willie Nelson as a main character. The difference with RPF is that the authors do not ask permission of their subjects, who in most cases would be unlikely to give it. This does, arguably, raise an issue and is why many readers of fan fiction will have nothing to do with RPF. The contrary argument from some RPF fans would be that what is in the world is potential fictional material and that there is a difference, which readers should appreciate, between the "real" material and its fictionalised version. Just as the "London" or "Cairo" in which a novel is set may not be identical with the place on the map on which it is based, so a character based on a real person and using his name does not necessarily inhabit exactly the same space as his "real" equivalent. This is a concept very familiar to fanfic writers and readers, who are constantly aware of the difference between the actor and character who inhabit the same body – or, indeed, between two people's concepts of a character. But they know many non-fans do not think the same way, and for those who steer clear of "real person" fan fiction on those grounds, the issue is more one of manners than morals.

And if it is similarly acceptable to use the fictional constructs of Charlotte Bronte or Thomas Hughes as a jumping-off point for one's own, then why not the works of living writers and producers? The obvious answer is commercial considerations: living writers must be protected from the possibility of work being passed off as theirs, to the detriment of their own income and reputation. Most also feel, reasonably enough, that having invented a fictional character (in so far as one can), they should be the ones to profit from him, or at least, if anyone else does, the original author's contribution should be acknowledged and paid for. This, presumably, is why J K Rowling, who does not object to fan fiction and in fact rather likes it, has recently obtained a judgement in the Netherlands to stop the Russian writer Dmitri Yemets from marketing *The Magic Double-Bass*, his spoof on Harry Potter, in the West. Like John Reed (see chapter 1), Yemets was claiming satirical intent, and he is not passing off his work as Rowling's. But he is making money from the Potter concept, which fan fiction writers don't do. Nor, of course do *they* try to pass themselves off as the original or claim ownership of the characters and universes they use; all fan fiction bristles with disclaimers making that clear.

Some might argue that even if fanfic authors discourage confusion with the originals and do not make money from their work, they could have an adverse effect on the original authors' trade, in that potential readers and viewers might choose to read fan fiction for free instead of paying for the original. But to anyone acquainted with fan culture, this is most unlikely. It fails to take account of the paramount importance of the canon – one major reason people read and write fan fiction is because they like the source material so much that they want more of it. However many *Discworld* fics are produced, it will not stop Pratchett's devoted fans from lining up to buy the next novel, far from it. And writers with a TV show as their canon could not debate body language and nuance of tone at length unless they had the videos. If anything, fan fiction, by maintaining interest between books, episodes or repeats, and by drawing in new fans, both maintains and increases the market for the original work.

But for many writers who object to fan fiction, commerce is not the point. It comes down to how they see their fictional universe and, especially, "their characters". If a writer takes Thackeray's line that the characters are her "puppets", created by her to do what she has ordained and express the views she gives them, then she may be very unwilling to see other puppeteers manipulate them, particularly if their view of them differs at all from hers. Such writers object to non-profit-making fan fiction as much as to ventures like Yemets's. Not all writers do take that line. As we have seen (chapter 7), Paul Magrs enjoys seeing "his" Iris Wildthyme in other writers' work, even citing published and paid work. In earlier times, Conan Doyle allowed William Gillette to dramatise Holmes and take him in new directions. Colley Cibber not only allowed Sir John Vanbrugh to use his character Sir Novelty Fashion in a sequel, but even played Vanbrugh's version on stage.

These two earlier examples both involved stage performances. It is tempting to suggest that seeing characters portrayed on stage and screen, brought alive by successive actors, adapters, producers etc, must make it harder, even for the author, to continue believing that there is but one "right" interpretation of them. Certainly such portrayals dilute the concept of the sole author, so that a TV version of *Pride and Prejudice* comes to be seen as "by Jane Austen and Andrew Davies" (see chapter 1). But in the end, I suspect it comes down to the mindset of the individual author and how proprietorial he or she is about fictional constructs and intellectual property. Anne Rice is "terribly upset" to see her creations used by others; J K Rowling is "flattered".

The poet Anne Stevenson dedicated her collection of poems *A Report from the Border*[11] to "the friends who have helped write these poems over the years". She meant, not that they had contributed actual lines or verses to the poems in question, but that their experiences, relationships, personalities, even, sometimes, their individual speaking voices came together with her own imagination and intellect to create the fiction. I am not sure the writer is a creator so much as a jackdaw or perhaps, more charitably, a bower bird, with a talent for assembling diverse materials and reshaping them into patterns. She takes material that was already in the world and shapes characters, sometimes universes, out of it, but the other thing I recall from school science was the law "during a chemical reaction matter is neither created nor destroyed". The writer does not bring anything new into the world; she arranges it in a new way.

This arrangement of material, rather than the material itself, is her creation, and it is right enough that her ability to profit from it and be known as its author should be protected. But to suggest that, for example, the arrangement of material to which she gave the name "Elizabeth Bennet" should, ever after, be unavailable as fictional material to anyone else strikes me as going too far. Indeed nobody does suggest that. Fiction out of copyright is fair game, and that, to my mind, makes it very hard to argue that even living authors' fiction should not be, provided always that the author's profit and good name are left untouched.

When I began reading fan fiction, (and I did so not because I was researching it but because I was a fan), I was reading fics based on TV shows. The idea of fanfic based on a single-authored book canon seemed more dubious to me, as a profic writer. I hardly read any until

I began to research this book and I was not sure how I would react to it. I am sure now that I share Rowling's mindset. If I, as a profic writer, managed to create a character who came alive so vividly for readers that they were convinced they knew him as well as or better than I did and wanted to continue his story, I would feel flattered and delighted beyond words. If they got him wrong, in the sense of making *factual* errors about him, I would feel mildly annoyed that they hadn't done their homework. If on the other hand they simply saw him otherwise than I did, I could say that their take on him wasn't mine, but I would no longer feel able to say it was *wrong*, as some authors evidently can. I said earlier (chapter 7) that I did not think fanfic writers altogether believed in the notion of the single-authored book. After being a fanfic *reader* for some years, I don't altogether believe in it either.

One thing I certainly don't believe is that authors, whether single authors of books or multiple writers and producers of TV shows, can put this particular genie back in the bottle. Michela Ecks, in the Internet article quoted earlier, balances the arguments of fan fiction readers and writers against the opposition of some authors and concludes, "There is a delicate balance and when it comes down to it, fans are the ones who will probably have to back off before the author". I can see no sign at all that this is liable to happen. Certain authors are well known to oppose fan fiction, but that doesn't stop their books generating it. Their opposition can keep it off umbrella sites like fanfiction.net, but individual sites can be policed about as well as individual minds.

Some TV domains have tried to come to an accommodation, encouraging gen fan fiction but making clear their opposition to adult material (often it was a specific opposition to slash). That made no difference either; it certainly did not affect the growing popularity of slash. Even J K Rowling's tolerance of fan fiction does not extend to adult and slash material, unsurprisingly since she sees her books as being written for children. A report in the *Washington Post* by Ariana Eunjung Cha[12] notes that Rowling's agents have been sending "sharply worded cease-and-desist letters" to sites featuring adult material. One can understand the author's reported alarm at the thought of such material falling in the way of child Harry Potter fans. But there are a lot of adult fans too, and I would not give much for the chances of stopping them using the source their way.

The latest owner of material (though in no way its creator) to express hostility to fanfic, again specifically to slash, is Andrew Sewell, a BBC producer who with Simon Moorhead acquired the rights to *Blakes 7* from Terry Nation's estate, with the intention of reviving a version of it as a made-for-TV film. In late 2003 he gave an online interview to Steve Rogerson,[13] in which he made his views clear:

> I think slash is distasteful. The actors that are represented do not appreciate it. And some produce this stuff on the web. I think it is bad taste. It has no reflection or bearing on what the show is and it is not a tribute to Terry Nation's legacy. I think it is an abomination. I think what is an abomination is the pornography. I have no problem with fan fiction, but I do have a problem with pornography."
>
> Asked what he planned to do, he said: "They will find out how I am going to clamp down on it. The moment you start doing something of an extremely dubious nature of the pornographic variety or for a commercial benefit without acquiring the rights, I and my partners will take a dim view of that."
>
> He acknowledged that slash would always go on. "If it is conducted in the privacy of your own homes, then we can't stop that. But when it is on the web, it is inappropriate. I will try to minimise it further than it already is. I won't have that representation of Terry Nation's characters given official sanction. Kids like Blakes 7 and I think it is inappropriate that they should come across that material under the guise of a celebration of Blakes 7. There are no gate keepers for some of this stuff, and that concerns me."

There are several interesting aspects to this statement, firstly the lack of understanding it demonstrates. There is no "commercial benefit" involved, and as for "no gatekeepers", if there exists a slash site which does not declare exactly what it is and warn off the unwary, I have not come across it in a great deal of reading. It is interesting too that though he cites the presence of a child audience in justification of his views (not that the series was ever written for children), he does not, like Rowling, object to all "adult" material but specifically to slash. This is an illogical but fairly common attitude. Some TV domains are tolerant of het adult fanfic but Joss Whedon, creator of *Buffy the Vampire Slayer*, remains exceptional in his tolerance of slash. Sewell's partner Moorhead later put a clarifying statement on the same website, in which he seemed to suggest that the pair were in fact objecting to *all* adult fanfic. But again it was couched in terms that suggested they thought "slash" was synonymous with "all fanfic with a sexual content", or indeed with "pornography".

Unlike Whedon or Rowling, Sewell was not himself a creator of the material he purported to protect, and many fans' immediate reaction to this interview was to question why in that case he thought he had any right to try to control what they wrote. His reasons of course are commercial; in the same interview he said "I am however against unofficial merchandise because it cheapens the product".

What he can do about it is another matter. His threats caused concern in the fan community, but they also noted the vagueness of "they will find out how I am going to clamp down on it" and "I and my partners will take a dim view of that." The fan speculation was that he might request ISPs to take down slash sites; the further speculation was that if he did, he or his lawyers would find themselves very busy and to little end. Law practitioners in the fan community pointed out on mailing lists that though many domains had over the years served cease-and-desist notices on fanfic writers, nobody actually seemed to have been sued for non-compliance. Fanfic or photomanips could be argued to be "transformative fair use" – i.e., even though someone else's intellectual property is used as a starting point, there has been at least some of the creativity that the copyright system is designed to foster, and it is not at all clear to what extent the owners of intellectual property can take steps against non-commercial derivative works. Others pointed out the ease with which a site closed down in one country could be moved to a server in some such country as Russia, where lawyers would have considerable trouble chasing it.

The suggestion of one fan – that writers in the fandom should simply busy themselves writing and posting to the web more material than any man could chase up in one lifetime – was facetious but expressed an underlying truth. The fact is that there are few headier pleasures than being an author, realising that you can create and manipulate a universe and give life to the characters in it. And a great many people who were once content to be readers have found that out. Many of them did so accidentally. It wasn't, at the time, that they particularly wanted to be writers. It was that they wanted some fictional universe and/or characters not to come to an end, or to develop differently, or to reveal facets that were hidden. And since the original writers would not or could not oblige, they had to do it themselves.

Naturally, for their own satisfaction and that of their readers, the best of them wanted to do it as well as they could. Reader feedback and the culture of pooling ideas among authors who were not in any kind of competition were their tools in this, and the Internet greatly improved both. Some fanfic writers had always been writers, of profic as well, but even those who had not written before often became very interested in literary technique, because they saw how it could help them achieve their aims. Some who had started in fanfic subsequently crossed the profic border.

But others found that their chosen genre enabled them to do what they wanted in writing without crossing that border. Belatrix Carter, in chapter 7, was startlingly candid on how she used her chosen genre to enable her to concentrate on doing what she found most interesting in writing and avoiding what she did not. Endings rather than beginnings, character rather than plot, twists on the familiar that do not depend on actually *creating* the familiar in the first place. "This intertextuality stuff", depending on an informed, involved audience who would enjoy seeing familiar things in new ways as much as the author did. Belatrix, unlike some, *had* always wanted to be a writer but had not, until she discovered fanfic, found a field in which she felt inspired to use her talent for words. Once she did, she found ideas "mugging her in the street" and so do many others. But those less beset by "plot bunnies" (ideas demanding to be written) can find them via interaction on mailing lists, challenges set on the same lists or, in another striking use of a web-based resource, random story generators which will provide characters, a location and props in a particular domain. This has now and then been dubbed "Cluedo online", i.e. X and Y, in such-and-such a place, with such-and-such an object.

Others found that fanfic could give them an audience without some of the concomitants the profic writer has to accept. They did not need to be in competition with other writers, and they could get the feedback which they, like all writers, wanted, direct from the audience they were trying to please. Criticised they may be, but at least those emailing the criticism will be readers, not critics or other middlemen. Most profic writers only get a taste of this direct feedback if they set up a website on which readers can leave comments, and I can testify from maintaining such sites that it is an enriching experience for any writer to have it confirmed that there are indeed readers out there.

Meanwhile, profic writers wishing to reach an audience must first convince increasingly cost-conscious publishers, or rather their marketing departments, not only that their book is a good one but that it will sell. This is frustrating enough under any circumstances, more so when the writer is herself convinced that the marketing men are wrong and that she *could* sell her vision to the readers, were she only allowed to get through to them. These are, after all, the marketing men who assured Richard Adams, on behalf of some two dozen publishers, that he would never sell a novel with a male rabbit called Hazel as the hero. And their criteria can be far removed from literature. It is unfortunately indisputable that a new writer is more likely to be accepted by a publisher if he or she is young and will look personable on book covers, not a consideration that has ever had to bother a fanfic writer. I have never yet seen a photo of a writer in a printzine or webzine, and that is only partly because many prefer to be anonymous. Mostly it is because their readers could not care less what the author looks like.

Those fanfic writers who choose not to try profic cannot usually be accused of an unwillingness to be criticised or a wish to work to less exacting standards. Fanfic editors are not afraid to criticise properly and beta-readers regard it as their job. But this takes place within a far more supportive community than most profic writers get to work with, even in these days of writers' groups and workshops. Partly this is because there is no element of competition, partly because writers in a particular fanfic domain are, due to their shared interest in the source material, far likelier to actually read and enjoy each other's work than many profic writers are.

All teachers of creative writing are forever stressing to students that good readers make good writers and that they cannot expect to improve at their craft without reading both their predecessors and their contemporaries. Yet still aspiring writers come along who will not read the work of others, for fear that it may "influence" and change their own style (which would generally result in nothing but improvement), and who seriously think they have nothing to learn from their contemporaries in the same field. It is as if a doctor should declare that he never opened a medical book or consulted his colleagues. These would-be writers are fewer than they used to be, but in fanfic they do not really exist: all fanfic writers are, almost by definition, readers, both in their own genre and outside it. This certainly makes them better writers than they might otherwise be; it also, I think, makes them more in tune with their readership and what that readership wants.

The main practical way in which fanfic differs from profic is not its intertextuality as such, but the fact that it gets intertextual with work still in copyright. Fanfic writers accept that having chosen to write in this genre debars them from ever publishing for profit – most of them aren't really interested in making money out of writing anyway. But they do sometimes feel bitter about the way their genre, which produces as wide a spectrum of quality as any other, is automatically dismissed and mocked by those outside the fan community who have heard of it. Sometimes this is because it is thought of as derivative (only litfic is allowed to be intertextual); sometimes it is because what is not done for money is assumed to be inferior. Litfic critics and practitioners find it hard not to associate writing published other than for profit with "vanity presses", which charge money to publish the unpublishable, or self-publishing, which is still in some quarters looked on as what you do when your work is not good enough to attract a "real" publisher.

Nevertheless, there are slight indications that this attitude may be changing, because of events on the profic side of the borderline. Most writers' guides no longer tend to assert confidently that "if your work is good enough, it will find a publisher", because the thing is no longer true, if it ever was. Instead they give advice on self-publishing, like the article 'Doing it on your own' by Peter Finch in *The Writers' & Artists' Yearbook*[14]. The attitude that writing which has not been submitted to some publisher's critical judgement must be flawed has been undermined by successes like Jill Paton Walsh's self-published *Knowledge of Angels*, which cut out the middleman and went straight to the reader, not to mention the Booker Prize shortlist. And this change in attitude may have persuaded at least some across the litfic borderline not to dismiss fanfic so automatically. At least one MA in creative writing has been awarded for a fan fiction novel, set in a universe still in copyright. It cannot be published commercially, but that has not prevented it from being evaluated as literature.

Not that dismissive attitudes from outside their community have ever discouraged fanfic writers and readers, or made them doubt the validity of what they do. There have been two relative explosions of fiction in British fanfic universes over recent years. One happened when a character (Archie Kennedy) was killed and his fans were not ready to lose him, and the other happened when a plotline which had, in itself, been popular with fans began in their view to cop out (the Craig Gilmore/Luke Ashton relationship in *The Bill*). In both cases the viewers were not only refusing to accept the creator's decision but doing something about it by becoming co-creators themselves. By and large, the nineteenth-century Sherlock Holmes fans who wore mourning bands on the London streets did not see this as a possible solution; the enterprising William Gillette was an exception. They did not want the story to end, but all most of them felt they could do was try to persuade Conan Doyle to continue it. The most that readers themselves have traditionally done in such a situation is continue the story in their head, rather than share their thoughts with others.

They may have stopped at this out of respect for the original author, or diffidence about their own capability as writers, or because of the difficulty of finding and communicating with other like-minded people. Or a combination of all three, of course. At all events, none of those reasons holds good now.

In a recent debate (2003) on an unarchived mailing list on reasons for writing fanfic, the *Bill* fanfic writer Sandi reports that her motives have changed somewhat, and her comments suggest a developing confidence which I think applies to many fanfic writers:

> In the old days it was a fun thing, usually to fill the gaps between seasons or once a series had ended. There were some characters I just couldn't let go.
>
> These days the need is driven more by the desire to treat the characters with the respect that the programme makers seem to lack. Craig Gilmore in The Bill is a case in point. If ever a character was mistreated by its creators, he was it. So I write Craig/OMC [original male character] to try to redress that.
>
> I really don't think that the programme makers these days realise how much the audience of a successful show is prepared to invest in certain characters, which is why we get such horrendous mistakes – characters being propelled into soap-style relationships where the other party is totally unsuitable, characters being killed off because the writers have run out of ideas for them, or in some instances the characters being changed completely to fit a storyline. As a fan with an insatiable desire to write, it's those kinds of things that I want to put right, if only in my own little non-published world.

In an echo of the mourning Londoners, many Archie fans lamenting his screen demise in the "Requiem" forum would mention in their tributes that they were wearing black for him. But they were not limited to such passive grieving, nor did they have to accept what the screenwriters had done. In the same way, *The Bill's* fans did not have to wait tamely for the screenwriters' next move, knowing from advance information that it was liable not to be to their liking. They could make it go which way they liked, and the Crumpeteers could busy themselves resurrecting Archie (see 'Long Live the King' on the

Archieology 101 website for the possible ways), because they were writers too.

Perhaps my own fascination with the genre is in the end related to my job. As I mentioned earlier, a slogan of creative writing teachers tends to be "good readers make good writers". In fanfic, more than any genre I know, readers took that literally and proved it.

NOTES

1. http://members.tripod.com/archieology101/home.htm 08.04.03
2. http://www.whoosh.org/issue62/ecks2.html 15.0303
3. Doubleday 1909
4. from the Fedonia Books edition, 2001
5. http://www.tbfanfic.com 21.04.03
6. http://sarahb1.tripod.com/hharchive.html 20.03.03
7. *Tales from Space City 4*, ed. Helen Patrick 2002
8. Nova, *Tales from Space City 4*
9. http://members.tripod.com/archieology101/requiem.htm 09.04.03
10. Ballantine Books, 1998
11. Bloodaxe 2003
12. 18th June 2003
13. archived at http://www.blakes-7.co.uk/b7e/b7eint.shtml 8.11.03
14. A & C Black, reprinted yearly

Appendix I: A Glossary of Fanfic Terms Used in this Book

Angst Writing which dwells on emotional problems, tortured minds and unconsummated relationships, and enjoys them immensely.

APA Amateur press association: also Letterzine; magazine of comments and/or stories produced by the members but collated and sent out by a central controller.

ATG Any Two Guys/Gals: derogatory term for a slash story in which the characters seem to be incidental to the sex.

AU Alternate universe: fanfic story which at some point deliberately departs from the canon on which it is based.

Avatar Character based on one from the canon but not identical with him.

Beta-reader Someone who reads and comments on stories before the author posts them to a wider public.

BUAR Beat up and rape: the more extreme end of hurt/comfort.

Canon The source property used as material by fanfic writers.

Character junkie Reader or writer for whom the characters are paramount.

Character rape What happens when a writer makes a character act in a way readers think against his nature.

Closed (Of canon): unable to be further added to by the originator(s).

Crossover Story in which characters from two different source properties interact.

Crumpeteers Group of Hornblower fans with a special devotion to Archie Kennedy.

Domlijah aka Domlij RPS pairing of Dominic Monaghan and Elijah Wood.

Fanfic Short for fan fiction.

Fanon Something not in the canon, invented by a fanfic writer but convincing enough to be adopted by others.

Fanzine Magazine of fan fiction, either in print (printzine) or online (webzine).

F/f (aka femslash) All-female relationship: see also m/m, m/f.

Fic Piece of fan fiction writing; a story, usually.

Filing off the serial numbers Rendering a fanfic story suitable for mainstream publication by removing obvious canon-based references.

Filk Song on a fan theme, written to an existing tune.

Gafiate Get Away From It All; move either from one fandom to another or out of fandom altogether.

Gen — Story suitable for a general audience – i.e. no sex or no explicit sex. Non-explicit het often counts as gen with editors, non-explicit slash hardly ever.

H/C — Hurt/comfort: genre in which one character is given a hard time physically, emotionally or both before being consoled/rehabilitated by another.

Het — Story featuring heterosexual sex.

HEXers — (B7) group of writers dedicated to providing positive endings (Happy Ending Expediters). See also SADists.

Illos — Illustrations in fanzines.

Jossed — (of fanfic): rendered incompatible with the canon by some later, unexpected twist taken by the canon writers. From the name of Joss Whedon, creator of *Buffy the Vampire Slayer.*

K/S — Kirk/Spock: the original pairing in slash.

Letterzine — see APA.

LKU — Hornblower: Live Kennedy Universe: alternate universe where Archie Kennedy did not die.

LOC — Letter of comment: critique of a fic either posted direct to the author or in a mailing list or letterzine.

LotR — Lord of the Rings: usually indicates film-based rather than book-based fandom.

LotRiPS — RPS fiction based on the actors from Lord of the Rings.

Mary Sue — Character based on an idealised version of the author.

Metafic — Fanfic story about writing a fanfic story.

Missing Scene — Story that focuses on something which was not shown in canon but could or must have happened.

M/f — Heterosexual relationship: see also m/m, f/f.

M/m — All-male relationship: see also m/f, f/f.

Mpreg — Story where a man gets pregnant.

Mundanes — Non-fans, people outside fan culture.

OC — Original character: character not in the original canon.

Open (Of canon): still capable of being added to by the originator(s).

OTP — One True Pairing: two characters who seem "made for each other"; stories which take this as a given.

PGP — Post-Gauda Prime: sequel story in the *Blakes 7* universe, set after the final episode.

Photomanips — Doctored photographs.

Plot bunnies — Ideas demanding to be written.

Profic — Fiction written for money.

PWP — Plot? What plot? Story in which character interaction, not plot, is the point, often a sex scene with no vestige of plot as an excuse.

RPF/RPS	Real Person Fiction and Real Person Slash: stories using real, living people as characters.
SADists	(B7) group of writers who prefer dark endings – see also HEXers.
'Shippers	Fanfic writers and readers for whom relationships between characters are paramount.
Slash	Story supposing a homerotic or homosexual relationship between two characters which was not present or not spelt out in canon.
Songfic	Fanfic story inspired by a song title or lyric.
Sparrington	Slash pairing of Captain Jack Sparrow and Commodore Norrington from the film *Pirates of the Caribbean.*
Trev	Generic name for bit-part characters in *The Bill.*
YAOI	Yama nashi, ochi nashi, imi nashi – no plot, no point, no meaning: Japanese equivalent of PWP.

Appendix 2: Fan Fiction on the Internet

This is not an exhaustive list but an indication of some good places to start for the fandoms mainly discussed in this book. All the sites also have links to others. The best place to find details of print fanzines in most fandoms is also on the Net, at Judith Proctor's *B7* site below.

General sites

http://www.fanfiction.net
Fanfiction.net is an umbrella site for any fandom except those where authors are known to object, and any kind of writing including adult and slash. It is not edited, so some of the fiction is very good, some semi-literate, and all standards in between are also represented. At the moment it seems to be the only place to find Discworld fics in any quantity. It is a good source for book-based fics.
http://www.britslash.co.uk/
Britslash is a site for slash fiction based mainly on British TV shows, plus some which originated elsewhere but aired in the UK.
http://cotillion.slashcity.org/
The Slash Cotillion is a home for historical slash, which includes not only TV shows set in the past, like Sharpe and Horatio Hornblower but also book-based slash from such sources as Shakespeare and Dumas, which you won't find on Britslash. Its remit is fairly elastic; it also contains fics from modern domains like the Buffyverse, if they happen to be set in the past.

Sites for individual fandoms featured in this book

Jane Austen

http://www.pemberley.com
The Republic of Pemberley is a large site with information on Austen as well as fan fiction.
http://www.austen.com/derby
The Derbyshire Writers' Guild is a purely fan fiction archive for Austen-based stories. Its guidelines are much the same as the Republic's and the fiction overlaps.
http://www.geocities.com/tinker_belladonna/directory.htm
Hyacinth's Garden Site – tolerates AUs and other departures from canon.

http://www.firthness.com/
Firthness. As its name suggests, the fiction on this site focuses on the TV adaptation of *Pride and Prejudice* starring Colin Firth as Darcy. Tolerant of adult fanfic.

Blakes 7

http://www.hermit.org/Blakes7/
Judith Proctor's site contains the Hermit Library, which houses a great deal of B7 fiction, gen, het and slash, and the site has links to a lot more. It is also relevant to other fandoms in that Judith acts as agent for print fanzines in many fandoms.
http://www.liberated.org.uk
Liberated is a site for specifically adult B7 fan fiction, both het and slash.
http://pinkasteroids.org.uk/
Pink Asteroids. Non-explicit slash and femslash.

Discworld

http://www.skyehawke.com/archive
Skyehawke, a multi-fandom archive, has some Discworld fics, both gen and adult.

Hornblower

http://sarahb1.tripod.com/hharchive.html
The Horatio Hornblower fan fiction archive houses stories submitted to the Hornblower fan fiction mailing list. No slash.
http://members.tripod.com/archieology101
Archieology 101 contains direct links to a lot of specifically Archie-focused stories (though not the slash ones). Archie-focused generally means angst-focused.
http://www.frolixers.com/index.html
The Frolix site is a Hornblower slash archive.
http://dmoz.org/Adult/Arts/Online_Writing/Fiction/Fan_Fiction/Television/Miniseries/Hornblower/
Links to various Hornblower slash fiction sites.

The Bill

http://www.tbfanfic.com
The Bill's gen fanfic site. It was home to more plot-driven fiction than most fanfic libraries I know. It is now discontinued but can still be found at the site http://webarchive.org
http://www.goldweb.com.au/~bessie/sunhill
The Jasmine Alley site hosts The Bill slash.
http://www.savegilmore.co.uk/index.htm
"Savegilmore" was originally set up to campaign for Hywel Simons, who played Sgt Gilmore, to remain in the show. He didn't, but in the meantime the Gilmore/Ashton storyline had generated slash fiction in unheard-of quantities and continues to do so. All the fiction on this site relates in some way to the Gilmore character. By the time of publication the site name will probably have changed to http://www.craiggilmore.co.uk/, though individual page references will otherwise not alter.

Some personal recommendations (individual stories)

http://members.shaw.ca/archbishopmelker/sleaze/tkodnl.html
'The Killer of Dole Nu Lin' by Penny Dreadful. (B7) One of the most powerful, thought-provoking fanfic stories you are liable to read. Some adult material (het).
http://www.geocities.com/ayafujimiya/mask/athos.html
'Make With Your Hands', by Maria Bonet. (Dumas) Gen, melancholy reprise on the Musketeers in old age.
http://www.goldweb.com.au/~bessie/
'Golden Boy' by Kel. (The Bill) Slash, Kel at her most brooding and atmospheric.
http://members.tripod.com/SarahB1/salus.html
'Salus' by Victoria Bitter. (Horatio Hornblower) Gen, classic Archie-angst.
http://www.geocities.com/london_lass/hiddendepths.htm
'Hidden Depths' by Susannah Shepherd. (Sherlock Holmes) Explicit slash, but with more stress on the emotional than the physical.
http://www.fanfiction.net/s/826031/1/
'Tyger, Tyger' by Grey L Bloom. (Discworld) Gen, manages to capture Pratchett's style while doing something of its own.
http://www.tilneysandtrapdoors.com/ff/acctc.html
'A Clandestine Correspondence' by Mags. (Jane Austen) Gen, epistolary missing scene from *Northanger Abbey*.
http://www.savegilmore.co.uk/Winter%20Blues.htm
'Winter Blues' by Eggbert. (*The Bill*) Slash story structured around the parallel relationships of Craig/Luke and Des/Reg.
http://www.viragene.com/ttba1/purple.htm

'Purple Haze' by Executrix. (B7) Some mildly adult material, both het and slash, but the focus of this fic is politics.
http://www.ravenswing.com/~mirrorgirl/servants.htm
'Servants with Torches' by Jane St Clair. (Romeo & Juliet) Mildly slashy, very atmospheric.

Appendix 3: Under the Waterfall: A fan fiction community's analysis of their self-representation and peer review by Kristi Lee Brobeck

This article was first published in issue no 5 of *Refractory*, the University of Melbourne's online media culture journal.

Preface

In the fall semester of 2003, my friend and fan fiction scholar, Dr. Amy Sturgis, allowed me to sit in on a class that she was teaching at Belmont University entitled "Fan Participation in Media and Culture." It was an interdisciplinary course which addressed exactly what the course title promised; fandom as expressed in myriad forms and within multiple genres, from the genesis of the first Star Trek convention to current writers of Labyrinth fan fiction, and much in-between: downloadable garage-band Harry Potter filking; watching and subsequently analyzing the messages portrayed in movies which highlighted fan culture such as "Free Enterprise" and "Galaxy Quest"; and papers presented by fellow students ranging from people who love all things Harley Davidson to groups who watch "The Andy Griffith Show" in syndication on a weekly basis. The purpose of the last project in the course was either to contribute to a particular fandom, whether in writing or artistic form, or to analyze one. As a relatively new, but prolific fan fiction writer, I felt that doing the first would be cheating, so this is my belated essay analyzing the online Tolkien fan fiction community of members of Henneth-Annûn.

> Though the internet may have begun to mainstream fandom, it has not necessarily created a single, unified fan position or practice.[1]

Henneth-Annûn (http://www.henneth-annun.net) is a public, member-driven archive on the internet which went live in May of 2002, where writers of Tolkien-based fan fiction can post, or "publish" their stories. The Henneth-Annûn story archive (HASA) is run by volunteers, all of whom perform the maintenance duties of the site in addition to real life day jobs and family responsibilities. This site does not simply house stories, however. Within the site's members section, there are multiple areas of resources and forums which provide a public space in which a member can access other writers' particular knowledge about geography, warfare, poetry, food, or any number of other aspects to life in what has been coined the "Ardaverse,"[2] the realm in which all Tolkien fan fiction is based. Writers can find beta readers, or proofreaders, to look over his/her work, as well as post comments about one's stories and await criticism or enthusiasm for one's works. The site has both a public and a members' exclusive section. There is no cost to becoming a member of the site. From the public area, one can read stories which have been accepted into the public realm of the archive after going through a nine-person, self-selected reviewing pool and have been accepted by at least five of the reviewers. From the members' area, one can read stories that are in progress, works which have not been submitted to the reviewing pool, and the Resources section, which includes Tolkien-based essays, character biographies, and URL links to other sites intended to aid an author who wishes to write within the rather complicated realm of Middle-earth.

From the Henneth-Annûn website, here are the final two paragraphs in the stated purpose of the archive:

> The site is set up to accept recommendations from the writers group, and to allow for author self-submissions. Every story that is recommended or submitted is reviewed through a standard process, and either accepted or declined based on our review criteria. Even our own group members must submit their work through this process.
>
> Our goal is to provide our readers with a selection of the best JRRT fan fiction we possibly can, and to inspire other authors to write more of it!

Having been active in this particular part of Tolkien fandom for a year, I had discovered that fellow writers and readers tended to be more vocal about this particular archive and held definite biases toward or against it. The archive is not merely a "bookshelf," or place where all fan fiction is posted without any sort of selection process (i.e. the FanFiction.net model), and therefore there is "...a profound tension in the site between the attempt to be inclusive in the members area and the need to be exclusive in the archive."[3] Implicit within the private and public side of the archive is an ever-changing, anonymous, self-selected group of people who have taken on the mantle of becoming objective judges of other people's writing. This is indeed an emotional and, to use a title of one of Tolkien's story collections, "perilous realm," whose sentiments are echoed in the words of this respondent:

> [...] I'm less concerned about the process than I am about those who participate in the process. Institutions (and yes, HASA is one), after all, simply are; it's people who make them fair or unfair, whether by perverting the original intention of the institution unacceptably or by instituting an unfair standard in the first place.(15)

mem•ber 2: one of the individuals composing a group

I have a deep and abiding love for the works of JRR Tolkien, and an equally deep appreciation of the people who have embraced me and welcomed me into this particular fellowship of wordsmiths. What more need be said? (28)

The Lord of the Rings trilogy and accompanying texts (including, but not limited to *The Silmarillion, The Hobbit*, and the *History of Middle Earth* series edited by Christopher Tolkien) may be described as "cult texts" as explicated by Matt Hills in his book Fan Cultures:

> Another defining attribute of the cult text is *hyperdiegesis*: the creation of a vast and detailed narrative space, only a fraction of which is ever directly seen or encountered within the text, but which nevertheless appears to operate according to principles of internal logic and extension.[4]

Such a rich density of texts, accompanied by Peter Jackson's overwhelmingly popular movie interpretations of the *Lord of the Rings* trilogy, has inspired an almost unfathomable number of people to write their own stories using Tolkien's works and/or Peter Jackson's films as a starting point. The Tolkien online fanfiction community ranges in the tens of thousands, using the number of authors at FanFiction.net as only a starting point.[5]

There are many Tolkien-based fan fiction archives on the web. Only a few are all-inclusive; most have particular guidelines or character focuses: slash only[6]; non-slash[7]; Legolas/Gimli stories[8]; Frodo-centric hurt/comfort[9]; R-rating maximum stories[10]; to list only a very few. HASA accepts all kinds of stories, regardless of time period, story genre, and rating level in regards to violent content or sexual explicitness. This attribute alone makes it unique within Tolkien fanfiction archives, though there are additional differences which set it apart from similar sites. At the time of writing this essay, there were around 460 active members at Henneth-Annûn.

Though almost all authors at the archive write under a pseudonym, those assumed names can be well known within the community. I wished for the people who replied to my survey to be completely candid and honest, so I specified that I would not use anything other than a numbering system when quoting responses in this essay. In November of 2003 I sent an email survey to everyone who had a member biography and a publicly listed email address. At the time, there were 183 people who I could contact, and from that, 50 people chose to reply to my questions, a response rate of 27%. As an active member of Henneth-Annûn myself, I recognized some of the names on the list that I knew had not contributed anything to any part of the archive in several months, and I do not believe that all 183 people on the list were still active at HASA when I contacted them.[11]

I felt I needed to have some benchmark questions, and length of active membership at HASA seemed to be a logical starting point. Of the 50 replies to the question, "How long have you been a member of the Henneth-Annûn story archive (not the yahoogroup list)?", 18 respondents or 36% had been members of HASA for 9 months or fewer; 18 respondents or 36% had been members for 10-15 months; and the remaining 14 respondents or 28% had been members for 16 months or longer. A few respondents indicated that they had been members since the inception of the site. The variety of months of membership in the responses of those who did reply means that the answers were skewed neither toward those who were relatively new to the archive, nor toward those who have been involved for well over a year.

The next benchmark questions had to do with what the members of HASA did at the archive, both in regards to contributions made and use of resources available. I asked, "What would you say is your primary activity at HASA – writer, reader, reviewer, admin, or some combination? (if it's a combination, please try to give a percentage or ratio of sorts, if possible)," and also, "What is your primary use of the archive? (for example: place to publish stories, place to communicate with other writers, find beta readers, etc.)" It was in these responses where some differing patterns emerged. Thirteen people, or 26%, indicated that they were not currently active writers, and of those, four specified that they were now mostly inactive in regards to HASA, though they had been more involved in the past. Four additional people indicated that at least 50% of their time spent at the archive had to do with their administrative and technical support duties. Fifteen people, or 30%, wrote that at least half of their active involvement was in writing, while 23 respondents, or 46%, indicated that at least 50% of their time at the archive was spent reading the stories there, whether completed or works in progress. In regards to reviewing stories, 21 respondents, or 42%, specified that they spent at least a tenth of their time as active reviewers.

Overwhelmingly, the people who replied to my survey use the archive as a place to house or publish their fan fiction. Of the 50 responses, 33 replies, or 66%, wrote that publishing their stories was either the primary reason for joining the archive, or it was one of only two reasons why s/he was a member of HASA. Fifteen people, or 30%, specified that one of their main purposes for becoming a member was to be able to communicate with other writers in the forums, and hopefully collaborate with like-minded writers. Below are some replies to the question "What is your primary use of the archive?":

> Place to publish & also communicate with other writers, mainly commenting (in forums) on favorite authorís stories, and getting feedback on my own W.I.P.s (27)

> Mainly to publish stories and sometimes comment on stories and stories-in-progress of which I've become familiar with the author. (18)

> Initially, it was to read, hopefully, quality fics that appeal to me, and I certainly wanted to publish there. (48)

> My primary use of the archive right now is as a place to communicate with other writers and to put beta stories/WIPs that I would like to hear comments on. (20)

> For me, it's mainly a place to publish stories and to find other people's stories without wasting my time with crap. (47)

The third part of the triumvirate of questions relating to participation in the archive had to do with members' use of aspects of the site that went beyond housing stories. I asked "Do you avail yourself of the forums, URL library, resources section, beta readers, etc?" All but thirteen people indicated that they did use the resources, forums and URL library at least from time to time. The remaining thirty-seven people, or a predominant 74%, use the archive beyond simply housing stories, or reading stories. Three respondents specified that they did use the beta reader section, and one writer specifically made note of his/her effort to get a beta writer, but to no avail.

feed•back
2 b: the information transmitted to a point of origin of evaluative or corrective information about an action or process

Since there are so many other Tolkien-based fan fiction archives on the internet, I asked the question, "If you are a 'published' (as in, have stories posted publicly on the internet) writer, do you have stories archived at other locations besides HASA, such as other archives or your own website? If so, why?" Two respondents indicated that they were not published authors within Tolkien fandom, and of the remaining 48, 11 people, or 23%, replied that they chose specifically not to archive their stories at HASA. These authors' reasons ranged from feeling uncomfortable or philosophically at odds with the stated goal of the archive of housing some of "the best" Tolkien fan fiction, to translation issues (one author was French), to having requested feedback and not receiving any, then removing their stories. At the other end of the spectrum, five authors, or 10%, revealed that their stories were available only at HASA. In those cases, reasons were not explicated. Most individuals who replied to my survey have stories both at HASA and other locales: other archives, their own websites, and in livejournal weblogs. An overwhelming 67% (32 people) fell into this last category. The answers to the question, "If so, why?" became repetitive, and being a writer myself, I was not surprised to see "maximum readership/additional feedback" come up multiple times – 22 times, or 69%.

> I find this an unusual question, as I tend to be more surprised when people say that they only post at HASA! (21)

> My basic philosophy is that the more people who can find and enjoy my stories the better. I'm not interested in exclusivity. I have my best-known story posted to many archives, translated into three other languages, and read by people all over the world. I like that. I'm not going to be coy and pretend it doesn't matter. (37)

> I have stories archived at FF.net, Stories of Arda, Open Scrolls and on my own website. I do not submit everything at HASA for publication, and I know people who do not know about or like HASA. Posting in other places helps expand my base of readers. (22)

A desire for more feedback or critiquing of works was a common theme voiced by several respondents, both in regards to the reviewing process, but also in general. Since almost one-third of those surveyed indicated that they hoped to have an active dialogue with other writers, such a pattern of comments was not unexpected, though the messages differed in perspective:

> I could never find a beta reader to take a look at my stories. Basically, the people of the site refused to help me better myself as a writer, yet expected me to write the best quality fic. (45)

> As for communicating with other writers, I did attempt to integrate myself in the beginning. But I found quickly that HASA was effusive only within certain conditions – to known denizens, writers who have made a name for themselves, and in clusters (i.e., friends and acquaintances). (48)

> I'm much more likely to leave a review or comment at HASA, because the fact that the person is an active HASA member tells me that they are genuinely interested in constructive criticism and discussion of their fiction – and might reciprocate for me! (8)

> I have always liked creative writing, but never thought I'd permit anyone else to read what I wrote. HASA changed all that for me. [...] HASA is still the place where I communicate with other writers, and exchange ideas and information re: the works that have provided inspiration for us all. (28)

am•biv•a•lence
1: simultaneous and contradictory attitudes or feelings (as attraction and repulsion) toward an object, person or thing

> HASA and its reviewers are caught in a neat little Catch-22. In order to achieve their stated goals, they must act in an elitist and judgmental manner, but they don't like the word elitist and get offended when "outsiders" call them on it. (37)

> Generally speaking I CAN see why the charge of "elitist" might be levelled at HASA and its methods... (38)

> Hasa is elitist and picky, and not very friendly... (40)

> HASA is wonderfully ordered community, and well kept. I like the professional environment of the writers in general... (35)

> ...it's a pretty well-behaved community – there are certainly spats and disagreements but I rarely see anything resembling flaming in the forums. Most members are very supportive of each other's efforts to write the best they can, in whatever form or genre best suits them. (11)

> I am very happy with this community. I feel I have learned a great deal from my participation here. Constructive criticism is often found here, but not flames or derogatory comments, as the readers here are more mature. (30)

> I usually compare HASA unfavorably to other fan fiction communities. HASA is conceited, vain, arrogant and anti-hobbit. (6)

> HA is very Hobbit and Men oriented. This is starting to make elf writers feel unwelcome, and slash writers feel like they are the plague! (26)

In the first chapter of Henry Jenkins' book *Textual Poachers*, he states that "The fans' response typically involves not simply fascination or adoration but also frustration and antagonism, and it is the combination of the two responses which motivates their active engagement..."[12] While that phrase is couched in the context of fans' relationship to mass media, I believe that it is equally appropriate for describing the inter-personal relations between fans within a particular fandom, and even within unique aspects of a fandom, in this case, the writers and readers of Tolkien-based fan fiction who frequent the Henneth-Annûn archive. This sentiment is echoed by Kirsten Pullen in the concluding paragraph of her article "I-love-Xena.com: Creating Online Fan Communities":

> Despite the aggressive, sustained fan activity visible on the Web, the internet should not be assumed to have created utopian fan communities. [...] fans do not always interpret texts, fan production, or fan positions and identifications similarly.[13]

I wished to find out how the members of this particular archive saw themselves, both in regards to the other members of the archive, but also within the fandom as a whole. To that end, I asked the questions, "Do you compare this community with other fan fiction communities, either on your own or with other fan fiction community members? If so, what comments do you have about HASA and other archives? Do you 'behave' differently in other communities?" Unfortunately the wording of the questions was not as explicit as it could have been, and some respondents indicated that they only participated within Tolkien fandom, as opposed to answering that they participated only at HASA, if that indeed happened to be the case. I next asked for a free-thought response with these sentences: "Please describe how you feel as an active participant within this community. If you are active in other Tolkien fan fiction communities, feel free to compare your participation and experiences within HASA versus those in other communities." The replies to these questions varied widely, as evidenced by the few quotations listed above.

Of the fifty replies received, I divided them into positive, neutral/no answer/ambivalent and negative. Twenty-five, or 50% fell into the positive category; fourteen, or 28% were in the neutral/no answer/ambivalent group, and the remaining 11, or 22% were negative. In the positive camp, many people wrote that they felt as though they were valued contributors to the community, or that it was a more mature community than some other fan fiction communities. Several respondents did voice sentiments that it was not perfect, while acknowledging that no community can be:

> What I like best at HASA is the forums; I haven't found the lively discussions in other communities I've been involved in, and HASA folks are a sophisticated bunch of writers – keep me on my toes. (7)

> I have gotten to know some wonderful people, found a writing collaborator, found encouragement and advice for my own writing, and had a great time. The level of both serious criticism and good humor suits me very well. (43)

> I feel valued, able to contribute, and frequently end up better educated! [...] I think HASA really is a community, though like most

> large communities it's made up of smaller "circles of friends" – which to others may sometimes look like cliques! – but the reality is simply that no-one can read and comment on everything on HASA, it's simply too big... (8)

> I feel somewhat "protective" of HASA; I get defensive when I read criticism of it from other fan communities (though I certainly don't consider it to be perfect). (20)

In the neutral or ambivalent group, some respondents indicated that they were only sporadically involved, which parallels the 26% who specified that they were not currently active within the community. Two people elaborated on their conflicting feelings about the archive:

> My experiences with HASA have been mixed, and so are my feelings about the community. Most of the members are fine, but in the past I've had unpleasant encounters with several key individuals... (24)

> Do I feel like I actually belong? Yes. Did HASA make me feel welcome? Yes and no, but the fact that I am not wanted hasn't always stopped me. (29)

The negative replies focused on feeling left out of the community, sometimes due to the author's personal preference to reading and writing in particular subsections of Tolkien fan fiction which were felt not to be accepted by most members at HASA:

> My fandom friends and I quite often joke about sending our AU fics to HASA to get shot down. [...] I spend my energies in forums in which I am respected and in which I respect the others in my group. (13)

> I feel mostly ignored and often annoyed. Hey I knew that before I joined and I have not been disabused of my opinion since I have joined. (40)

> I think a lot of people at HASA take themselves too seriously. Every little disagreement seems of monumental importance. I don't need that much grief over a hobby, so I don't stay there much anymore. (39)

re•view
1. a critical article or report, [...] on a book, play, performance, etc.; critique

As mentioned earlier, one of the primary differences between Henneth-Annûn and other Tolkien fan fiction archives is that it is composed of two parts: the members' section, which is private but has no requirements for membership outside of joining a public yahoogroup; and the public side, which showcases fan fiction which has been evaluated by a nine-person, self selected reviewing pool. Any person who has been a member of the archive for thirty days is eligible to be a reviewer. Reviews are encouraged to be anonymous, though some reviewers include their pseudonym and email address in their comments.

My final question in the survey was an open-ended one to encourage the respondents to think about the reviewing process and articulate their feelings about it. I wrote, "A unique attribute of this archive is its 9-person, self-selecting reviewing process to approve or decline stories for the public side of the archive. If you have been involved with this process, whether as a writer, reviewer, or both, please describe your feelings about it."

The comments I received about experiencing the judging end, being a writer submitting stories to HASA's reviewing pool, varied significantly. I categorized the replies into those who felt primarily positive, predominantly negative, and those who either did not address that aspect of the question or were not published authors. Twelve people, or 24%, were in this last category. Of the remaining 38 respondents, half wrote that they felt mostly positive about being a writer and having submitted works in the reviewing pool. The other 19 people felt that their experience in the process was a negative one, or as one person replied, "It's a mixed blessing."[16]:

> I wasn't horribly impressed because the first thing anyone asks when they are rejected is "Why" If you can't tell me that much then if I really felt my story was appropriate I'm going to be both upset and angry. [...] Now it's optional that reviewers leave a reason. But they don't always [...] (39)

> I've had one of my stories reviewed and it was fine. I was impressed with the depth of a couple of the comments. (7)

> I think sometimes it's a pain in the ass, because one person will say you have awesome writing and approve, and another reviewer for the same story will decline with the reason that the writing is undistinguished. I think it's a real lottery/crap-shoot/whatever you want to call it. And trying to get people to elaborate on their reasons for declining is quite frequently a waste of time. (22)

> As a writer, I think twice before submitting, where I publish on ff.net without a second thought. It has thickened my skin to the 'decline' votes, and even many of those are encouraging in the long run. (32)

Most people who replied to this survey, if s/he was a reviewer, indicated that s/he took the responsibility seriously, while others explicated their conflicting feelings about the process:

> As a reviewer: I take it very seriously. I know what it's like to get criticism. [...] I try to be as objective as I can be in the subjective realm of writing/reading. I follow the guidelines and don't just vote on my own whims. (2)

> I try to be constructive when reviewing because that is how I would want to be reviewed. (10)

> I like the reviewing process myself but take my duties as a reviewer very seriously and do not allow friendship or favoritism to interfere with my choices. [...] I write a long critique (when necessary) and try and help the author to write a better story. I do not kid myself that other authors do this. (6)

> I have some serious qualms about the HASA reviewing process, [...] because I am wary of the idea that there can be self-evident parameters of taste. One man's Mozart, after all, is another man's screeching cat. [...] this is not to say that the reviewers at HASA are cliquish or insular, only that they may be perceived as such. (4)

> As a reviewer, I have shifting feelings about it. [...] I do bear in mind that HASA guidelines call for 'excellence,' and I'm encouraged to keep reviewing when I see things that I consider flawed get voted in (an experience common to everyone, I'm sure!). (21)

> As an infrequent reviewer, I like the newer combination comment box/capsule decision, although it does open up more possibilities for difficulties. For one thing, each anonymous reviewer is essentially assuming an official position in taking on the responsibility of reviewing – to the author whose story you review, you (and eight faceless others) are HASA, and I think reviewers really should remember that when they comment and vote, and if they cannot remember that, then they ought to abstain. (15)

In some of the quotations already listed, the sentiment was voiced that the people doing the reviewing are biased for or against particular genres of stories or even whole races, such as hobbits or Elves. Many respondents, however, addressed how they felt the reviewing pool actively discouraged this bias, while acknowledging that reviewers can opt to be selective in what they review, or "cherry pick" particular genres or story focuses.

In early March, one of the site managers posted a public plea to HASA members either to become reviewers, or to review more often. Since the reviewing pool and stated purpose of the archive have proven to be points of contention within and outside of this particular community, and one of the purposes of this paper is to reveal how the members of this community interact with each other, I feel it is not inappropriate to include this additional insight outside of the answers to my survey questions:

> There are 243 reviewers eligible to submit reviews. However, only 174 of them have done a single review since July 2003. Of the 174 that remain, fewer than 50 have reviewed 20 or more submissions.
>
> So, speaking from a strictly statistical point of view, a relatively small group of people is deciding what does and does not get accepted. I am convinced that the people in this group are well-intentioned and are submitting considered, reasoned opinions. I'm also convinced that they do not know whom the other involved reviewers are, i.e., I do not see patterns of collusion in the voting.
>
> They are also doing a heck of a lot of hard work. There have been over 500 hundred stories submitted since August, requiring over 4,000 reviews be performed. You do the math. Simply through the accident of non-participation, story decision making is being done by a small and dedicated group of reviewers. [...]
>
> You can't vote on your own stories, but you can do for other members what you hope they would do for you – become a reviewer, check out a few stories a week, and evaluate them. In doing so, you will broaden the perspectives in the reviewers pool.
>
> And that is a benefit to all.
>
> So, be a good HASA citizen – review something today.[17]

'Come, come!' said Gandalf. 'We are all friends here. Or should be [...]'
–*Lord of the Rings*, "The King of the Golden Hall"

> "I have read all the FAQs and stuff about what Henneth Annun WANTS, but what are we trying to do here? Make better writers, better fiction, better Tolkiens?"[18]

The Henneth-Annûn story archive is a multi-faceted community of fan fiction writers and readers who participate with varying levels of involvement. I wished to find out, from the members' own words, how they saw themselves in relation to each other, and the archive as a whole, as well as comparing their experiences with this community with other Tolkien fan fiction organizations. As the quoted responses reveal, there are widely divergent views, and any sense of an overarching sentiment could not be gathered from the replies I received. A further difficulty in this process was my inability to contact every member of the archive, as well as my dependence on people taking the time to reply to my survey. While there are over 450 active members, I was able to contact fewer than half of them, and of that, under 30% chose to communicate with me.

Henneth-Annûn is not the sole archive in cyberspace whose goals are to house quality works of Tolkien-based fan fiction. The definition of quality, however, differs from person to person. HASA is most definitely an ensemble of individuals who are there to write, and to learn, and to share ideas. Included in the stated aims of the archive is this sentence: "The purpose of the site is to collect the very best examples of JRRT fan fiction writing from around the Web, and to provide a collaborative work environment in which site members can appreciate and create quality JRRT fan fiction." The archive is there to promote all writers to improve their craft, as well as freely share a wealth of detailed analysis of Tolkien's characters, languages, politics, and much, much more.

What it is not, and I believe this is what addled many people who replied to my survey who were frustrated by a lack of personal attention to his/her works, is an educational institution. Like all archives with which I have been involved, Henneth-Annûn is administered by, and prolifically attributed to, volunteers. My impression from the replies received is that most people who become members of this archive do so to house their fan fiction. That is only a part of the reason, however. They wish to learn, and to collaborate. I did not get the sense that people join HASA for the sole purpose of improving other people's writing, which creates yet another Catch-22 for the archive. Newer writers are there to solicit constructive criticism and feedback, but the more established writers are still at work on their own stories and have a higher profile, therefore there are more writers seeking their advice. From my personal experiences at the archive, I do firmly believe that no new author is purposefully ignored. There is an adage which sums up this situation, though: "perception is reality." Even if what is revealed through surveys and statistics is that overall, members have a positive experience in the archive, what each unique writer undergoes during their time at the archive is what remains the ultimate truth for that person.

Despite a shared commonality of a love of Tolkien fan fiction, whether as a producer of works or a reader of them, the members of the Henneth-Annûn archive are neither unified in their perception of the archive itself, nor in their observations about their participation in the archive. Given how many people are involved with the community, and the differing backgrounds of the authors (age, culture, length of time in the fandom), this is not surprising. This community, as with all communities which are internet-based, is also in a constant state of flux, which makes analysis a challenging endeavor. While the information garnered from my survey hopefully illuminates the many complex and contradictory purposes and emotions which surround this particular fanfiction archive community, it is obviously only a few trees in a forest the size of Fangorn.

Works Consulted

Hills, Matt. *Fan Cultures*. London and New York: Routledge, 2002.
Jenkins, Henry. *Textual Poachers: Television Fans and Participatory Culture*. New York: Routledge, 1992.
___. "Why Heather Can Write." Technology Review, Inc. February 2004. [http://www.technologyreview.com/articles]
McCormack, U. '"How can it be transgressive if it's been on Woman's Hour?": Online fan communities and the politics of slash.' (Unpublished manuscript.) 2004.
Pullen, Kirsten. "I-love-Xena.com: Creating Online Fan Communities." *Web.Studies: Rewiring media studies for the digital age*. London: Arnold, 2000.
Rust, Linda. "Welcome to the house of fun: Buffy fan fiction as a hall of mirrors." *Refractory: a Journal of Entertainment Media*, Vol.2. March 2003. [http://www.refractory.unimelb.edu.au/journalissues/vol2/vol2.html]
Sabotini, Rachael. "The Fannish Potlatch: Creation of Status Within the Fan Community" [http://www.trickster.org/symposium/symp41.htm]

Endnotes

1 Pullen, Kirsten. "I-love-Xena.com: Creating Online Fan Communities." Web.Studies: Rewiring media studies for the digital age. London: Arnold. 2000, p. 60.

2 "In the language of the Elder Days, 'Arda' signified the World and all that is in it. Arda was created through the Music of the Ainur to be a dwelling place for the Children of Ilúvatar (that is, Elves and Men)." from The

Encyclopedia of Arda, http://www.glyphweb.com/arda/, original date pf word creation unknown. A Google and Altavista search on the word on 3/24/04 revealed its use four times.

3 Respondent 3

4 Hills, Matt. Fan Cultures. London and New York: Routledge., 2002. p. 137.529,826 when accessed on March 26, 2004 (Lord of the Rings only; if one adds in stories based on The Silmarillion the number is increased by 1,125.)

6 Library of Moria [http://www.libraryofmoria.com]

7 Open Scrolls [http://www.scribeoz.com/fanfic]

8 Axe and Bow [http://axebow.hakaze.com]

9 Frodo Healers [http://www.rosiesamfrodo.com/~frodohealers/about.html]

10 Parma Eruseen [http://www.parma-eruseen.net]

11 Per email correspondence with the site administrator, sent February 19, 2004: "There are 800+ people on the list at present time, @ 460 of whom are active. Starting this year, people who have no activity after one year will probably be removed permanently, simply to keep the list to manageable levels. We have had 59 new members sign up since February 1, and almost 100 since January 1."

12 Jenkins, Henry. Textual Poachers: Television Fans and Participatory Culture. New York: Routledge, Chapman and Hall, Inc., 1992. p. 23.

13 Pullen, ibid. p. 60.

14 "FAQ #3: Who can review? Anyone who has been a member of HASA for 30 days is eligible to be a reviewer." [http://www.henneth-annun.net/members/faq/faq_list.cfm?FAID=5]

15 Author's personal experience. As of March 30, 2004, I had 13 works accepted into the archive and two which had been declined. Most reviews were anonymous, but not all.

16 Respondent 41

17 "Review Process" forum, posted March 9, 2004 [in order to keep this response private outside of the members' section of HASA, I am not list ing the actual URL].

18 ibid. Reply posted March 20, 2004.

★

The significance of the title of this paper refers to the name of the archive. As quoted by Faramir: "This is the Window of the Sunset, Henneth Annûn, fairest of all the falls of Ithilien, land of many fountains." *Lord of the Rings*, "The Window on the West."

The definitions used at the beginning of the different sections came from Webster's *Ninth New Collegiate Dictionary.*

Appendix 4: Reading Between the Loins by Executrix

I thought that an explanation of what I thought I was trying to accomplish as a fanfic writer might be interesting. We're all familiar with the phenomenon of grotesque disparity between intention and achievement. We've all seen S4.

Probably the normal route is to become a fan of a show, start writing about it, and then start writing slash. In my case, I bought a set of B7 tapes as a present for my boyfriend, who said that he had enjoyed the show on broadcast TV.

Several years later, under the influence of Jenkins, I borrowed back the tapes (I still have them, about three years later – he really prefers *Dr.Who* and B5 to B7), and started watching them, because it sounded interestingly slashy. At that point, I had no involvement in organized fandom; very seldom read science fiction or fantasy; had watched perhaps one episode of ST:TOS and a couple of episodes each of *Dr. Who* and *Babylon 5*. I have never felt impelled to watch any more.

Sometime in January or February of 2000, I started watching B7, and sometime in March I started writing fanfic. Precipitate as always... but then I only slotted the first tape into my VCR because Jenkins made B7 sound like a fascinating starting point for the stories of a homoerotic romance with plenty of irony and antipathy to temper the saccharine.

He also made slash sound like a playground in which the story belongs to those who watch it (and add to it). Jenkins-plus-Joanna-Russ prepared me for slash as a queer-friendly zone of non-commercial woman-controlled pornography, which I thought (and still think) is a pretty cool idea. IMO, there's nothing wrong with pornography as such – to the extent that pornography is dehumanizing to its subjects, it's because of the preexisting nature of the fantasies of the consumers, it's not inherent in the production of materials that serve as a sort of Hamburger Helper for sexual fantasies.

Some of it worked out that way and some of it didn't, which I guess is about all you can expect (the emergence of some sort of worthwhile compromise after a loss is a major E'trix theme).

I still haven't figured out why the vast majority of fanfic writers – and especially slashwriters – are female, especially given the traditional belief that science fiction is a "masculine" genre. It's not that I would expect – and I certainly wouldn't wish for – fewer woman writers, I'm just surprised that there isn't at least an equal number of men. (And it's not just that slashwriters are character junkies – there's no huge group of male genwriters.)

I'm also surprised by the paucity of hetsmut on FC – looking in from the outside, I would have predicted a lot more stories reflecting women's sexual experiences. However, Tavia's figures show that there's a lot of het material in printzines, and perhaps FC's reputation as slash-friendly creates an expectation that it is not equally hetsmut-friendly.

I like most of my stories, but I have to admit that they're usually kind of strange. We had a thread about re-reading your old stories – it seems only natural that you'd like them, they're always about something you think is interesting and they reflect what you consider to be a valid view of the characters.

Morrigan once said that Executrix stories are about two standard deviations off. [Oh, I don't know. Light bondage and something with whipped cream, I suppose.] Some of it stems from being a trouble-maker. If we had a profound respect for constituted authority, we'd probably be Trekkers.

I've been known to cackle "Classify THIS!" as I finish a story featuring various implied, past, consummated, and unconsummated sexual and quasi-sexual activities involving both same-sex and other-sex activities, sometimes on the part of the same characters.

Some of the air of deviancy comes from sheer inability to plot, but most of it from having sort of off-center intentions. It seems to me exactly as natural for same-sex characters to interact sexually as mixed-sex couples (although some pairings seem a lot more plausible than others). However, even though I don't think there's anything unusual about homosexual activities, I don't think this is the Federation standard, so I get in a lot more soapboxing than most slash writers. In other words, just because I don't think it's a big deal doesn't mean that I think the characters don't think it's a big deal.

Ideally, I'd like to write stories with a wide variety of physical events, emotional events, and interesting and well-characterized dialogue (spoken and unspoken), in line with the "same-sex sex scene as everyday event" theory. Admittedly I very seldom manage this, but I don't think that's a limitation of slash, it's my limitation as a plotter.

A lot of the time, I feel like I'm looking through the other end of the telescope: that I'm observing the story as it unfolds from a distance of about two inches, so I'm writing extreme closeups when most people are writing master shots. Not to mention money shots.

This doesn't bother me at all – actually I think it's a strength of B7 fanwriting is that not only are there a lot of damn good writers, there are people with quite different objectives.

VOICE FROM THE PASTICHE

The two things about B7 that really interest me are My Client and what kind of place the Federation is and how a frazzled and declining Empire is managed. I once had a long and quite civilized conversation with Neil Faulkner between 1 and 4 am in which we agreed on the importance of world-building, although I consider it an adjunct rather than a replacement for Character Drug-Pushing.

I'm really proud of being one of the inspirations for "Stealing's Quicker" as a Party topic, given my history of writing a lot of pastiches, prequels, and for that matter prequel pastiches. Part of it is genuine interest in figuring out how the characters got that way. Some of it comes from being much more interested in things like the Liberator washing-up roster and Federation mass transit than in techno-neep. (The fact that I never bothered to learn to drive a car probably has something to do with my attitude toward the technology of space travel.) Also, the further back in time I can go, the further away I can get from Season 4, when it's just all too damn sad.

But then, strictly speaking I can't be classified as a science fiction writer, and not even really as a B7 writer – most of my output was either installments of an unauthorized Avon biography, or a bunch of little sub-*New Yorker*-y stories about a couple of guys having an unhappy love affair in a big spaceship in stationary orbit over the suburbs. There's probably a good reason why nobody ever tried to become the John Cheever of B7 before.

Nova suggested to me a long time ago that actually I was writing a serial novel. Since then, I've felt faintly guilty: some stories do fit together in sequence but most don't, and I have to convince myself that irreconcilable facts from story to story are "experimental" and not "contradictory." (I'm pretty sure that Blake is an eldest, whereas Avon is a middle child, but the ttba2 story required Blake to be a middle child too. The names of his siblings also tend to shift – canonically, they're in the Servalan and Travis no-first-name camp.) But then I also have to convince myself that when I see similarities between two of my stories, that that's "development" and not "being too lazy to come up with another idea."

Traditionally, tragedies are about gods and heroes and kings – someone far above the audience. And one theory is that comedy is either about people at audience level or below it. I've been assiduously mining a previously unrecognized seam of B7 drawing-room comedy. This also involves a certain degree of normalization, deglamorization or, it might be argued, dragging things down to my own level. I think it's fair to say that the melodrama level in E'trix World is quite low. (Being down-to-earth, for a science fiction writer, is like a defense attorney having the courage of his convictions.)

Because I'm so literal-minded, I can absolutely imagine the characters as real people (albeit, in some cases, *boring* real people) which implies that they must have back stories, families, etc. I also really, really try to write for the entire repertory company, but my imagination has never been able to catch fire when it comes to either Jenna or Cally.

Although fanfic has given various accounts of Avon's childhood, usually describing it as horrible but rather glam, I think it's a safe bet that no one else posits him being raised in a semi-detached in an executive estate by a social-climbing tinned-pineapple abuser. Or, for that matter, that his favorite food is not chateaubriand but chips.

Doubtless I write about trivial things because I'm a trivial person, or frivolous at any rate. Certainly, even before various contemporary RL tragedies, Executrix stories were predominantly non-violent, either because they don't have any exterior action at all or because I made an effort to come up with a credible mission for the crew that advanced revolutionary objectives but didn't involve violence. Other people don't seem to worry about this much, but I don't think it's good for the characters to have to spend all their time killing people. In other words, in E'trix World, the word "blow" is seldom followed by "up."

THE PINK TRIANGLE THING

Everybody's Mileage Varies, but as noted above, my initial interest in B7 was as a very slashy domain, and my initial interest in slash was as a Brighton Rock artform in which the queerness ran all the way through.

I doubt if anyone would disagree with me that "Romeo and Juliet" is about a rather unsuccessful love affair, ending up with 100% dead protagonists, with a feud going on the background. It would be more controversial to suggest that B7 is about a rather unsuccessful love affair, ending up with 100% dead protagonists, with a rebellion going on in the background. Nor would "Big Spaceship! Big Queers!" rate a lot of votes as the official B7 motto (if only because Louise & Simon had a long thread about whether the Liberator is actually all that big a spaceship).

My assumption when I had read ABOUT slash but hadn't yet started reading or writing it was that it was about characters who (whether or not their environment was supportive, and whether or not they were happy about it) thought of themselves as gay. Imagine my surprise to find that a significant portion of the slashwriters and audience members define slash as being about same-sex relationships between HETEROSEXUAL canon characters.

I don't think it's impossible that someone could first experience, or first recognize, same-sex desire in his or her thirties or forties instead of his or her teens, so I don't find it implausible that canon characters could be having their first same-sex relationship. (Depending on the way you think mind-wipes as working, Blake could certainly THINK he was having his first same-sex relationship even if he wasn't, or conversely have been conditioned into remembering a heterosexual past that never actually existed. But then I'm not 100% sure he had a brother and sister – the whole thing could have been a wind-up. TWB is sort of like Henry V, somebody who eventually becomes powerful but in the meantime just gets pushed around by everybody.)

I usually don't write First Time stories, because it's been done so often (and I must have written more Avon Break-Up stories than anyone, ever). I don't think Blake and Avon could have resisted going to bed together given the quantum of optimism on one side, and bad luck and worse judgment on the other. I just don't think they could have made a go of the relationship, but I'm interested in "watching" them not do it.

Which is my basic rationale for crossovers: who would I like to see together? My first thought in that direction was Avon/Angel, but that story also had Avon/Giles, a pairing I repeated in another story. IMO Spike certainly counts as a bit of all right, but they don't seem to go together.

Every story seems to dictate its own amount of sex, although I haven't written any huge number of gen stories. I was very flattered by Predatrix calling me "the cleanest slashwriter – ever!" (and might indeed ask for permission to put it on the back cover if there were ever a Big Book o'E'trix). However, the problem with sex is that, even though I have a high opinion of it in general, it's very hard to describe without making it sound awful.

Also, things have certainly changed since 1985, when Joanna Russ pointed out that nobody in slash had ever heard of "lube" – nowadays, what nobody's ever heard of is "refractory period."

I just don't see the point at all of 0-60 in 4 seconds sex scenes, and I take an above-average amount of interest in foreplay and in sexual modes other than anal intercourse – probably because I'm writing this stuff in part for my own amusement, and that's my least-favorite sexual practice out of any that I've actually bothered to try. Admittedly if I had a prostate gland I'd probably feel differently about it.

THE SAME ONLY DIFFERENT

In several instances, I've written variations on someone else's story – I think of this as either an "over the shoulder" (i.e., the other angle in a two-shot) or a "carport" (i.e., it leans on an existing structure). The interesting thing about these stories is that they have virtually nothing in common with their "substrates," and sometimes it wouldn't be obvious when read side-by-side that they're "the same."

The one reliable constant is that my version can be counted on to be much shorter, and will probably be lighter in tone (e.g., Nova's "Much Ado" story vs. mine).

MARYLITIGATION

It could be argued that my endless absorption with My Client is simply a long-running Mary Sue.

So, let's look at the facts:

* More or less the same size
* Dark hair, light skin
* Loads of black gear
* Fondness for sound of own voice
* Generous willingness to share omniscience with entire Universe

* Poor physical coordination
* Sentimental about money
* Dedication to smart-ass remarks and insubordination in all forms
* Extremely serious sexual interest in men without thereby lacking sexual interest in women.

Looks conclusive, so far. But as to the other side of the coin:

* Easy mastery of all mechanical objects
* Astonishing physical courage
* Volcanic sexual attractiveness to individuals of various species, nationalities, gender positions, etc.

HAHAHAHAHAHAHA!!! Get me to the Liberator, next thing you know I'd be joining Vila under the bed as dust-bunny inspector.

Although someone once e-mailed me, "Oh, I love your Avon, he's so sweet," which simultaneously gave me a warm glow and brought home the fact that I'm really missing the point.

Nearly all Executrix stories are about something (albeit perhaps something very far from admirable) that Avon does – I mean, not only am I willing to indulge his bizarre tastes, I give him a degree of control over his environment that I suppose one can only envy in RL.

THE SYMPATHY VOTE

"Ask-Tell-Pursue," the Travis/Avon, is one of the first B7 stories I ever wrote and, as the intro on the Liberated version says, I've felt a degree of sympathy for Travis ever since. But more lately I think that he and Blake must have some kind of personal history, or at least a serious attraction, explaining why they can never close the sale. (Neither can Avon and Servalan, which is what made me think of the parallel.)

But maybe Blake's hesitation is like Hamlet's – if Claudius has managed to achieve Hamlet's Oedipal objectives, then Hamlet has reason to envy the jammy bastard, but not to feel morally superior. So maybe Blake wishes he could duplicate, on behalf of the Cause, Travis' unbending devotion to the Federation, even though he can't give his full endorsement to Travis' unbending devotion to bumping off Blake.

Before I met Fran (online and in RL) it would not have occurred to me that Servalan would have a constituency, and at first I found it impossible to write about her. Now I'm a little more comfortable, but still don't feel I have a handle on her early life, or why they let her wear evening gowns to the office. I haven't written very much about Jenna or Cally. I don't at all subscribe to the theory that we write slash because we don't think women are interesting (as M. Fae Glasgow said, 'I have a strong female role-model – it's called a mirror') but I don't think the female B7 characters, as distinct from

RL women or women in fiction in general, are particularly interesting.

I try to give all the characters quality "screen time," but God knows it's difficult, no matter how I try. I've never come up with anything really interesting for Gan, but then has anybody except Nova, ever, anyway?

Of course, the greatest obstacle to my development as a B7 writer is My Blake Problem. I suspect Nova nailed it ages ago when she said that I have a problem with authority. Indeed if My Client existed (or I were fictional) I bet we'd bond along an axis of sheer primitive anarchism. Not to mention inept ballroom dancing.

I know it's swimming against the tide, but I can't help thinking that Avon's family (except for his older brother) is nice and Blake's is horrible, which is why Blake is able to get further from his upbringing.

I also have a regrettable fondness for stories about Who Knew Who Pre-TWB (always did, even before the Festival was announced), but I rationalize it by saying there may have been a small elite who naturally would get to know each other.

SONGS ABOUT BUILDINGS AND FOOD

Any B7 story featuring both money and food is guaranteed to be written by me (and in fact, any story featuring one of them probably is, although it might be by Manna, and any story with a lot of puns is either by me or Marian in one of her various incarnations).

There's very little canon evidence about food, and one reference to "concentrated food" (Horizon), which could just be emergency back-up supplies. Palmero grows tropical fruit, or anyway did before the Star One disruptions, and grapes, wine, and coffee "from real beans" are available as luxury items. I'm very taken by my own conjecture that Gan installed a hydroponic farm in some of the vast amount of (presumably empty) space on the Liberator. I accept the fanonical institution of "agricultural worlds" and assume that the Liberator stocks fresh as well as concentrated food and that food, seeds, growing medium, etc., can be purchased with Treasure Room funds. (BTW in that the Liberator stores enough concentrated food for a thousand person-years, the expectation must have been that there'd be a helluva lot more than six people on the damn thing.)

Several stories ("the Roj & Kerr Travel Bureau") were written specifically with the idea of sending them someplace nice for a change. One thing that leads me to label a story as disappointing is that its setting doesn't seem to be very clearly visualized. One of the nice things about fanfic is that you can instantly build a rose-red city half as old as time, and it doesn't cost any more than sending them down another naffing quarry.

WHERE DO YOU GET YOUR IDEAS?

Ideas? What are these things of which you speak? They probably have something to do with Plots, those other mythological creatures. A lot of the ones that I don't swipe are visual. For instance, the impulse for "Wanderjahr" (the Cabaret pastiche) was thinking that Servalan's haircut, eyelashes, and general style look a lot like Sally Bowles' in the Bob Fosse film, and wanting her to sit on a piano and belt out "Tomorrow Belongs to Me". Usually, the way I write a story is by a kind of videoless video editing: visualize it, and then keep "running tape" in my head until I like the way the scene looks. Then I write the first draft (I wrote my first few books by hand, in notebooks, then typed them on an electric typewriter – now I always, only, ever write on the computer.)

I don't really write stories in running order – I write the things that seem most compelling, and try to remember to put down the bits that I think are particularly clever but might forget if the story takes a long time to write. Then I rewrite the first parts over and over, and gradually filter in more and more of the story, and finally get fed up and do the last parts – usually the sex scenes come into this category.

Finally, I go back and see if any of the scenes should be rearranged (e.g., you can't lose something before you steal it) and whether I want to put anything into a flashback or take something out of a flashback into chronological order. Then I go through again and take things out – I really want the story to move fast, and for every word to serve as many functions as possible. I'm trying for black-hole density, but bouillon cube is OK too.

ANALYSIS: TERMINABLE AND INTERMINABLE

It took more than a year for me to finish the first B7 story I ever started (whereas I've written lots of other stories over a period of a couple of days), and I have another WIP that has been dragging on even longer than that. But then again, that one includes both a door-slamming-farce plot (and I have difficulty trying to keep track of where the plates of sardines are) and Tarrant, inclusion of whom is guaranteed to at least double the in-progress time of any story.

This essay has been in progress for yonks. As Douglas Adams said, "I love deadlines... that swooshing sound they make as they rush by."

On the other hand, I've written some fairly long stories in just a day or two. I'm very prone to plot bunnies, so much so that I've prefaced stories with an apology because I know that at least someone in the audience is going to get pissed off, or that something in the story contradicts fannish consensus.

I really am very concerned with audience reception. I know that several fanfic writers say that they really write for themselves anyway, but I must respectfully disagree with My Learned Colleagues on this point. I mean, it's one thing to have a story idea, or even to think them through a little, but writing (even for someone with as little concern for craftsmanship as I have) is bloody hard work. As far as I'm concerned, there's no point in undertaking the effort unless someone else is going to read it, and I like giving pleasure and I don't like being flamed. (Actually I don't like being legitimately criticized either, but that's my problem.) I can be genuinely apologetic about writing a story that I suspect will annoy a reader, but then again the bunnies deliver what they deliver, and if the readers don't like it they can write their own damn story.

Or indeed their own damn essay.

Dateline: Everyone-upon-Avon, December 2002

Fandoms referred to or quoted from

Fanfic authors referred to or quoted from

Index of fanfic stories referred to or quoted from

General Index

The Author

Poet, novelist, critic and translator, winner of an array of prizes, including the Forward Prize for Best Individual Poem, Sheenagh Pugh lives in Cardiff and teaches creative writing at the University of Glamorgan.